HORSEKEEPING

Horsekeeping

One Woman's Tale of Barn and Country Life

Roxanne Bok

TWIN LAKES PRESS: 2011

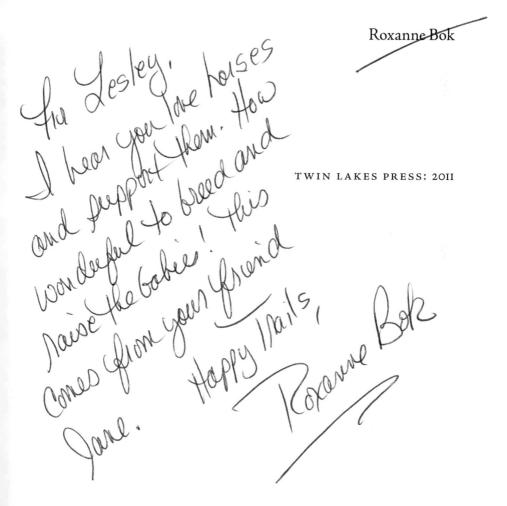

For Lesley,
I hear you love horses and support them. How wonderful to breed and raise the babies! This comes from your friend Jane.

Happy Trails,
Roxanne Bok

A TWIN LAKES PRESS BOOK

Published by Prospecta Press, an imprint of Easton Studio Press

P.O. Box 3131, Westport, Connecticut 06880 (203) 454-4454

www.prospectapress.com

Book and cover design by Thomas Whitridge/Ink, Inc.

50 White Street, New York, New York 10013

Hardcover ISBN: 978-1935212-52-2

E-book ISBN: 978-1-935212-77-5

FIRST EDITION

Printed in the United States of America

First printing: October 2011

For Scott,
for the farm,
and for the time and space to ride and write

And for Bobbi,
for teaching me the language of horses

Contents

Acknowledgments

·❦——————❦·

ALL OF THE FOLLOWING EVENTS ARE TRUE, and were first penned as they happened; yet, my memories are seen through my own wavy glass and may differ from my characters' recollections. I have changed the names of some people in this story while keeping those who agreed to be so designated.

I wish to thank Scott, my loving husband of thirty years, for his support both financially and emotionally throughout the living and the telling of this experience. I also thank Bobbi for her consistent hard work, the amazing talent that she shared unstintingly, and her friendship. I greatly appreciate my many readers, editors and friends who have offered valuable advice and moral support at various points in this book's genesis including The Gotham Writers' Workshop—especially Amy Sickels, Chip Carleton (thanks for sharing!), the late Bill Binzen, Riga Meadow Equestrian Center, Susan Wallace, Gretchen Lengyel, Ronald Jones, Michael Morphis, Matthew Smyth, Alexandra Lange, Amy Reiss, Laurie Egger, Christopher Hewat, Mari Ann Fortuna, Carol Kalikow, Dan Dwyer, Cynthia Knabe, Charles and Sara Bachman, Kitty Benedict, Gregory Miller, Stephanie Emerson, Aimée Bell, George Massey, Mickey Pearlman (who taught me a thing or two about memoir and line editing), and Thomas Whitridge for his beautiful book making.

Lastly, I am deeply indebted to the superb horses and my growing family of equine-devoted friends who labored, remade, repaired, volunteered countless unpaid hours (especially Terri Licata), boarded and rode at Weatogue Stables throughout its rebirth. I am thrilled to have shared this journey with you. Horses, and horse people, are special, indeed.

CHAPTER ONE

Green Acres Is the Place to Be

·◁══════════▷·

DID I HARBOR AN UNFULFILLED DREAM and not realize it? Was a life entwined with equines a wish from way back, even to my childhood, one I submerged as impractical in suburban New Jersey? I knew no one who kept horses, nor did I know anyone who knew anyone who owned horses; I was triply removed from that world. Or, did I conveniently invent this dream of horsekeeping once presented with the actuality, the opportunity? Whichever the case, in my forty-sixth year, when the fact of a farm trotted into my grown-up life of wife and mother, a weighty stone dropped deep into my psychic well with a distant, satisfying clunk. I became aware that this unconscious, patient calling beckoned as a long-awaited adventure—hazy, parched and weak, but there nonetheless. I felt destined to manifest it.

I knew the faded blue exterior of the El-Arabia Arabian horse farm in Salisbury, Connecticut, well, being a neighbor to it for five years, though I never expected to own it. Tired and failing slowly, both its moniker and appearance brought to mind an under-used military training camp. A few lethargic, mute farmhands sporadically tended dilapidated, low-slung buildings graying into mud-slicked acres. Dirt-caked, ignored horses limped aimlessly around vaguely fenced, balding paddocks. Some stood in ankle-deep water. Originally housing some fifty horses, only a few scraggly brood mares and some out-to-pasture geriatric stallions remained as ghosts of Mrs. Johnson's once-thriving farm.

Neville and Janet Johnson started the business in the 1970s, breeding Arabian horses for sale. In the United States, small, sturdy Arabians were renewing in popularity: they excel at the fancy stepping required for saddle seat and uniquely possess the physicality for endurance riding. Success rewarded the Johnsons' hard work and dedication: over the years glowing articles were written and awards won. They held parties to celebrate the foals and their mares. Their horses upgraded the Arabian gene pool. The couple lived across the street in an old farmhouse, painted baby blue to match the farm's colors. Perhaps an Arabian-inspired choice, the blue was untraditional for a New England farm, arid like a desert sky. It had been toned down by wear, interrupted more often than not by weathered grey. The house sat above the road with a view over the roof-line of the El-Arabia barn and across the fields to Canaan Mountain beyond. The land behind reached up to nearly nine hundred feet in altitude and connected to hundreds of acres of forest held by a few neighbors.

Mr. Johnson was elderly, ill and rarely seen by the time we moved to the neighborhood, though he had been a ceramics expert, musician and restorer of English motorcars. In her seventies, Janet Johnson, one of three first women scholarship graduates of MIT, did not squander her talent or her education. A double PhD in physics and metallurgy, she and her husband designed and manufactured piezoelectric ceramic elements for ultrasonic sensing and metering instruments, often used in medical equipment, at their factory further afield in Connecticut. But her life became the horses, and she increasingly valued her privacy, so few local residents knew her well, considering her aloof, even odd. One neighbor told me that Mrs. Johnson would emerge from her house once a year to deadhead her day lilies that lined the road. She'd lie down in the patch of green and chain-smoke through her garden chores, pulling down the slender stalks one by one, pinching the expired petals, and not say a word to passersby. I had traveled that road frequently the last five years, and I'd never laid eyes on her, but the increasingly weedy day lily bed still conjures an image as clear as a memory.

The factory burned down in 2003. Caught without adequate insurance, Mrs. Johnson needed to sell a sixteen-acre parcel of the El-Arabia hay field. Since it bordered our property, my husband Scott and I bought it and leased it back to her for one dollar, to deter the developer who had been sniffing it out for a spec house. This advantageous transaction preserved the field, protected our property and Mrs. Johnson still harvested the hay and kept her farm. It required money, but no work on our part. The lawyers and brokers handled the deal, so we never met either Johnson. The break up of any farm parcel tugs at our nostalgia for the simpler life of old, but by the time we moved to the road in 1998, El-Arabia had already passed its prime. If in need, maybe our cash infusion would help.

Friends who had once rented an adjoining house overlooking the farm opted not to stay because their view of bedraggled, uncared for horses broke their hearts. I had heard that lax breeding meant many unsold foals were left to mature wildly in the pastures. The breakdown was a pitiful end to a once cutting-edge, top-of-the-line operation run by a woman who adored horses. I'd like to think she was let down by her farm manager and staff, but it was hard to reconcile this with her proximity to the farm: directly across the street, she had only to look out her front door to see those horses, even if she avoided the grounds directly. Only illness and lack of funds could account for what had happened. It's a tough business.

Despite the farm's run-down state, my family and I grew to love the land itself: forty-five acres of gently sloping pastures with a few well-placed mature trees. "There's no tonic like the Housatonic," quipped Oliver Wendell Holmes, Sr. about the meandering river that lines the eastern edge of both our property and El-Arabia. Its waters seep a hazy mist over the valley many mornings, a cover that keeps us guessing while it slowly lifts, often to reveal a surprisingly fine day. Hawks, eagles, songbirds, deer, bobcats, coyotes, turkeys and black bears populate our river valley arcadia nestled between the Taconic hills and Canaan mountain: but in contrast, every barn, run-in shed, garage, outbuilding and bit of fence at El-Arabia sagged and tottered. Relics littering the southeastern property line included the fiberglass hull of a speedboat, a peeling, prop-less Mercury outboard motor, a hulking, broken-windowed multi-stall horse trailer turned condo for squirrels and chipmunks, a "marble/slate" truck shrugging on rusted rims, the carcass of a car resting on its right side, and an antique television poised on a stump.

The main structure stretched longer than a football field: twenty-two thousand square feet of weathered boards wedged into the land's slope up to Weatogue Road. With fifty-eight stalls, this barn was designed to service many needs—6 x 6-foot stalls for ponies and smaller hacks, 10 x 10 for larger riders and geldings, 12 x 12 for brood mares and stallions, and 16 x 16 for draft horses that stand eighteen hands high and can weigh over two thousand pounds. I learned all about stall-to-horse specifica-tions later. For five years I only viewed our neighbor's operation from the outside and knew *nada* about the horse business, not even a gelding (a castrated stallion) from a mare. But there is something about horses, an inner voice whispered. I was seduced by the idea of them, like so many little girls, and even these sad ones intrigued me. Were they wonderful to know once cleaned up? In the way each dog that I meet is cute, but becomes quite a complex "personality" upon further acquaintance?

Once, on a walk past, I inquired about the pretty white horse always isolated across the street.

"He's the teaser," the farm hand said.

"A teaser?" I queried, eyebrows innocently raised in interest.

Horse man stared past me into the thin air. "He gets the mares ready."

"Ready for what?"

"For the stallions." He looked me straight in the eye.

I leveled another squinty-eyed look at this petite animal and only then noticed his preposterous penis that recharged the simile "hung like a horse." Oh, I thought to myself, I get it. Finding firm ground, I dug deeper.

"But he's over here and the mares are over there. Plus, he's only one horse; does he impregnate all those females?"

Horse man considered me with contempt. "Nope."

On I blundered: "You mean he never gets to… you know, do it himself?"

"Nope." He was firm and unapologetic.

"Oh," I said, and moved on.

Just one more aspect of cruelty to animals, I thought. It reminded me of those crass Viagra ads warning men with erections lasting over four hours to head for the hospital. This poor horse spends years "erected," rendering even gelding a more humane option. Maybe it's a blissful state? If not, should I crusade to improve his lot in life? What do I know? This practice probably dates to the early Moroccans who first tamed horses; like so many other aspects of horsemanship, maybe it's hallowed ground. So I continued on my not-so-merry way and resolved never to look at the pretty white horse and his unsatisfied manhood again.

As it turned out, a few years later the threat of development forced me to look closer at El-Arabia, though in retrospect I see that my destiny was already printed and bound. My family and I treasured our patch of fields and woods in Connecticut, and often talked about annexing land as needed to preserve diminishing open farmland and slow the pace of development, all while protecting our privacy. In 2003 a local realtor notified us the rest of the farm land was for sale.

"How much?" I looked at Scott's scribbled notes as he hung up the phone. "Are you sure?"

"Yep, that's what the man said," Scott answered. "It certainly can't be worth that; the place is a wreck. It doesn't even have a place to live; the Johnsons are keeping the house and land across the street."

"Then what do we do? Let it go to whoever walks through the door? Don't you think a developer will go for it?"

"Well, the price would seem even higher to speculators. They'd have to tear down the buildings, improve the drainage and the site in general, and then resell or build without any guarantee of sale or profit. It's a risky venture at those prices."

"But the market is pretty strong. Everyone says it can't hold up, but so far it has." I paced our kitchen island. "Do you think they might try to break it up into smaller lots? Offer more than one house site?"

"Legally it can be subdivided once, so probably two house sites max. But these land deals are often shady." Scott stashed his notes under his Blackberry, and sorted the mail pile on the counter.

"The land is certainly nice, but there are neighbors in view and few trees. It's hard to judge its value. What should we do?"

Scott's deep brown eyes looked out the window to the open field and woods across the road. I willed his thoughts to form a coherent plan and shifted my weight left to right, a rocking horse of fruitless agitation.

"Well, what do we do?" I asked again.

He surfaced from his inner consultation.

"We should float a lower offer. They may just take it. If they don't, at least we're in there. If other buyers come forward, they'll return to us for a counter offer and we can weigh it again. We can't even see the property from our house so we have no reason to be desperate."

As unsatisfying as this half-measure tactic seemed to me at the time, Scott was right. The property sat. Nearly two years later, Mr. Johnson died and his widow quickened her pace to sell. The broker gave us heads up that they were about to accept an offer for the rest of the farm, at a lower price than the ask but not as low as our original bid. Taking the bait, I stood ready to pile on as I had worried and daydreamed about the place the entire time. Scott registered my barely contained excitement with a deep breath. He well-knew my tendency to mindlessly forge ahead, but he always hesitated to be piggish in that weekender way of throwing money around. Maybe someone else would take it on and restore its former glory? Or, were we about to be staring at two or three reproduction country manors? Few people eking out a living in the horse business could afford the cost of the real estate, let alone the repairs.

We felt somewhat guilty, recognizing ourselves as part of the problem—weekenders pushing up the price of real estate with friends that follow in our tracks, some of who replaced old barns and farmland with McMansions and guest-houses. We had taken care to fit in rather than burst through, and had predated the more recent soaring popularity of the county. Salisbury is not the Hamptons, but some of our neighboring towns to the south like Kent, Litchfield and Roxbury verge nigh. Now we were victims of the robust prices of a market we helped create. But our chance with El-Arabia is here and now, we realized; no more theorizing. Developers hovered, the market sizzled and the El-Arabia land laid choice. We called the real estate agent with a higher bid.

A WEEK BEFORE OUR FORMAL TOUR of El-Arabia, Scott and I took our regular walk through our field and into the woods. The bright late October day encouraged optimism; the burnt sienna leaves showered a woodsy version of ticker tape with us the celebrated heroes. The wind whipped swirling eddies amongst the fallen. *Go for it,* nature persuaded. We paused at the border of our property and peered out over the Johnsons' hay fields beyond to the tired barns and horses. A canvas of blue sky arched across it all, shrinking the enormity of the project.

"Wow," I said, squinting into the lucid openness. "Big sky country. Look at the clouds racing." I pointed, appreciating a deep inhale of clean air. "What beautiful land."

"Wouldn't it be terrible if the farm was sold and the land subdivided into spec houses?" Scott mused.

"Yes, that would be the only thing that could make it sadder than it already is, but what would we do with a horse farm?" I parsed, hiding my own land lust to show Scott I was responsibly weighing the situation.

"We'd get into farming," he replied as casually as he kicked aside the stone under his foot. "Maybe horses."

Was he serious? I held my breath.

He frowned. "Can you imagine two new houses, one sitting right here along the edge of our path? As you've so often said yourself, we hope to die in our house, and then pass it on to our kids, so could you really imagine years and years of saying 'we should have bought that old Johnson place when we had the chance?'"

He came by his decision as emotionlessly as he did all his business transactions, but he also knew how much I wanted this farm. We each dutifully expressed our worries about the expense, about squeezing another project into our full lives, about over-straining our already time-pressured marriage. But beneath this lip service my heart pulsed with delight, knowing that we would go for it at anything close to a reasonable price. Two days later, under pressure from another shadowy buyer, and without even having seen the inside of the barns, we agreed to a purchase price. The double meaning of the term "we bought the farm" was not lost on either of us.

Some of our neighbors had counted on us to rescue our road from the tyranny of the developer. John Bottass, the cattle farmer at the far end of Weatogue Road, guards his acres and watches over what he passionately believes is the last well-preserved valley in Salisbury. A dedicated farmer who laments the loss of local agriculture, he waxes eloquent about our road and the surrounding land. Cautious about us at first, he eventually trusted that our common land interests were in sync and now we share a curmudgeonly skepticism about change. His family and mine bookend Weatogue, and we fret about the next lot in between us to fall. Like two mother hens we catch up and keep tabs; me draped over my bicycle, stroking my miniature black poodle Velvet perched in a basket at my handlebars, and John hanging his head and farm-work dirty arm out of his old green tractor while we trade our gossipy knowledge about the good guys (farmers, land preservationists and unpretentious neighbors), and the bad guys (developers and neighbors who sell to developers). We always agree despite our local/weekender dichotomy.

One day John hailed me down.

"Did you and Scott really buy El-Arabia?"

"Yes John, I'm pretty sure we're getting it."

"Are you keeping it a farm?" he asked, anxious.

"Yes sir, I think we are. We'll keep the land open at any rate," I fired back, happy to report some solid action to fortify our heretofore verbal lines of defense. His effusive gratitude embarrassed me: much of the purchase being made in self-interest after all.

Another neighbor, Bill Binzen, is an accomplished photographer whose home borders El-Arabia at the northeastern end. He is elderly, and an impossibly thin six feet four, but he gave me a hug that lifted me off my feet when he heard.

"If I were a little younger, I'd saddle up Western-style and help you out."

I tried to envision it. In May he had collapsed at the town Memorial Day celebration: a modest parade of fire engines, the ambulance squad cars, daycare kids in wagons throwing wrapped peppermints to the crowd, the elementary school band blaring marches and the seventy-five year old Salisbury Town Band in their gingham-ribboned cane hats keeping them on key, the giggling Brownies, the self-conscious Boy Scouts and the not so modest roster of Salisbury veterans, crisply uniformed, armed, and humbly serious with memories of time served. The scene never varies: a hush falls on the townspeople as they follow the soldiers into the old pine studded cemetery. The master at arms reads the names of all the Salisbury war dead, Episcopal and Congregational ministers and a Catholic priest invoke God's blessing, a local child recites the Gettysburg address, Taps hangs in the air twice—to begin near the crowd, and to end, poignantly far away, an anguished cry from deeper in the cemetery. Four guns salute. The shock of the blasts sets a few babies wailing and nervous dogs howling as the older kids pounce for a prized shell casing.

It is a time to be grateful for these soldiers' sacrifices, whatever one's politics. A few feeble veterans ride in fancy convertibles, but most still march, including Bill as he had done for over thirty years, handsomely outfitted in his full khaki WWII regalia, under an airless, sunny sky. He regally stood at attention in the cemetery until the premature May heat got the better of him, buttoned up tight in his uniform. Down he went, stretched out lean in the dandelions and fragrant wild thyme. Conscious and loathe to go to the hospital but unable to fully rally, he was ambulanced by the on-hand EMTs. I sadly wondered if Bill's time had come.

Two days later, Scott and I watched him ride along our road atop a vintage bicycle, arms vigorously working the handlebars to stay vertical. It seemed dangerous, but I deeply admired his perseverance in filling life to the brim. I hoped I'd have the guts to do the same.

Relatively young if not as vigorous, Scott and I cottoned to the idea of our kids hanging around a working stable. Some parents pay good money for their coddled offspring to experience "farm life"; here we'd have the real thing in our own front yard. I waxed romantic about the sound of horse whinnies in the distance and pictured our five-year-old pixie daughter, Jane, helmeted and smiling on a white pony with a flowing mane. I imagined our ten-year-old nature-loving son, Elliot, growing muscular and competent mucking out stalls. I sighed over visions of the sun gleaming on the river, the restored-to-their-former-glory barns, and solid, perfectly aligned fences corralling fit, contented horses kicking up their hooves in emerald green pastures. I considered all the animals I could justify having—chickens, goats, pigs or whatever else fills up a barn. They wouldn't be in the house, so how could animal-averse Scott object? My vision beamed vivid Technicolor until my dark side, the monochromatic pessimist always alert to lurking disaster, concocted a scene of my silly ten-pound poodle kicked in the head to fly across the barn into a too-still heap. But this was minor in my schemes of calamity, and the only negative I could conjure.

Like Bill, I decided to get on, and enjoy the ride.

CHAPTER TWO

Farm Livin' Is the Life for Me

·⟨⎯⎯⎯⟩·

THE DAY CAME FOR US TO SEE exactly what we had already agreed to buy. Excited despite the soggy grey air, we drove through eroding mud and parked in front of the barn's open doors, its grinning maw ready to gobble us up.

"Ready to see what you're in for?" asked Pat, our real estate agent, who smiled and swept her arm across the scene, her auburn highlights shining despite the lack of sun.

"We have to be the easiest clients you have: we agree to buy sight unseen and don't even negotiate," Scott joked.

"Yeah," she laughed, "you probably win the prize."

Pat and I serve on the board of the local musical theatre company in an old barn of a playhouse, so we are good friends. This wouldn't be the usual smarmy real estate tour, all of us being novices when it came to horse farms.

We stepped through the middle of three double sliding doors and a few paces into the mammoth building. I could not see a thing. Thinking I was temporarily blinded by the limp November sunshine, I blinked to adjust to the abrupt change in light, but the place remained practically pitch black at high noon. A long slit of a weak glow intervened where one wall met the roof-line on our right: a "window" of mustardy corrugated plastic yielded, once our eyes adjusted, only a miasmatic gloom. The close air smelled old-person-poorly-groomed musty. As Pat fumbled for

the lights, a thickened atmosphere pressed down on my shoulders, and though not mystically inclined, I registered a malevolent energy. Damp cold emanated from the dirt floor through the treads of my hiking boots and penetrated the bones of my legs. My back began to ache.

Several hot-wired tubular fluorescent lights blinked to strobe a miracle of cobwebbery that echoed a horror film version of the snow-filled country house in *Dr. Zhivago*. Dust-laden spider houses hung like fishing nets opaquely thick from ceiling to floor, pillowing webbed balloon shades from every rafter, peg and seam, so weighty and abundant, I imagined them gathered up and sold as fiberglass insulation. Generations of insects industriously worked many undisturbed years to build this webbed metropolis, and I considered renting the place out as a movie set before a much needed power wash would flush them away.

The lights decided to hum a slender illumination.

"I'd definitely have an electrician check out this wiring," Pat said.

"I thought the inspector initially gave it the okay?" I complained, flipping the switch a few times.

"It's probably not the only surprise," my usually upbeat husband scowled, hands in his fleece-lined pockets for warmth and maybe to protect his wallet from this money pit.

We focused our attention on the double rows of ten stalls leading to an open cross hall and then more stalls beyond. I saw the barn continued on, but against all our neck-straining peering the light reached no further. The splintered sliding doors hung askew on the empty stalls, their rusted, bent metal bars suggesting a prison from which rebellious inmates hurriedly escaped. *What could have bent those bars?* I wondered, only to conjure frantic, desperate animal strength.

Our wandering revealed another row of twenty or more stalls running the entire length of the barn on an aisle to the left, interrupted by a cozy pinewood tack room that recollected happier days, a few spooky storage closets we all backed away from, and two beat-up wash stalls. Split hoses hung flaccid, and bent black rubber buckets lay upended. This cavern of barn held a whopping fifty-eight stalls, and I traded my early prison impression for the more comforting one of an equine Motel 6.

The far end of the barn was capped by an indoor riding ring with the same cobweb castles but also some of the lovely honey-colored wood I'd glimpsed in the tack room. The ceiling dripped some viscous liquid, pooling in the dirt. I sneezed.

"An indoor ring is a real plus for our cold winters," Pat offered. "It would certainly draw boarders if you decide to go that route."

One end of the ring held a metal fortified wooden door that we unbolted and stepped through. A horse whinnied loudly and thumped his feet, shaking the floor. The three of us cowered, raising our arms in self-defense: its cries and ours echoed through the empty dark. Pat fumbled with some lights. Not two feet away paced a white horse, his bulging eyes defiant. He kicked at the stall walls with a ferocity that scurried us down this long side aisle that was mostly underground against the hillside. We squinted through the small barred plastic windows at the top of the back walls of the stall, eye-level to the grass outdoors. This buried barn side whispered tales of troubled inmates and solitary confinement. A damp rot seeped into our nostrils, clothes and hair. I shuddered. The wooden posts and stall walls were whittled with teeth marks, hieroglyphs from the secluded who gnawed away at insanity. I re-edited my equine Motel 6 image to that of an asylum.

The vibrant snorts and whinnies of the lone white stallion still cut the otherwise dim quiet. His agitation was understandable. He was the farm's last prized stud Stanislav, imported from Europe in El-Arabia's heyday at great cost, but now half-crazy with neglect and an even more isolated than usual stallion life. The farm hands, first too lazy and then too afraid to deal, locked him away in that interior chamber, the creature rarely encountering the outside except through the yellowed plastic eyebrow of a window. *Could this place ever have been good,* I wondered?

Speechless and depressed, we hastened from the barn to the small office building that the help camped out in when not working. It was well-worn from mucky boots and barn-male non-hygiene. Only the inhabitants proved remarkable, sitting amidst a layered fog of smoke. Two loose-skinned men slanted on two legs of their respective chairs, feet stacked on a rickety table, staring blankly at a soundless, static-screened TV rigged with a cockeyed rabbit-ear antenna. These good old boys acknowledged our hellos only by dragging more deeply on their cigarettes, blowing rings. Their contempt indicated they knew their days were numbered—the new *bourgeois* was moving in. I hated that feeling of pushing them out, of my better circumstances: *Why couldn't they be nice? We'll need help here and might have hired them*, I thought. Taking the high road, Pat cheerfully informed them that we'd have a look around, and so we did.

The little house needed an overhaul, but the layout made sense: a living room, a bedroom and two grossly offensive bathrooms, one we decided could be converted to a kitchenette. Just enough room to house a stable hand on round-the-clock duty for nighttime emergencies, when horses supposedly morph into equine drama queens. I already vaguely understood how they excel at developing infections, colic—the coverall term for myriad intestinal/digestive problems, panic attacks, and simply get their feet, heads and bodies stuck in the most unlikely crannies, usually when no one is around to help. Their legs are ludicrously delicate given their size, enabling them to run like the wind. More of air than land, they are exquisite creatures when all goes right with their polished hair shining in the sun and their manes blowing in the breeze, but they are also labor intensive and pose consistent challenges to their owners and handlers. Given the expense and the heartache and the wear and tear they impart to a barn, I began to wonder why on earth anyone bothers with them.

Scott, ever systematically practical in his due diligence, had already purchased some books about running a horse business. I dutifully read them. The unending list of crises even the experts can't avoid intimidated me. I also had experienced enough "projects" to know that we only knew the half of it. Doubtless this one belonged to the camps of renovating a house and having babies—if we knew fully what was coming at us and for how long, we might never have undertaken either. Scott was interested in the land, but the idea of large riding animals gripped me such that I subtly persuaded him over the coming weeks to keep the farm operating rather than demolish the buildings in favor of crops. Sure we had a lot to learn, but with the right help, maybe we could pull it off.

My confidence was short-lived. About this time we met the horse-farming Billingsly family. Tammy and Ken parent Keira, my daughter's schoolmate. Shared interests of school, weekend territory and now horses brought us together. It started off pretty swell. We paid a visit to their farm in Hillsdale, New York, just northwest of Salisbury, on Christmas Eve to sing carols amidst their horses on a cold, moonless night. An immaculate barn cozily housed their fuzzy, winter-insulated Icelandic horses. With manes braided and tails beribboned, they snorted and nuzzled us as long lost friends. Warming up with mulled wine and steaming cider, we sang *Frosty the Snowman* and *It Came Upon a Midnight Clear* led by two neighbors, an elderly trumpet player and a robust opera singer. We chatted with interesting people bundled in festive scarves and hats. Children and dogs, powered by their snatchings of truffles and chocolate chip cookies with each end run around the food table, completed what could have been a film set. *This is perfect*, I thought to myself, picturing a similar shindig someday in our own cobweb-free, renovated barn.

A couple of weeks later Tammy and Ken met us in Salisbury for a dinner at The White Hart Inn. As Tammy, Ken, Scott and I huddled in front of a crackling tap room fire, the talk quickly turned from kids to horses. Ken and Tammy had ownership in a large Thoroughbred breeding operation. In deep, they imparted the nitty-gritty: how unmanageable the stallions can be, and sometimes vicious; how some masturbate in their stalls: how some brood mares are hobbled when the stallions mount them to avoid injury, mainly to the valuable stallions; how the best time for a mare to become pregnant is only seven to ten days after giving birth; how dangerous it is for the handlers; what a factory it all is. *Not much different from those dreaded puppy mills*, I thought.

"You wouldn't want to come back as a brood mare, that's for sure," Tammy said.

I quizzed them about the darker aspects of racing life, about the doping of horses and unscrupulous trainers who knowingly run them unsound, the controversy of running two- and three-year-old horses before their bones and ligaments are fully stable, the betting fixes and the sad afterlife of too many washed-up, but still young Thoroughbreds. Losing racers are shifted to ever lesser tracks as their winning prospects dim. Some get rescued and patiently rehabilitated as pleasure horses, but many remain unaccustomed to life off the track and make troublesome companions. Few horses in any discipline enjoy lifelong security but the racing industry pushes the envelope. I had gleaned these ideas from newspaper accounts that appear around the big three races—the Derby, the Preakness and the Belmont Stakes—and also from Jane Smiley's account of her adventures in this great sport of speed and bravery, but my friends' experience had been a good one overall, and I imagine that the Billingslys' operation is humane and well-run. Many others aren't so. It is akin to factory farming—once remote, large scale specialization "improves" productivity, cruelty and nonsensical practices can creep in. If we witnessed the brutish life of cows, pigs and chickens, we'd force change for our own physical and mental health. But we don't see these feedlot animals—the barbaric conditions and slaughter. In the case of expensive horses bred for the track, the mare's plight of live cover while confined in a stall is not even alleviated by artificial insemination, a good practice banned for no reason other than tradition.

Back in Manhattan two days later, I ran into a morose Tammy. Her horse, one that she had nursed back to health after an infection two months before, relapsed and was put down. *Oh, boy.* I can already hear the sobs of my children prostrate over the stiffening body of some ill-fated pony; not to mention my own agony. I mourn every chipmunk I roll over, and brake for frogs. More pets mean more love, but I have also opened my family's hearts to more pain. Many mourning owners opt for a pet-less future, eschewing any more grief. I need animals in my life and make that compact, but I know Scott would prefer to avoid them and their dramas altogether.

Two weeks after our visit to El-Arabia we awaited the inspector's full report. Braced for the worst, I half-hoped a bad verdict would rescue us from our folly. How could it be good? But Pat called with surprising news: a sound main building, but some boards would have to be replaced and improved doors and a new roof put on. The inspector deemed the electrical wiring safe, but advised better light fixtures. The beams and interior woodwork, if ragged, stood stable. Most of the work tended toward cosmetic. Suspicious but willing to suspend disbelief, and despite our poor qualifications, we were green-flagged to buy fencing by the mile, have our kids' fingers mistaken for carrots, and probably go broke in the horse business. Optimistic businessman Scott considered himself that one in a thousand who could make it work.

Our imaginations about the possibilities for our "farm" ran wild. My kids thrilled at the idea of baby animals—from horses to piglets. Jane would finally get the cats her father forbade in the house, and I pictured black-and-white downy chickens and speckled brown-and-blue eggs. Clucks, oinks, neighs, baas and cock-a-doodle-doos orchestrated in my head. Elliot would learn about sex surreptitiously through animal husbandry. Goats and cheese sounded fun. And I've always liked the sage look of highland cattle—those orange shaggy coats and long horns. We'd find safe, grateful horses that Scott and I would ride around our property like Ron and Nancy Reagan, and as a family we'd gallop off into the sunset. We could play as gentleman farmers, and maybe, *just maybe*, not get our hands too dirty and our hearts too broken.

CHAPTER THREE

Keep Manhattan, Just Give Me that Countryside?

E L-ARABIA BORDERED OUR PROPERTY TO THE NORTHEAST, and we had been walking and biking past it for six years, since 1998, the year my husband Scott and I traded up our second home. Our rural village of Salisbury was founded in 1742 with the quintessential Congregational Church established on the green. About five thousand souls are spread over sixty square miles, a community remotely wedged into the northwestern corner of Connecticut where the Litchfield Hills graduate into the Berkshire Mountains of western Massachusetts.

New Yorkers during the week, we have been spending blissful weekends and chunks of the summer here for sixteen years. Our friends introduced us through a house they rented on Lake Waramaug a little further south. We visited Bob and Laurie four times, saw our city-circumscribed shih-tzu joyously leap and roll through a tender, greener-than-green spring hayfield, and fell hard for New England—the soft mountains, the distinct seasons, the Puritan remnants, the privacy. Though still renters in the city, when we saved enough money we decided to spend it on such a retreat. During our reconnaissance trip, we drove down curvy Route 41 from Sheffield, Massachusetts, into Salisbury, almost killing ourselves gawking at the undulating spread of forested hills and lake dotted pastures fully in May's fertile burst. We

agreed that the beach, a more conventional choice among NYC thirty-somethings, couldn't hold a candle to it: this was the most beautiful place we had ever seen.

Our first house purchase, made when we were childless, did not later suit our then-toddler son so we moved from our (now we can admit it) three-story, box-ugly, out-of-place A-frame contemporary into a "real" New England country house, a two-hundred-year-old colonial. Previously nestled up a long dirt road along with five neighbors against a reforested mountain, we would now dwell in the pastoral, flat, long-inhabited, pasture patch-worked, misty river valley. This house holds family histories we can only surmise, long predating paved roads, strip malls and gas stations. It is a needy house, still standing but requiring lavish attention.

Unenlightened urbanites think they want a quaint antique house until they crack their noggins against the low ceiling beams, locate that "country" kitchen unsocially hidden away at the wrong end of the house, and, most irreconcilably, see that the house sits smack up against the edge of the road. Convenient in the snowplow-less days of horse and buggy, roadside agility is not a modern-day asset given that country roads are no longer the sleepy, meandering lanes we romanticize. Country folk speed just like time-pressured urbanites, flying over hill and across dale with chainsaws, leaf-blowers and tools of every variety banging around the beds of their pick-ups. Lacking bypassing highways, the two-lane country roads also support a steady nighttime parade of tractor trailers and, combined with the absence of sidewalks; this means you risk your life by venturing a stroll. Be ready to pitch yourself into the rough at each rumble of an oncoming vehicle.

Though our house was extensively renovated and enlarged by former owners, an old house is an old house: quirky and expensive problems continually manifest themselves no matter how much money we prophylactically sacrifice to plumbers, painters, tree experts, caretakers, handymen, gardeners, pest controllers, roofers, and various other "experts." Pipes seize up in winter in spite of the thousands of gallons of fuel oil that the forty-year-old furnace sucks down. Ice dams along the roof gutters and slowly melts, working a puddle through the ceiling of the living room requiring re-plastering and a new roof. The workhorse gutters marginally prevent the cascading H2O from turning the foundation into a soupy muck and flooding the basement into a moist mold that rots the gapped pine floorboards of the uninsulated library. It is the kind of damp we are over-blessed with in merry old New England for three-quarters of the year, and we have to power wash off the external clapboards every few years before each paint job.

Since our house is so aged, with hand-laid stone walls and a dirt floor as the foundation, water in the basement shouldn't be a problem—except for sinkage: ship-like, a soggy footprint can list a house this way or that, mis-aligning the timber structure, cracking walls, bending floors and otherwise wreaking havoc from roof to attic. Not to mention the dead people I've heard were sometimes buried in basements back in the day, residents of our distinguished homestead I would not care to upset. A wished for ghost in theory beats one in practice. Despite the heroic gutters, some water and much else still manages to intrude because an old house is porous, perforated like lace. This has its advantages, I persuade myself, in terms of healthier indoor air. When the price of fuel oil soared in the seventies, people built shelters so tight that they poisoned themselves with the gasses emitted by mundane items like carpet, upholstery, Windex and hairspray, not to mention natural toxins like radon.

But impenetrability is not our problem. Water, mud, cold air in winter, hot air in summer, mice, shrews, bats, chipmunks, snakes, squirrels, frogs, mega-spiders and insects of every variety—creeping and airborne, a large noisy toad or two, and only Noah knows what else, regularly invade our space through attic, uninsulated walls, one-hundred-year old windows in two-hundred-year-old casements and of course, the crocheted stone walls of the basement. My supposedly sturdy, two-hundred-year-old, time-tested dwelling all of a sudden seems a rickety house of cards with a life of its own as regards weather and creatures. I don't begrudge the animal kingdom its bit of shelter, and mainly I let it be. I try to accept the bats as my friends: one tiny Chiropteran can devour six hundred bugs an evening while flying above my yard, so even when they graze the split ends on the top of my head when diving single file out of the eaves like machine gun pellets shot from a WWII Spitfire, I simply duck. I know better than to get my hopes up for a bug-free picnic the next day, but I imagine five mosquito bites instead of ten on each leg of my two children.

Other visitors get to me when I am cold and huddled in my high-off-the-floor creepy-crawler fortified bed (I'm in denial that anything would dare crawl up the four bedposts, despite their carved footholds). Outside, the coyotes howl it up while tearing the flesh from the bones of the neighbor's sheep, chasing away sweet dreams. The nocturnal flying squirrels perform their housekeeping at 2:00 a.m. in the attic recesses overhead. At 3:00 a.m. I lie awake imagining the elaborate condo complex they construct. As I wait for their rustling to quiet and envy my husband's soft snoring, my blood pressures as I plot vigilante tactics that rival Bill Murray's against the gopher. Furry, cute and innocent my ass: not in the wee hours they're not. I see red-rat eyes and sharp, salivating teeth. Poison? Metal traps? Death cages? Rifle? I picture myself grease-painted, my hips hoisting a sagging belt studded with Raid cans: *bring it on fur ball—I've got camo and ammo.*

But to complain is churlish. This old house is lovely with wainscoted and plastered walls and wide-board floors cut from pine trees that were already ancient when our house was long ago hand-hewn with axes, square nails and muscle. Burnished for years by mops and socks, these floors appear marbleized in places. Built for a Mr. Averill around 1801, the house boasts two-stories and higher ceilings than most and was periodically added onto and tastefully modernized since. At one low point, perhaps a century ago, it served as the police barracks. We know one of the "boys," now my age, whose parents lived in our house for forty-five years, until the early nineties. Each time I run into John in the village coffee shop or pharmacy I am treated to another anecdote of his siblings' high jinx. I learned how the kids tiptoed around the squeaky floorboard outside his parent's bedroom door on their midnight escapades. Now I smile when I slip in to give my sleeping son yet another good-night kiss, making these boards speak.

I heard about the barn the boys burned down, explaining the mysterious bits of concrete foundation I pondered at the base of the huge willow. We respect the tomb of the family Newfoundland interred beneath the stand of tall hemlocks outside the pine-paneled library bay window, and have a visual of the old dormitory-style layout of the children's bedrooms, now a spacious master bedroom suite. The pantry bell panel still carries the Borden family designations—"John's room," "parlor," "library" etc.—evidently still in use through the fifties. Some still function, not that anyone remains to do the servanting. My husband tried ringing for breakfast once, but remained hungry, feeding only upon my "yeah, *right*." Several years ago John and his family returned to scatter his mother's ashes on the property of the house she treasured.

Onto this history we have layered our own experiences. I wielded my thick black notebook of room dimensions and fabric swatches in eagerness to do justice to the beauty the house, one we never dreamed we'd ever be able to own.

"Can you believe this is ours?" I asked Scott as we wandered through the empty rooms after the closing.

"It is hard to believe. We've come a long way, baby," he joked.

As we admired the molded archway segmenting the long entry hall I pictured kissing him under the Christmas mistletoe.

"Let's not muck it up," my lovebird added.

And it was Scott's desire to start from scratch, incorporating few furnishings from our first house. Undaunted and true to our sign of Taurus, Scott and I are nesters. We moved frequently as kids, and neither of us had the pleasure of adhering to a long-established homestead, so this house was for keeps. We wanted a permanent familiarity for our kids and set about filling the house with art and personal knick-knacks accumulated from twenty-plus years of life together while adding ongoing collections. We decorated to please ourselves. We took angled photographs and countless measurements, and I lost myself in fabric books emulating the professional we didn't hire. Weekdays, Scott met me for lunch at ABC Carpet and Home and Ethan Allen to debate rugs and sofas, neglecting food. Combing local antique stores, both the precious and the junky, occupied us weekends for two years. We each seriously took ownership, with a sharp eye for every detail—I'd turn the carved snow goose on the dining table one direction and on his next walk through Scott would reverse it, or even shift it to the sideboard, the nervy bugger. I would put it back. *Why did I have to get a husband who cares so much and notices everything,* I wondered, when my girlfriends complained their husbands couldn't care less. But our battles for decorative control resulted in an eclectic home of tender care and affection, and we can both point to every "treasure" in our house and recall its provenance.

Faced with filling up this overwhelming house on a limited budget, our first purchase was a purely decorative, two-hundred-year-old wooden slatted, oval-shaped barn vent still attached to a portion of the New York state barn that once proudly held it. An artful piece of Americana, built when nails were hand-forged and square, we splurged when we really needed mattresses, chairs and curtains. It holds prideful place inside the main hall and reminds us of those early exciting days creating our first real home, one that our children will grow up in, revisit after they are released into the wild and perhaps return to marry in, one in which we hope to grow old, entertain our grandchildren, and, when tired and ready, die in. Encompassing our family mythology as a living museum curated with love and memory, the "Borden House," as it is still known locally, makes us extraordinarily happy. We may live, work and school in New York City, but Salisbury is our home. Our house feels almost alive in that it predates us, transforms with each new occupant and, barring fire, will survive us. I imagine it two-hundred years hence absorbing another family's triumphs and tragedies. As our lives wear it down a little more around the edges, maybe we will etch it into "the Bok House."

Located at the eastern end of the long Twin Lakes Road, our house sits three-winged and nine-gabled on land studded with evergreen stands of mature hemlocks and white pines. Our eight-acre plot is bordered behind by hundreds of acres of mixed forest: northern hardwoods of beech, birch and maple as well as the eastern broadleaf species of oak and hickory that are more southern. One immense weeping willow resides solitary in the middle of our back lawn gracefully holding a dream-perfect tree swing. A plain wood plank is tied to the ends of two fifty-foot lengths of rope plugged via cherry-picker to a high, uneven branch. Housing purchases tend to be emotional, and I believe we bought this house because of this swing. Elliot and Jane love arching dangerously high into the gracefully hanging softer shoots, kicking down confetti of petite leaves. Because the long ropes narrow at the top, the seat spins like a carnival ride, minus the safety belt. More worrisome, our tree man advised me that the willow is weak, unlike the muscle-bound maple or oak.

"What does that mean?"

When willows fail, they fail spectacularly," Skip answered.

We gazed up at the tree's massive horizontal arm, perfectly aligned for unobstructed swinging... and slamming a human into the ground as easily as a hammer would drive a thumbtack into corkboard.

"But we don't have a maple or an oak."

"Then you take your chances."

We cabled the willow's bicep against catastrophe, and I tried to think that the likelihood of that one trunklike, brain-crushing branch fracturing during the few hours a year my kids fly, spin and giggle into the breeze was miniscule, but my dreamy swing is now tinged by a harsher reality.

Across Twin Lakes Road, over the years we had annexed another sixty-four acres along a sluggish length of the wide Housatonic River. Sixteen of these produce hay harvested for El-Arabia's horses, twenty is woodland, and twenty-eight sprout alfalfa grown by the local farmer, Mr. Duprey, as feed for his dairy cows. Every five years he substitutes corn to replenish the soil. Once or twice in my Christmas card I had asked the Dupreys if they could plant sunflowers as the rotation crop. I pictured southern France with acres of yellow fringed, seeded black faces bobbing eight feet high to the sun. I mistily envisioned my kids running breathlessly through their thick, fuzzy stalks in the ultimate game of hide and seek; of waking up, country-relaxed and sleepy-eyed, taking my warm teacup outside to survey a spectacular golden carpet, sighing with the wonder and beauty of it all. My fantasy remained root-bound. I suppose that sunflower seeds are expensive, and not appetizing to a milk cow's palate. Oh well. My naïve request probably provoked guffaws from cows and farmers alike at the Duprey holiday repast.

It is dawning on me that farming is hard, dirty work. Once I took Elliot, then a tender four-year-old, to see the milking at the Dupreys': the 4:00 p.m. milking since we slumbered peacefully through the first at 4:00 a.m. Mr. Duprey's stout son maneuvered these bulky, hygienically challenged animals into two lines on either side of a narrow barn. The cows obliged their longstanding routine. Duprey the younger, outfitted in high rubber boots, cast an amused glance at our feet. I pretended not to care that our white sneakers were lace deep in mud and cow effluvia— "big poopie" according to Elliot—and that dozens of buzzing flies, fat black ones and translucent babies, were lighting on every moist surface, including the wide-eyed and open-mouthed face of my son.

I swatted surreptitiously as the lowing cows had their teats splashed with blue disinfectant and sucked into tubes that coaxed milk from their bulging udders into not-so-gleaming silver tanks. Duprey expertly managed six cows at a time, taking about fifteen minutes to get them in, drained, and out again. Since the farm had one hundred cows, the job took four hours, and he did this two times a day, with plenty of other jobs in between. A man of few words, he let the action speak for itself, and after a few polite questions Elliot and I bee-lined to the car. I set to work sanitizing all thirty-three inches of him, using a full bottle of Purell and the better half of a box of diaper wipes. He finally balked when I tried to swab the inside of his mouth.

Mr. Duprey the elder harvests the alfalfa in our field three or four times a summer. Timing is everything as it takes about two days to chop, churn to fully dry, and then scoop up the cuttings. Rain necessitates several more days of fluffing. The deer pray to the rain god and come nightly to feast away a good chunk of the yield. Once we counted fifty-eight bucks and does in our field: lithe, graceful beasts grazing our own open plain. We'd sigh in awe as these timid, gentle herbivores would catch a warning on the wind and, with white tails held high, collectively high-jump into the cover of brush and trees. Many passing drivers slow to view this New England version of a wildlife park. Some haul out binoculars. One car drove out across the alfalfa for a closer look, stampeding the herd.

Our family was anxious to witness the process of harvest. One July daybreak, we awoke to an old-fashioned dull red tractor with a wide series of blades circling our irregularly shaped field, working from the outside in. The completed geometry of cut greenery swirled a giant's thumbprint. But Mr. Duprey's satisfying neat sweep of the field took two days of tedium in the beating sun atop a steaming, noisy, smelly machine, and ours was only one of many fields to be tended. And, a closer look took more of the beauty out of it.

At dusk I strolled through the newly cut alfalfa. Only a few steps and I noticed some squirming in a groove of denuded soil. Four hairless, gooey creatures blindly rolled in search of cover and mother. Roughly two inches long, these babies were the color of raw salmon. Opossum, raccoon, mouse, I couldn't tell. I could not bear to touch their vulnerable half-formed skin, nor could they bear handling. *Should I stomp them out of their misery or let nature take its course?* In cowardly despair I left them, doomed as they were to death by exposure.

I later learned that naturalists request farmers hold off on the first cutting until the ground-laying birds have abandoned their nests. Even so, plenty of other creatures take time to wean, and the farmers have no choice but to occasionally plow over fawns, turkeys and other smaller unfortunates whose desperate parents can only flee the path of the steel grim reaper. The farmers say they can't see the hidden animals, only feel the "thump," and I suppose this is both the good and bad news. Farmers do not have the resources or the time to be in the rescue business, though they do it when they can.

How would I adapt to my new role of farmer? Certainly I wouldn't be milking cows in the wee hours like Mr. Duprey or dragging a plow across the fields, but I would be more than a casual weekend onlooker. Could I grow a thick skin, look death in the face every day, treat animals as commodities and not as kin? What category is horse? From what new angle of vision would I reconnect to the land as food rather than ornamental backyard? Would I sink in deeper, tilting the urban/rural balance even more in favor of the country? Could I continue to regularly flip the rural/urban switch, a debate I already had each Sunday night when I'd rather be curled up with a book in Salisbury as the sun dips down, rather than crowded for two-plus hours in a child- and animal-filled Suburban hurtling our way down the perilous Saw Mill Parkway back toward the concrete jungle? Back to school and homework; the bleating Blackberry of Wall Street work; the elbow-jostling crowds racing along the sidewalks to beat the traffic lights; the pedestrian and driver rage; the economic competition and social one-upsmanship; the stressed-out people on foot, in subways, buses and cars; the exhaust fumes; the noise, *noise*, noise, NOISE; the effort required to squeeze in a museum, a play or a dinner at a nice restaurant on occasion in order not to waste living amidst such a brilliant offering of culture and cuisine; the time tension that makes Scott and I unnecessarily cross with one another.

The country supposedly offers respite, the weekday world at bay. Riding up Fridays unfailingly relaxes and excites, the start of our time in the place we prefer, rather than its end. Once we hit the Red Rooster in Brewster for non-processed chicken tenders, perfectly unhealthy fries and ice-cream heavy milkshakes that require strenuous sucking, we breathe easier into the second half of the journey. We greedily track the interim five days' worth of change that occurred in our absence. In the spring we race the darkness to see the latest blooms, especially that one profuse daffodil field along the roadside hill in Amenia. "Isn't it beautiful?" we sigh every time. We watch for the annual migration of frogs and salamanders that first rainy, forty-five-degree Fahrenheit night in April, arguing about Scott's speed—"You hit one," "No, I didn't, that was a leaf"—and roll down our windows to get the full effect of the peepers' cacophonous mating chirps in the wetlands at the foot of our road. "Do they make you feel like a horny old toad, dear?" I'd tease, and he'd "peep" back at me with a guttural mating croak of his own.

The autumn is not outdone by spring's prizes. We keep tabs on our favorite flashy trees, comparing their color to years past and debate what makes a vibrant foliage year, the experts' theories different every year and no closer to reliability—dry year or wet, cold snap or a slow cool? The blustery wind that whooshes us, still dressed in our city duds, through our front door into sheltered warmth, the welcoming waft of the extinguished fireplaces reminding us their useful time is near. In the winter we watch the temperature gage drop as we head north, a degree variance of twenty or more that our family bets on at various landmarks—"I say eighteen at the top of Smith Hill" Elliot guesses, but Jane goes for seventeen and wins. I especially like the black, dark nights when it is impossible to see without high beams that search mile after mile for a quick-darting opossum or swooping owl. Or, those deep hours of low, fat moons that wake me and through the skylights cast my large shadow as I tiptoe, shivering out from under the down comforter and across the cold tile floor where I gratefully reach the rug only to face the freezing toilet seat. Returning to my bright-as-day bedroom, I find Scott also awake and ready to snuggle me into his heat. "How do your feet get so cold so fast?" he asks.

But the ride back on Sunday is a push against the tide of the dream into the wakefulness of work, school, city stresses.

"Do you think we could live in Salisbury full-time and be happy?" I sullenly asked Scott as we flowed from route 22's two lanes onto 684's six.

"I think so, but timing is everything. We're too young, and we still like New York. At least *I* still do." He arched his eyebrows at me. "Most people who make the switch have tired of the city, or at least its expense."

"I still like the city, too. But it's so beautiful here, and I never really want to leave, while I always look forward to coming up here Friday nights. We sleep so well in our Salisbury bed and are often ornery during the week."

"Yes, but that is because we work and deal with school in New York, while all we do in Salisbury is play. If we lived only here, it'd be different."

I sighed: it was true. I didn't want to stale our Salisbury life, its fresh snap perpetually newly born of its part-time status. Yet we "play" to a fault squeezing a full life into each forty-eight hours so that we go south exhausted and often grumpy. Our Connecticut weekend life slowly became even fuller than our NYC one, disabling it as a retreat to regroup like most weekenders. Friday nights we hustle our clan and belongings into the car, charge the traffic, stop for kid food, arrive, unload, tuck the kids in bed and hurry to our dinner-date at The White Hart before the kitchen closes at nine-thirty. Then an hour or so unpacking the two LL Bean bags of stuff we can't seem to avoid even after eighteen years of buying two of absolutely everything, going through the mail, listening to the phone messages and reading the local papers. We are usually up around 6:00 a.m. Saturday, out by 7:00 for an early walk before breakfast, and rush around to farm visits, tennis and basketball time with the kids and bike rides with and without them, the kids' singing lessons, church, time on the swing, backyard baseball, swimming at the town lake, boating on the other lake, our Saturday night date of a movie and dinner, planting the veggie garden, skiing trips to Butternut a half hour north, hikes with friends, cocktail parties and charity events, weeding the veggie garden, and, and, and!

It's a crazy pace we know we shouldn't sustain, and the constant busyness frazzles our marital relationship on occasion—days of the silent treatment, a frosty co-existence requiring energy we don't have to thaw. We pledge to slow down but balk at giving anything up. And summers pose another challenge. With Scott working in the city weekdays and the rest of us living it up in Salisbury, the weekends are fraught with him refitting into our new routine; we're still busy, I'm tired of dealing with the kids single-handedly, and he is understandably resentful that it's not always a forty-eight hour Kodak moment. Lacking day-to-day face time, we spend ten weeks vaguely out of sync with one another. This new farm could only add to our time pressure: one more thing to create, fit in, take care of and, supposedly, enjoy. Scott handles the shifts better than me and is more refreshed by the weekends than drained. But when I am really shattered on Sunday nights, my solution is "Don't you think it's time to move?"

"You poor mutt," Scott refrained his favorite line from John Updike's Rabbit series. I have always hoped irony makes it a term of endearment as opposed to Harry Angstrom's contemptuous pity for the wife with the gritty bottom he no longer loved. "You really can't take it, can you?"

I wasn't provoked. "Do you think the schools in Connecticut are as good as they say they are?"

"It's hard to know," Scott shrugged. "The kids would probably get a fine education almost anywhere because they like to learn. But I wonder if Salisbury would lose its luster when no longer paired with New York urban life. Maybe we'd take its beauty for granted."

"The winters *are* long in New England" I conceded. And those muddy months of pre-spring—you know, all of March, April, and even sometimes May. Museums, plays and movies certainly help when we're in the deep freeze."

"Anyway, I still like my work and don't want to quit yet. Plus, if we're getting into farming we'll need the money."

"But can't you imagine long walks every day, time to do all we like to do and to sit and relax? Maybe even sex in the middle of the day?" He looked at me like *yeah, right.* "Would we get sick of each other?"

"No. We'd fill our time just the same, and be just as busy. We're not happy doing nothing."

"I wonder if we'd go feral. Some people I see around here don't seem so well-groomed, kind of like the great unwashed. Maybe without the city competition to look good, you just give up."

Would I still bother with make-up, I wondered? A slave to eyelash curlers and mascara since the age of fifteen, my country weekend routine had pushed morning showers and full facial attention to the evening, if then. Maybe one cold winter day just slides into the rest, the house too drafty to bare skin, nothing to dress up for. Truly practical clothes are not fashionable, and in the lashing cold everyone looks grey and parched, their skin tissue-paper crinkled. Under flannel, puffy coats and hair-crushing hats, who'd notice any effort?

"Maybe we should stick it out a little longer, keep Salisbury that special treat," I persuaded myself as I thought of the times I debated wearing my still warm PJs under a long coat to my son's pre-dawn hockey practices.

"Yes, let's. At least for now," Scott concluded as we turned onto Lexington Ave toward "home."

THOUGH I STILL TALKED of trading the city for the country, I remained wary based on my study of English and American literature undertaken while Scott and I lived in London from 1990–1995. Writers have been accused of killing the notion of the American Pastoral since literature began; weekenders can be accused of the same land grab in trying to have it all. I thought back to my work on Nathaniel Hawthorne,

Herman Melville and Edith Wharton who cast aside Boston and New York City for rural life in the Berkshires, just a stone's throw from Salisbury. They showed me the lay of the land: the dream and the reality of both exterior and interior landscapes. They conditioned my expectations of all things rural.

I identified with each of these writers in different ways, and taken all together they gave me depth of field. Hawthorne, a parent like myself, showed me country wonders through children's eyes in his diary of a few summer weeks alone with his son Julian in Stockbridge. In Pittsfield, Melville, a "gentleman" farmer like me, pointed out the beautiful industry of stone walls, the pleasures of a crackling country hearth, and the serenity of a cow simply moving her jaws around a cut-up pumpkin. Wharton, a domestically inclined person like me, unapologetically celebrated the deep satisfaction of staking a home in Lenox: planting a garden, setting up house, taking friends, dogs and horses for upland adventures. Our shared experience of locality highlighted the woods, the hills, the pastures, the stone walls, the industry, the artistry, and the echoes of old in rural New England life that I had newly encountered there.

Their past still informs my present. I associate the history of place and people with myself and the land now under my feet. These artists depicted themselves puzzling over their landscape and culture. Reading their Berkshire-based fiction and biographies I delved through past layers of my environment, and added my own pictures, words, memories. In Hawthorne, Melville and Wharton's metaphors, scenes and stories, I recognized what I saw around me and intuited what was gone, a more informed engagement than I could have managed through my own surface vision.

Though all three authors at times gushed over the beauty of the place in their letters and fiction, they ultimately zeroed in on the darker side of country life. Hawthorne's Faustian character Ethan Brand turned fiendish when he looked too directly into the fiery lime kilns, the author's pointed warning against the annihilation of the heart by an over-intellectualized head, all in the midst of a "pastoral" environment. He questioned mechanization and progress—the new factories producing iron, paper and textiles popping up alongside rushing rivers and remote hillsides that would denude the entire region of ninety percent of its trees. Do we sin against nature? Can nature protect us from ourselves? Are we, like Brand, driven by forces beyond our control? Is evil a choice?

Melville also worked these themes into his short story "Tartarus of Maids," "inspired," or at least enhanced by his visit by horse-drawn sleigh to a Berkshire paper factory to purchase writing stock. Blank faced factory girls produce blank paper, and the monotony of assembly line mechanization is roundly criticized. This all suited my curmudgeonly fear of suburbanization and sprawl, dismal by-products of our nation's industrial past and current wealth. Fortunately for western Massachusetts and northwestern Connecticut, the smoky industrialization of the nineteenth century blew out before it irreparably ruined the land, but poverty and depopulation followed in its wake and contemporary menaces newly threaten. McMansions pave over farmland, metal barns replace old wooden beauties, chain stores and strip malls render Main Streets obsolete, and I often despair.

Melville and Hawthorne understood that the country life was not a hideout from the "real" world. Both Hawthorne's Ethan Brand and Melville's Pierre characters were country boys afforded little protection by their rural upbringing. Life and choices drove them from their childhood pastoral into suicide. And neither author remained in his New England country idyll—they both returned to "civilization," Hawthorne back to Concord within twenty months, and Melville back to the docks of New York City after thirteen years.

Wharton high-tailed the country life too, though it long continued to define her alter ego. Despite her society upbringing and the intellectual company she preferred, she doggedly protested she was happiest in the country and should have remained the country hermit. Yet, skittish of country isolation after ten half-years in Lenox, she moved to France, never returning to the place she prized. In her autobiography, *A Backward Glance*, she wrote: "The Mount was my first real home, and though it is nearly twenty years since I last saw it (for I was too happy there to ever want to revisit it as a stranger) its blessed influence still lives in me." Should I believe her words or her actions? Despite her personal country experience, her fiction portrayed silently suffering characters trapped in hidden rural poverty. Though heavily criticized by her Berkshire neighbors, her novella *Ethan Frome* remains one of her masterpieces. Its less well-known sister story *Summer* is similarly bleak.

I wonder whether these authors' fictional creations persuaded them to leave. Full-time country status ultimately didn't work for these rural sojourners, and I do not want to go similarly sour on Salisbury. Maybe truth lies in the old adage "too much of a good thing." The slide into country life can defeat as well as inspire, though for most of us the experience encompasses a middle ground between awe and terror. I have felt the petrifying aloneness of a late autumn sun dropping below the edge of a vast and impersonal forested hillside; a few minutes of such existential angst can last a lifetime, rich or poor, writer or plumber. And, any romantic version of nature was quickly dashed once I got lost in the woods; its seemingly benevolent face turned a sinister cheek. I both yearn for my country idyll and fear its isolation. Maybe it is best I stick with what I've got and continue to fantasize about an alternate life.

CHAPTER FOUR

Animal Kingdom

·⊂══════⊃·

MY NOTIONS OF COUNTRY LIFE sprouted from shallow roots in American suburban soil. In childhood I followed a well-trod path through fairy tales and backyard, woodsy adventures only to depart nature and the imagination to study Economics at college and work ten years in the retailing business. In my thirties, I returned to a more formalized study of nature as part of my British-based nineteenth-century literature degree and emerged the other side of Romanticism fully versed in its pastoral tradition of the country as the seat of innocence and adventure. To dim the stars in my eyes, postgraduate study taught me to be wary of an anthropomorphic approach to nature and that transporting nature encounters are often slippery. They happen surreptitiously, almost by osmosis, or as Hawthorne described, when you are lucky enough to catch nature unawares, obliquely from the corner of your eye. If you resort to force, or, if you'll excuse the feminized metaphor, try to grab her by the throat and shake the life out of her, you will be sorely disappointed. Any deep appreciation of country life is an acquired skill hard-won by knowing a place well, penetrating beyond the desired spectaculars to more unexpected subtle surprises. Not every encounter is lovely, not every pleasure void of pain.

But once back in Salisbury I only half-expected reality to adjust my "rose-color spectacled view," to borrow Wharton's borrowed phrase. I still held my youthful visions and had to earn a more mature knowledge,

not through books, but up close and personal. And New England nature did prove elusive to my suburban-untrained body and mind, requiring patience and time—not something that this instant gratification-addicted American was good at. At first, Salisbury did and did not live up to my high expectations. Sure, it was picture-beautiful upon my first visits—the greens, the blues. But once we settled in, nature's revelations proved minor and occasional.

An eager beaver that first year in 1989, I awaited a grand flotilla of natural beauty, song and especially wildlife: that perfect idyll, that serene arcadia. I sat back to enjoy the parade. But I made a poor witness, my sensory awareness dulled by the animated Disney and TV of my youth in nature-parched northern New Jersey topped off by fourteen years pounding the pavements of Philadelphia and New York City. Simple contrast was not enough to yield true appreciation. After the first blush of amazement had passed, I tried to deny my disappointment. I looked so hard and saw very little from my imagined preview.

There were exciting moments, like a bobcat on the deck of our first house, stealthy, short-tailed and catlike, but wild. Or the fawn that slept against the hillside in our yard for the entire day, until, out of fear for its health, I approached it with a carrot. Of course it upped and fled, rendering me naïve and ridiculous. Apparently, does often park their newborns in a "safe" environment while they graze nearby if not exactly within sight. This mama did not anticipate do-gooder urbanites wielding orange sticks at their progeny. Stubbornly childlike, I still worked at my adventures to take things up a notch.

One night in our first house I awoke to a strange keening. The dark and the night had both enticed and terrified me for many years. Night noises are fearsome in the "quiet" of the country, not conducive to sleep for the neurotic. I had often awoken those early years, convinced that some animal or an escaped maniac was about to get us. It is unnerving at first to be so exposed. I was accustomed to living in a high rise apartment inaccessible to intruders, the building entrance policed by vigilant doormen, and my own front door satisfyingly bolted with steel. In a country house, locking doors seems silly with ground floor windows in abundance and no near neighbors to attend my screaming SOS. Ditto security systems: by the time the lone state trooper patrolling sixty square miles arrives, my assailant could have me carved up, roasted on a spit, the dinner dishes done, and be well on his way to Foxwoods casino.

So I avoided staying by myself in Salisbury, and the few times I braved it, breathless panic courtesy of my overly keen attention to what was not in every shadowed corner I investigated spared me little sleep. It wasn't until my forty-fifth year that I stopped being afraid alone at night. It took two kids and a husband to convince me that any "alone time" was too precious to waste a second of it worrying about some backwoods Joad trying to kill me. Kids helped me get over a lot of things in life, if not exactly grow up, and I replaced my irrational fear for my own safety with more rational ones regarding my kids. Now when I am alone in the country, I lie in bed worrying about Jane or Elliot in a taxi accident or an apartment fire, the homicidal lunatic on my own tail be damned.

Well, back to the strange noise. It was the wail of a lone child in the woods.

"Scott, wake up," I whispered, propped on my elbows with ears tuned.

"What? What's the matter?"

"Did you hear that?"

"Hear what?"

"A scream or a screech."

"I don't hear anything. Just go back to sleep," he yawned. "It's probably just some animal."

"SHHH," I cupped my ear. "Listen."

We turned our heads toward the open window. The cry echoed again, clear and eerie.

"That. It sounds like a baby," I said, certain.

"Why would a baby be out in the woods?"

"I don't know. Lost, maybe?"

We heard it again, loud and clear. It had to be human.

"Let's go find it." I was wide awake, heart pounding toward a rescue mission.

"You've got to be kidding." Scott locked my eyes to check my mental health.

"Well, I'm going," I said, petulant.

I fumbled on my robe, slipped into Scott's Docksiders and plodded out into the dewy night. Billions of crickets and frogs chirped and bellowed. The night is *loud* around here. What do they mean "dead of night"? Everything is not just living, but partying. A misnomer equivalent to "sleep like a baby": if you've had one, rocking and singing to it for hours before stealthing back to your own forgotten bed, you know the truth. "Sleep like a teenager"—try waking one up in time for school—would be the more appropriate saying.

I didn't think to pack a flashlight, but no matter, I was pumped. I strained my ears toward the desperate call. *Come on*, I urged, *Where are you?* I jumped off the deck into the brush. *Snakes?* I high stepped to perch on a rock. It was very dark. That's why I needed Scott—power in numbers. I'm big on ideas, but cowardly in follow-through.

I strained with listening.

Nothing.

The sound ended as mysteriously as it began. Foolish once again, I swatted at the mosquitoes planting bites on my ankles and temples that would plague me for days. I crept back into bed, inching so as not to wake my husband who, with a little luck, would forget all of this by morning. My expectation of tending to some ethereal changeling or injured, grateful animal lay fallow. Some years later a radio program informed me that certain nocturnal animals sound just like babies crying, and many people just like me have gone a'hunting for to save them.

One autumn night several years later, Scott and I joined a group of Nature Conservancy-led hikers to call for owls. Only a few hardy souls signed up, but this smacked of adventure—dark and wild, yet with a protector who knew the territory. I had read *Owl Moon* to my son, a lovely children's book about a boy and his father summoning owls, and I have always wanted to communicate with any animal on its own terms. Frank led us across protected land to a fen, swampy with dead, leafless trees. Their bleached trunks silhouetted starkly, even against the moonless sky. On the way, Frank gamely suggested we douse our flashlights. Blind in the black dark, we intuited the verge of the trail with the edges of our shoes. It was slow-going, and I instinctively looked downward to spy the trail.

My eye caught something aglow.

"Frank, what is that?" I asked, uselessly pointing to the verge.

"Where?"

Feeling for his arm, I led him to a white, irregular rectangle, motionless but brightening under our gaze. Frank squatted to better identify.

"Wow, that's cool. It's a fungus that makes phosphorus. It's quite unusual to see one so large."

I glowed with pride at my find.

Of course we didn't disturb the glowing fungus of our nature hike, but we all had a good look, and it proved the highlight of the night. For all our expert and inexpert calling, no unwise owls flew over to astonish us with their graceful beauty. Again, I would have to wait to see one of my favorite creatures. To this day I have only seen a few in the wild, swooping across the road at night, too quick for me to see their big eyes and charming head swivel. Occasionally I hear their nightly hoots in the woods behind our house though, and I reply my own toward conversation.

All in all, Salisbury was not as exciting as I had imagined with nonstop adventure, action, stunning beauty, animals in abundance, creepy woodsmen and peasanty women. Isn't that what we've been fed through wilderness epics, pioneer stories, and fairy tales, not to mention notions of romantic environments and the sublime still filtering into us through literature, paintings and the movies: raw nature, red in tooth and claw, and beautiful like the candy-colored Land of Oz? Instead, my new country life, lived only on the weekends (part of the problem), flowed awkwardly. Flashes of brilliance only intermittently punctuated long periods of ho-hum that I strove to gussy up into my literary-romantic, Wild Kingdom wardrobe of "the country."

Only after years of slow understanding, when I stopped working so hard, relaxed and let it happen, did I begin to find the under-layer of wonder in the ever changing, far from perfect, often smallish miracles that make up New England country life. Individually these moments may seem paltry—like that first hummingbird that arrives at my feeder the same week each May. But over time and with patience they added up, and I sensitized to them. That ruby-throated flutterer became spectacular when I figured him possibly the very same individual from last year, counting on my reliable refreshment after an arduous migration from the Yucatan Peninsula. And this year he lingered by my ear, drinking from the hanging petunia blooms as I read and dozed in the shade of the porch. Or the Monarch butterfly that enjoyed a long rest on Jane's knee; or the chipmunks that play hide and seek with our dog along the tunnels of the stone wall.

Such encounters filled the freed-up space my departing dullness availed, and nature and I inched toward each other. Eventually I reached a level of fullness, an accumulation of experiences, ordinary and exceptional, such that I was often overwhelmed by all I increasingly witnessed. When I *waited*, this environment offered up simple and complex high notes to my more sensitive and receptive self. Never diminishing or growing tedious, every new and repeated experience elicited more satisfaction and deeper happiness. I was taught to read this particular place: the exquisite nature I sought in the beginning was there all along—mine now, not because I muscled it, but rather received it as a gift to my now humbler self.

With my adjusted powers of awareness, Salisbury's genteel profusion of renewable beauty often hits me with exceptional clarity. Especially in the summer I experience an almost chemical happiness when I drive along the many familiar scenic routes, both main and back roads. These emollient days—the sun blares but not in my eyes, warming my skin. The trees' highest leaves, encouraged by the west wind, tickle the expanse of blue sky, their rustle a lively chorus. The road is smooth, clear and clean from yesterday's thunderstorm. Feeling light and perfectly content, even dying might be acceptable. I'm in the now, the moment, not bothered by the past or anticipating the future—so exquisite, it's enough for one lifetime. It lasts about a minute or two if I am lucky. Ahhhhh... but hold on.

What's that?

Oh no.

Please don't let it be....

But there it is.

Road kill.

A once robust, happy-go-lucky raccoon, now freshly dead, its back half smeared along the macadam, red and raw, an extended intestine, a petite black paw curled in; or, a week old carcass, bloated beyond belief, arms sticking out like the fingers of an inflated surgical glove; or the flattened, soggy fur of one such balloon recently exploded.

I will never harden to road kill, and could shed tears for each and every one if I let myself. I had read about the naturalist poet Barry Lopez, who pulled over to retrieve every flattened critter he came across, make-shifting a grave and whispering a prayer. I feel the urge to be so noble, but am usually time-deprived, or not dressed properly, or afraid of disease, or I tell myself *I'll get it on the way back*, or, or, or.... Instead, I well up from helplessness and try to save the overflow of emotion for the damaged-but-not-yet-dead, *about-to-be-*road kill: the ultimate bane of country life. With so much driving amongst copious wildlife, murder happens from the best of us. While it is amazing how many chipmunks and squirrels manage to race themselves around the obstacle course of four tires on the move, the raccoons, opossum and deer aren't quite so gymnastic.

BAM!

One minute we were heading contentedly home from a summer stock play at the Sharon Playhouse, late afternoon, refraining *My Fair Lady*— *All I want is a room somewhere, far away from the cold night air . . .* —the next we faced death. A large deer tore out of the tall corn stalks lining the road on our right. Only a fraction of a second's glimpse of brown fur in motion out of the corner of my eye preceded our plowing into it with the front end of our small Honda.

"Oh my God, oh my God!"

The impact pushed us left into the oncoming traffic lane, mercifully clear of vehicles. My friend Paula gripped the steering wheel and wrestled us back into our lane, all the while shoveling that poor animal about half a mile down the road. It fell away fifty yards before we managed to stop.

"Oh my God, oh my God!" Paula repeated.

"Paula! It's okay. You did great. We're all okay. Are you okay Elliot?" I'm pretty good in a crisis.

"Yeah. What happened?" he asked, wide-eyed.

"We hit a deer. Did you fall forward or hit your head or anything?"

"No. I mean I came forward but didn't hit anything."

"He came out of nowhere," Paula moaned.

"I know, I know. There's no way you could have avoided him."

I looked out the back window. The deer lay still. I again checked that we were all intact and shakily exited the car. The driver behind us had already stopped where the deer was sprawled out. *Please let it be dead*, I silently begged, knowing a bad scene could be exponentially worse if we had to deal with a slowly dying, panicked animal. I didn't want myself, but especially not my son to witness anything so dreadful, not yet. I instructed Paula to wait with Elliot. I jogged back meeting a man from the house across the street who had heard the collision and ran out to help.

"Is it dead?"

"Yes. Are you all alright?" the neighbor asked.

"Thankfully, yes. It was pretty scary."

"This happens all the time here. At least twice a month we hear tires squealing. I'll call the police so they can get it picked up."

I took a last glance at the largish doe, trunk scraped up and legs tangled, her strong neck and head gracefully arched. I wondered why their long tongues always loll out, a last indignity. With nothing left to do, we retreated home.

Paula and I tucked Elliot into bed and bemoaned our fate and raised a glass of tranquilizing whiskey to any and all guardian angels. The car sustained a broken headlight but otherwise seemed unscathed. Yet two days later, as Paula gassed up, the traumatized Honda refused to start, debilitated by a slow leak of fluids. Now when I travel that stretch of road, I remember that deer. Still tender to that spot, I beg Scott to slow down, as if our chances of a run-in are higher there than anywhere else in town.

The next time, Scott was behind the wheel. Elliot and Jane slept peacefully in the back of the Suburban, but Elliot's friend Max, an inner city kid with little country experience, was too excited to sleep. He sat in the middle of the back seat with big eyes staring out the front windshield as we plowed over a fawn following behind his running mother who we had just barely missed. The creature rumbled gingerly under the chassis, front to back, and sick gathered in my stomach. A baby! Our high beams torch-lit the entire scene—a ghastly movie set. My distress grew realizing that Max was alert to every second of his country adventure. Worrying that it might not be dead, I persuaded Scott to turn around to check, and also to make sure that the doe did not hang around endangering herself, and, if necessary, warn other drivers. An image of a mother nosing around her dead fawn had me on the brink of tears, held back only for Max's sake.

"Did you see what happened, Max?" I asked, keeping my cool.

"Yeah. We ran over that animal."

"It was a deer, Max. Unfortunately it happens in these parts because there are so many. I'm sorry you had to see it."

He remained silent as we circled and saw the fawn dead-still with the mother nowhere in sight, though I imagined her big doe eyes accusing from the dark woods. As Bambi's mother whispered: "*Man* was in the forest." I wish Walt had spared us that film.

Being a fairly young fawn made it more like hitting a raccoon than a deer, but we sustained some front-end damage nevertheless. Unfairly, I took my helplessness out on Scott.

"You shouldn't have been driving so fast. You *always* drive too fast."

"I wasn't driving too fast. They just came out of nowhere. Anybody would have hit them. Don't make me feel worse than I do already."

He was right, and we had Max to consider.

"Are you alright, Max?"

"Yeah."

DEER ACCIDENTS cement in your mind forever. It's like remembering where you were when Kennedy was shot or when the Twin Towers crashed down. Like the one we helped get euthanized on New Year's Eve; and another time, on our return to the city, when I spied a downed deer just short of the village.

"Oh no," I cried. "Scott, did you see that?"

"What?" Elliot asked.

"An injured deer."

"Yeah, I saw it," said Scott wearily, knowing what he was in for.

The young deer sat oddly collapsed, upright on its torso, head up and alert and eyes perplexed, in no obvious distress. But all four legs were splayed outward in a double split. My eyes welled.

"Pull into The White Hart so I can ask Larry to call a trooper."

Exiting the inn I passed a man striding in with purpose.

"Did you see that deer, too?" he asked.

"Yes, I just asked the desk manager to call it in."

"That's good," he said, turning back to his own potential assassin of a vehicle. "He's paralyzed for sure, and there's no sense in his panicking for very long."

"It's so horribly sad," I couldn't help saying, hoping for a humane trooper. I had heard many don't like to discharge their weapons because of the paperwork.

"Yeah, but it happens. They come out of nowhere," he said, repeating the common refrain from anyone who has hit a deer.

WE HAVE ALSO RESCUED SOME ANIMALS or tried to anyway. We returned a baby bluebird to the house from which it tumbled, relieved to see the mama still bringing food. A few weeks later we watched the youngsters' first flights, taught incrementally by their parents until one day they vanished. An empty nest: *what will it be like when my kids leave?* Another summer the four of us were playing baseball in the back yard. The sunny day revved our endorphins, and even Elliot was kind about Jane's swinging misses with the bat. As Scott pitched and I played out-field we noticed a hawk circling low and lower over our heads. Its crazy pattern chased us together and set us thinking Alfred Hitchcock. With our eight eyes staring, it crashed straight into the side of the house, just alongside the window of a gable, bounced off and fell to the roof motion-less; two thumps.

"What the heck?" Elliot asked, his hands shielding his eyes from the glare.

"I don't know," replied Scott. "Maybe he planned on going through the window."

"What's the matter with that birdie?" Jane asked.

"I don't know, sweetie. Maybe it saw the sky's reflection on the glass and got confused," I said.

Many small birds have crashed into our paned windows over the years, even though we've made window art to deflect them. Usually, after a bewildered rest they autopilot away. But I was already anticipating the damage control Scott and I could deploy about this large dead flyer that had not aimed for the window.

To our surprise, the hawk resurrected. It flew off and returned, circling haphazardly and, with all our eyes glued, it dove straight into the side of the same dormer, knocking itself again into stillness on the slanted roof.

"Oh no," cried Elliot. "Not again."

"There is definitely something wrong with that bird," I said.

We watched for a long time, fully expecting Lazarus to fly again.

"Will he be alright again, Daddy?" Jane asked.

"Maybe Janie, but I think we'll have to leave him alone for awhile and give him some time."

"Shouldn't we try to help him?" Elliot asked.

"I don't know much about birds, El, and that one may be sick in a way that we don't want to touch it," I said.

West Nile virus had been reported among birds in the area. Later I heard a theory that birds commit suicide in this manner when unwell. That is certainly how this appeared, but I generally curb my anthropomorphic tendencies.

"He may need a good long rest," I said, giving Scott the nod which means the deep sleep, and we better think fast how to handle this.

"I hope he'll be okay," Elliot said. "Here, Mom, catch." He threw me the baseball.

Our continuing glances did not work any miracles. We headed in for lunch and planned a funeral for the bird should it fail to fly again. Sure enough, the next day it remained, stiffening, until our caretaker George climbed a tall ladder to retrieve it with gloved hands. He dug a hole in the tall grass at the edge of our yard, and we buried the beautiful bird.

"You were a good birdie, but now you're dead," Jane said, her voice sad, her lip pouting, a dramatic little mourner.

"I hope you had a good life," Elliot rejoined. "I wish you could've lived longer."

Jane sang a made-up-on-the-spot song, Elliot sprinkled a handful of torn grass over the mound, and that was that. No tears. No existential angst. But the bird funeral proved popular. When next a smaller bird hit a window and didn't revive we staged another, more elaborate burial. We took turns holding the little sparrow and admired its intricate design—rubbery clawed feet, patterned feathers etched in infinite shades of brown, silky white breast—so delicate, soft, perfect.

Jane sang more songs, a stone marked the plot, flowers were picked and laid in memoriam, and stories illustrating the bird's imagined life and family were concocted. I wished I remembered my Tennyson. Both kids repeatedly visited the grave that day and tried to dig it up the next, but I put the kibosh on that, citing respect for the dead. In a few days it was completely forgotten.

Bird trauma dogged us. The next summer a game of badminton edged us from the lawn toward the tall grass. A movement caught my eye, only about ten yards to my left.

"What's that?" I asked Scott, moving slowly toward it.

"Is it a cat?" He thought of the feral opportunists that hide in the bushes under our birdfeeders.

"I think it's a turkey." I motioned the kids to keep back.

It is unusual to get this close to a turkey. They have keen eyesight and are swifter of foot than you might guess for such large, awkward fliers. When we moved to Salisbury sixteen years ago, turkeys were rare. The few released onto Canaan Mountain twenty years ago slowly multiplied, and now a large group often crosses our yard, nervously bobbing and weaving through their reclaimed territory. They espy every movement, even our still, barely breathing bodies through the glass in the house as we watch them, and our fast little dog Velvet doesn't have a chance even when she happens to be lying in wait in the grass.

This turkey sensed me and ran a few paces. At each sound of my creeping it raised and cocked its head in my direction.

"It can hear but I don't think it can see me," I reported.

A crust covered the top of its head, including its eyes. I inched within two feet, and it scurried only slightly away. This was a blinded turkey.

"What do we do now?" I queried.

"I guess we just let nature take its course," Scott hit the badminton birdie back to the impatient kids. WHACK. "You know the animal control people" WHACK "aren't particularly interested in helping." WHACK. "You'll never get anywhere" WHACK "with them."

He was right. Once we called about a limping, mangy coyote staggering around our field in the middle of the day. We started with the police and chased a long sequence of phone numbers from the EPA to local animal control. No "authority" could help. I remembered John Bottass, our neighboring farmer telling us, "You're best off just shootin' it yourself."

We do not own any firearms, but occasionally we hear a few shots go off nearby. Our next door neighbor, Mrs. Kilner, was known to prowl nocturnally, aiming an ancient rifle at coyotes who menaced her rescued greyhounds. I am not in favor of guns in most circumstances, but the one good argument for weaponry is to be able to put down, quickly and efficiently, an injured and suffering creature. That we euthanize animals is one way we are more humane to them than to ourselves.

We left the turkey alone, allowing some space to avoid stressing it. But later that afternoon it remained, having scarcely moved. I thought of the possible nighttime scenarios. It could be quickly dispatched by a couple of coyotes. That would be the best. Or it could make it through the night, and the next and the next, panicky and ill until it starved to death. Either way, I knew I couldn't rest with inaction. We eventually trapped the turkey with an overturned recycling bin and transported it thirty minutes to the Sharon Audubon Center where they examined and euthanized it. Our adventure had taken about three hours, and I hoped Elliot had learned something from it. A sad outcome, but we did our best and alleviated some suffering. Dying animals are tough for most people, and as my kids increasingly cozy up to our pets, from our wonderful seven-year-old poodle Velvet to the menagerie at the farm, they will suffer too. I hope they will agree, beyond the illnesses witnessed and losses keenly felt, that the presence of animals, their unconditional love and companionship, is well worth it.

My husband Scott, however, has steadfastly kept his distance from our pet canines, and though he now denotes the first dog of our married life his favorite, this affection latently bloomed after "Peanut's" demise. My stepmother surprised newly wed Scott and me with this shih-tzu puppy straight from a puppy mill in New Jersey. Only four months after graduation from college, two months of marriage, and two months of law school for Scott and work for me, we were already parents. Scott bristled at his mother-in-law's imprudence, but I secretly delighted, and our little "Nutter," inbred and crazy, barked and chewed her way through our new teak furniture and the baseboard moldings of a series of rental apartments for the ten years it took her to outgrow her puppyhood.

Peanut never learned a thing: would not come, sit or stay and ran just out of reach every time we needed to catch her. Never fully trained, I scrubbed a lot of carpet, and my impatient father almost killed her several times—she was that infuriating. She craved water and would leap from my dad's speedboat at forty miles an hour to take a swim: we would scoop her up in a fish net, eventually outfitting her in a tiny doggie life jacket with a handle on the back for easier retrieval. What she lacked in brains she made up for in kooky charm, and she saw us through the first sixteen years of our marriage, surviving six months of quarantine during our move to London, my first pregnancy, and the first two years of Elliot's life. Putting her down was one of the hardest things I have ever had to do.

It took five pet-less years for me to realize I was not as happy a person without a dog in my life. More careful this time, through a breeder I found our current Velvet, a smart and slavishly affectionate poodle. Meek and sweet, she lacks Peanut's high-octane personality, but is much easier to live with. Whereas Peanut would inevitably vomit in the car, Velvet dreams peacefully as we stop and start through New York traffic, sticks to me like glue, comes whenever I call her, and as the quintessential lap dog, contentedly drapes her black furry body across my thighs, resting her head on the armrest of my desk chair to keep me warm while I write. But Scott focuses on her only fault: she begs at the dinner table. Scott *always* sees the bright side, so how does he only see the bad in Velvet, I wondered?

Unlike Scott, I had been weaned on dogs. A largish white miniature poodle "JouJou" loudly growled his teeth into my diaper to tug toddler me from the freedom of the front yard. Unfortunately, once I was safe in my mother's care, JouJou would take off after his true passion—chasing every car on the road. He limped home from his last rampage to quietly die on the back door rug. Our subsequent small white toy poodle "Tigre" ate only table scraps and lived twenty-one years, toothless and blind but still perky to the end. Llaso apso "Boucher" served as child substitute to my empty-nester parents when I left for college. Alongside my immediate canine companions, my grandfather's sleek black mutt Velvet hid deep in the closet under the eaves when it thundered, and my aunt's clumsy rust-red Irish setter and my grandmother's series of graceful afghans showed me the pleasures of the larger breeds. I remember them all fondly.

Even the mean ones that scared me I revered. My cousin's grandparents had a boxer-pit bull mix named Butch to protect their one-room home down the port in Elizabeth, New Jersey. Butch would just as soon tear your head off as look at you unless called off in Polish by Bubba or JaJa. But that dog adored the old lady, and I can still see Butch with his front paws up on the chipped lip of the porcelain kitchen sink smiling broadly while Bubba brushed his gleaming white, lethal teeth.

Scott had only one childhood experience with a pet. Before he fully embedded into the household, a frothing springer spaniel named Rusty bit the neighbor kid's bottom and was shipped off to the pound. Too bad: if only his parents tried another dog, maybe Scott would be more interested in our growing animal family. But we are formed by early experiences and follow our own inclinations. I make do with one house pet when I'd prefer several, and Scott had endured our problem child Peanut in our new marriage and now suffers my over-enthusiastic affection for our excellent Velvet. So in tune on almost everything else, we stare across a gaping divide when it comes to pet adoration. I envision other couples cozy on the couch, with a cat and a dog squeezed in between, waxing eloquent about their furry children, just as we do about Elliot and Jane.

I have not given up: someday he may surprise us all with a deep and abiding affection for a dog, a bunny, a cat or even a horse.

CHAPTER FIVE

Not Much of a Plan

A S OUR MAY IST CLOSING DATE for El-Arabia approached, we fully registered our limited experience. Our romantic excitement did not quite prepare us for the responsibility of operation. Now what do we do, just up and run it? Plug in a few horses and throw them some hay occasionally?

We had enough on our plates already—two homes, two kids, too busy. Moreover, we were not horsey material—we liked things neat, clean and safe. We are sensible, practical people, and horses are not sensible, practical animals—they are expensive, delicate and needy. Scott, a lawyer turned investment banker, grew up in small town Michigan, dresses in hand-tailored suits and works all hours not dedicated to me, the kids and sleep. While he can readily put together a merger of two titans of industry, he crumples when faced by a six-year-old's unassembled hot wheels track or a "fun to do together" Lego space station. Talk of building a tree house turns him visibly pale. Although he claims to have picked cherries and asparagus for a nickel a pound as a kid, after twenty-plus years of marriage to the man, I still find it hard to believe.

Scott had ridden horseback only once, a trail ride I bullied him into when we first moved to Salisbury. As we raced along a wooded path, Scott's massive smart-aleck horse ran his knees into every close tree trunk and his head into all low-hanging branches.

"Duck," our fifteen-year-old leader repeatedly yelled.

Scott's wrathful eyes bored into my back as we recklessly flew along the mountain trail.

I boasted a bit more experience. As an invincible teenager I rode western a few times at one of those backwoods operations where they took your money and cared little for your life. The horses meandered all pokey heading out from the barn, but look out once they turned for home. They would full-gallop back, and if you lost your grip you got dumped in the dust and left for dead. Later, when Scott and I lived in London, I hacked a few times in Hyde Park. The stable girls do not baby you there: their rule of thumb is that you are not a real rider until you've spilled a dozen times. Once mounted, ten or so of us would cross an unforgiving cobblestone lane and a honking London ring road to reach the park. The Dickensian charm attracted tourists, many who were riding virgins. "How hard can it be?" I imagined them asking their friends and spouses. "The British are so polite, so civilized." Well, the British and their horses hide a wild streak—they invented fox-hunting after all—and few of the uninitiated could anticipate the Rotten Row, a half-mile stretch of soft dirt where the horses like to let loose.

At the top of Rotten, our guide barked in Cockney English: "Those of you who fancy a gallop go on ahead. If not, hold your horses back and trot along."

A few of us nervously cantered off. Horses sense incompetence in a nanosecond, and incompetents are useless at containing a thousand muscled pounds of herd animal hard-wired to stick with his buddies. So off everyone explodes in a pack resembling the Derby, faster and faster because once they get going, horses love to race. A few bodies go flying, and I had dismounted more than once to help collect the rider-less horses that wandered off to eat the emerald grass amongst the picnickers. One Japanese woman, who spoke no English but communicated fluently through the universal language of hysteria, refused to get back on—who could blame her—and the two-leggeds led the four-leggeds in slow and dismal return to the stables, those quaint cobblestones clopping a more gothic music.

Once Stateside, I rode occasionally at local barns in Connecticut, content to hermetically seal myself in riding rings concentrating on how to walk, halt, turn, trot, and, to a limited extent, canter. But I had only minimal technique and had yet to tack up or groom a horse. My son, on the other hand, started riding at eight. He immediately possessed balance, rhythm, confidence, respect, and listening skills: an ideal rider young enough to take the punishment, like when the grumpy lesson horse Sultan bit Elliot's finger. He cried, hard, and I berated myself for encouraging him to feed the friendly horse. He also weathered his first fall, again courtesy of Sultan, a slow motion topple when the trot abruptly halted, and that mercifully I didn't witness. Shook up, but with more respect, he climbed back on.

After each of Elliot's half dozen lessons, we would hold Jane up on the saddle and walk her a few paces.

This was the sum total of our checkered past in the horse world.

And now we owned a horse farm?

What had we done?

Buyer's remorse took up residency in the stalls of our brains if not our hearts. A horse farm is reputed to be a black hole for losing money, a close third to roulette and the lottery, maybe tied with inn-keeping, a business Scott and I know a little something about. Since 1990 we have owned The White Hart Inn, the local watering hole that shelters leaf-peeping tourists and parents visiting their kids boarding at the resident prep schools, not to mention the regulars who imbibe at the popular tap room bar. Over two-hundred years old, it holds court on the village green as the foremost historic landmark in town. Its twenty-six rooms and restaurant have served the town well. The broad columned porch anchors a comfortable building with a patina that welcomes the casual and the posh. It seems everyone has a story about their experiences there, and no matter where Scott and I go in the world, we find six degrees of separation circling back not to Kevin Bacon (who has a house in the area and is an occasional customer), but to The White Hart Inn.

The White Hart "family" echoes a soap opera and it is probably best we do not know even half of what else goes on alongside business, but, all in all, inn-keeping has been fun. We further integrated into the community and, though the business will never support us, it steeled our nerves to our next unplanned adventure of horsekeeping.

In three months we would close on the horse farm property and have to hit the ground running with repairs and renovations on that May 1st or lie dormant over the long winter. Not the types to postpone gratification, intuitively Scott and I objected to years passing with the farm horseless. But even the basics were undecided: should we lease the farm outright, maintain total control, or some combination?

What we needed was an expert: a competent, take-charge, honest, likable farm manager who could ultimately run the business but start immediately advising us how to set it all up. Logical yes, but Salisbury offered a limited employment pool. This job required someone multitalented, dexterous and independent. On the one hand, we didn't want to turn the place completely over to someone who ignored our input and evaded control; that was why we bought it in the first place. On the other, we could never educate ourselves, find the contractor, and oversee the planning, let alone the construction, from New York City in three short months. Scott may have purchased all the how-to books, which I gave a thorough read, but wisdom is realizing what you don't know. We wised up rapidly.

Word of our impending purchase grapevined through our small community.

"Have you heard that the Boks bought that old Johnson place? What do they know about the horse business?"

No doubt their chuckles descended to belly laughs with "They paid *what*? For *that*?"

In the eyes of the local population, weekenders possess more money than sense, spending it lavishly on the real estate (thereby pushing up prices and the cost of living) and then expecting the locally provided services to come cheap. I am acutely conscious of the full-timers' angle of vision, their long witness to the forgotten years of slow-moving properties and declining values. But we've been here long enough to remember and to have been burned. We lost money on our first house in Salisbury. Buying at the top of the market in 1989, we resold ten years and many improvements later at the same price. But since 2002, it has been a stretch of rising prices. The vast sums people cough up for their Litchfield County real estate is general knowledge with all transactions, including names, listed in the local newspaper, along with fender-benders, bad checks, domestic disputes, and "doo-eys," the vernacular for DUI and DWI citations.

The newspaper's police blotter is innocuous most of the time. A famous actress long-residing in Salisbury once read excerpts from it on *The David Letterman Show* to prove she's a country girl. But the threat of finding one's self on the "who did what" list keeps most of us honest and law-abiding, though it is off-putting when a friend's escapades end up in print. Do you mention it amidst small talk at the deli counter or pretend you didn't see it, unlikely as that may be with our slender newspaper? In a small town, the fact that everyone knows everyone else's business ups the ante. Likewise, property ownership and transfer is the local spectator sport, and full-timers and weekenders alike indulge for the fun of it, but also to reassure themselves about the value of their sizable investments.

But the gossip around town served us well in one respect: everyone had a friend we should talk to about running a horse business. Kissing a few frogs would be worth the free advice. Our neighbor John Bottass called immediately with a recommendation. Grateful that we took on El-Arabia, he might also have felt he owed me for saving his cows. Riding my bike last fall, I capped the hill at Shady Maple Farm, enjoying the long descent only to cruise into dozens of cows, fretting in the road and skewing every which way into the woods. I u-turned and pedaled hard back over the hill to sound the alert. John jumped in his truck, and his son Danny ran down the road to rustle up all that had now mysteriously disappeared. John kept driving, thinking his cows had followed the road, but on foot Danny and I spied a few confused heifers in the woods. Sounding a bell and banging a feed bucket, Danny coaxed about twenty of the worried from all directions. Seeing Danny lead a herd of relieved bovines up the middle of the road to the safety of home was reward enough. Danny and John knew each animal individually and accounted for all MIAs. While I could not imagine doing otherwise, John painted me the hero, believing that most people would not take the time to save a few tons of beef.

John put us in touch with the Hanovers. Knowing they would be good people like John, we visited their small farm where they buy, train and resell horses. Real life horse traders, they needed space to expand. Their farm looked old, but it was clean, and they obviously cared for their animals. Scott and I guarded against expecting a horse barn to mirror our meticulous living room, but I wondered if I could ever get used to the inevitable farm messiness. The Hanovers had their hands full with a tough business and a disabled younger child, but their older daughter enthusiastically described her life on the farm, and they all freely parsed "Horse 101." An appreciative audience, we absorbed our first mini-education. Though a match between us wouldn't work—they wanted a leasing opportunity and were not able to relocate closer to our farm—they might be able to find or sell horses for us when the time came. Furthermore, the horse world is a small one, and most of its inhabitants are just plain nice to know.

The Hanovers recounted a remarkable story. Their farm lies in the softly curving, lush Great Barrington valley that got walloped in 1989 by an awesome storm. Technically labeled a wind shear, most people called it a tornado even though the weather experts hesitate to acknowledge that tornadoes strike New England. Twenty years later, its path still registers on the side of the mountain where the trees lie flat in the same direction like so many matchsticks. The Hanovers lost several horses during the storm, including a draft horse that they never found.

Now a draft horse is huge and can literally weigh over a ton. At eighteen hands, they stand six feet four inches tall at the withers, the top of the shoulder where the neck meets the back. Strong as oxen, historically they pulled the heaviest loads in hilly terrain and dragged iron plows across fields. It is hard to imagine one being swept away or so torn apart by wind as to simply disappear. Chuck Hanover understood my incredulity.

"I couldn't believe it either until I found his shoes stuck in the ground where I last saw him. I knew they were his because I shoed him myself that morning, and I adjusted them to his peculiar feet. We looked everywhere for the body or something, but never found a trace of him."

The poor fellow was yanked right out of his mud-sucked irons, similar to pedestrian accidents where still-tied human sneakers are strewn, incomprehensively to onlookers, near the wreck.

STILL IN SEARCH OF A FARM MANAGER, my second call led me to Bobbi (short for Roberta) Carleton. Not only has Bobbi been on the back of a horse since the age of nine months (she is forty-four), but she lives only a mile away, as the crow flies—three miles by car—on our own winding Twin Lakes Road. Moreover, she has been on the lookout for an interesting horse opportunity since relocating from Dutchess County in New York, where she ran a large stable for a Rockefeller, to marry Chip. Bobbi and Chip erected a six-stall barn and riding ring on their property for Bobbi's horses. A day after a promising introductory meeting at our house, we loaded up the kids to check out their place. We found their light blue colonial farmhouse appealing and the barn and horses immaculate, just as she had described. Chip warmly shook our hands and welcomed us into the barn where Bobbi wrestled with a horse.

The tack room bulged with ribbons (even though Chip said most rested in boxes) attesting to Bobbi's expertise as an "L" judge and advanced dressage rider. I liked the idea of dressage more and more. I saw it as ballroom dancing with a balletic horse rather than the un-rhythmic shuffling around my husband and I call dancing. And I could lead, or so I thought. Requiring pinpoint agility and speechless communication between horse and rider, it is sanely contained within a ring. It is so quiet and slow, how hard could it be? Hunt and jumping courses cover so much more ground, and the speed tilts wild and dangerous. I like control. Atop a fifteen-hundred-pound, muscle-bound, speedy herd animal, I like it even more. Let's face it: the Christopher Reeve accident inclined many of us to rethink this sport. Superman's death after years as a quadriplegic adds not a little to my anxiety both for my family's safety and as a liability issue. Most horsey people do not mention the "P" word, but that doesn't mean they don't think about paralysis, probably more than they'd admit.

Without prompting, Bobbi stressed safety and the cleanliness and care of the horses and their environment, priorities that calmed my aging, worry-about-my-kids-all-the-time, animal-loving heart. She and Chip had also rescued several hard to manage dogs from the pound. Canine-ites also, we eagerly asked to see the beasts we heard barking from the house.

"They are two wonderful shepherds, absolute sweethearts, but they aren't great with strangers. Who knows what happened before we got them, but it couldn't have been good."

As if on cue, "bing" chimed a timer from the house.

"Oh, that's the special food I cook up for them. Twice a day, they know it's coming."

This woman is conscientious with a heart of gold, I thought. As an extra bonus, Chip volunteers for the local fire department and is a motor head, loving nothing better than mucking around with tractors and heavy equipment. With no shortage of that kind of work on a farm, these two were a find.

Their horses clamored for attention, and Bobbi introduced each one with more ceremony than I did my children. All five friendly horses clearly adored her and Chip, nudging and nickering. Half-blind Theo shied at Elliot's touch, so Bobbi, ruffling his mane, explained to approach from his seeing side.

"One time old Theo banged his other eye, swelling it completely shut for a whole day. Completely confused, he walked into everything. I spent a full day leading him around wherever he wanted to go." Closing her eyes and goofily bumping around, she had both my kids giggling and play-acting two blind old racehorses.

I admired Bobbi's skill at maneuvering her seventeen-hand (six feet at the withers, where the neck meets the back), young horse Toby through a shower and into his fresh straw-bedded doublewide stall. Chip referred to this silly young gelding that hardly knew his own strength as the "Big Galoopas," and suffered "the Tobster" with the humor generally afforded a brawny, thick-headed younger brother. Bobbi bred Toby for eventual sale but found she couldn't part with him. She chattered all the while with a ready white smile and crystal blue eyes. Latvian, athletic and "blonde by choice," she exuded grace and confidence even though Toby shied and pranced indelicately about. Her hands were intelligent with skill, guiding this rambunctious horse and his complex arrangement of gear even as her mind was focused on us. She openly shared her evident knowledge about all things horse-related and our conversation flowed full and easy. We all envisioned the same horse farm—casual, very clean, safe and up-to-date, but definitely not fancy.

This is a good match, I thought to myself, and I heard Scott's answering sigh of relief signaling *yes, she seems just perfect*. Our side of the partnership was clinched as we witnessed Chip enjoy a head massage from Bobbi's prized horse. "Dream Weaver," also known as "Angel," is Toby's older sister. As Chip leaned his sinewy shoulders against the stall door talking away, Angel poked her head through the metal yoke and worked her thick, surprisingly soft whiskered lips back and forth over the entire surface of his scalp. Angel kept her teeth safely closed but vigorously articulated in between each hair from Chip's forehead to the back of his neck and from ear to ear. It was an act of intimacy possible only through loving care and time spent, an earned camaraderie of man and beast. As my kids looked on with mouths agape, Chip laughed, his voice smoker-deep.

"It feels really good, but you need a hair wash afterwards."

He came away not in the least self-conscious with his gooey hair sticking up in all directions, a saliva-gelled Mohawk gone awry. Angel whinnied and nuzzled his plaid flannel shirt gently, and Chip absent-mindedly pulled at the bits of chewed grass and hay braided into his hair. Their contentment was palpable.

The next day, our kids' sitter Marie mentioned that fellow-fireman Chip designated Elliot and Jane the nicest and most well-behaved children he had ever seen. *Hmmm, taste and honesty to boot,* I laughed to myself. We quickly determined Bobbi's salary requirements, and she eagerly took the job. Bobbi would line up the workforce to hit the ground running as soon as we closed in May and help us decide what to demolish, renovate and add. Once we opened for business, she would manage all aspects of the farm, from taking care of and training up to thirty-eight horses as boarders, to finding, training, and caring for horses for our family's use, giving lessons and maybe even staging some shows. This grim farm was signing a new lease, and Arcadian visions of its transformation danced merrily in our heads.

Bobbi lost no time choosing quality barn builders, plumbers, electricians, painters, fencers, well-diggers and septic system experts. As often happens with home purchases, what seemed possible to live with before ownership became impossible afterwards, and the redo list grew by inches. By the second week of April, the "while ya's" had infected us all—"while you're changing the roof, ya' may as well add skylights; while you're replacing the plastic windows, ya' may as well use glass; while you're sprucing up the indoor riding ring, ya' may as well build out a viewing room." Our while-ya's were spawning while-ya's like some out-of-control DNA experiment. In the end we planned to rip out and replace all the stalls, re-roof the main barn and refit all the outbuildings with new, commercial grade gutters. Copious water runs off a twenty-two-thousand-square-foot barn roof, pouring a lake in the outdoor riding area we had renamed the skating rink. We decided to replace all the electric wiring and lighting that the inspector condoned but that everyone else had emphasized was extremely hazardous, having actually sparked a few fires. Finally, we could not resist renovating the pleasing but dilapidated peg and groove round pen to serve as a viewing venue for shows (here we really were getting ahead of ourselves), and as a shade haven in the summer.

"We can make some money from food concessions out of the refurbished gazebo once it's fixed up," I said, confident in my income-producing reason to renew my favorite structure.

"That's a lot of hotdogs, pal," Scott teased. "And who's going to cook and serve? ... You?" He gave me the "you poor mutt" head shake.

The list grew like the mold creeping up from the bottoms of the stalls: for the indoor ring, add glass windows along the one wall to brighten the dark interior, go for dust-free footing (rather than a sand/dirt mix that needs watering), and consider a heating system to achieve thirty degrees when the mercury plummets.

"Why bother with that?" I asked Bobbi.

"Well, riding in thirty feels pretty good when it's minus ten outside."

I figured I would flash my "gentleman farmer" card then—if I'm the one shelling out all the money, I'll opt to stay in my toasty kitchen with a cup of steaming tea when it hits zero—a fair weather rider.

Then there were the mundane but essential items: lay down concrete in the barn aisles to keep down dust, add another heated tack room, build up the lower pastures and replace all the fencing: *buying fencing by the mile just sounds wrong*, I thought. This in addition to new sliding barn doors (that actually slide), the removal of dead and dangerous trees, new plantings for shade and aesthetics, the replacement of rotted wood from and the staining of all buildings, and a complete renovation of the cottage, including a new bathroom and kitchen, for the on-site farmhand.

Bobbi came by in mid-April with the estimates clutched in her hand. We sat on the back patio, all of us nervous. While the spring birds twittered, Bobbi solemnly revealed a total twice that of the generous number Scott and I had filed in our heads as "couldn't possibly be more than." Our "head number," we thought, gave us ample room for a hot tub or some other crazy indulgence should we think of one. We carefully padded our head number to cushion ourselves against the blow of a high estimate. Yet we knew Bobbi had done her best and that there was no getting around the cost for what we had chosen.

"What do you think, Scott?" I asked, heart pounding.

"It's a lot of money."

"I know," Bobbi winced. "I could keep working on it, get some more bids."

"Maybe Velvet and I should get a paper route?" I joked.

Silence.

How could it be so expensive, I wondered? *It's an ugly old barn.* "I guess you better keep your day job, Scott."

Silence.

"Let's sleep on it. If we see our way clear tomorrow morning, we'll send in the deposits," he frowned, already working numbers out in his head.

"I'll do my best to trim costs," Bobbi assured, serious.

We parted with queasy guts signaling that this was no longer an amusing hobby but a serious business venture with much at stake.

Scott and I jumped on our bikes both to release the adrenalin of "the number" and to discuss what to do.

"Any second thoughts?" he asked as we puffed up our first hill.

"It IS a shocking number."

"If I had known what's involved..."

I didn't want him to say it—that we should turn this ship around.

"Maybe it's like having children," I interjected. "If you knew all that was coming at you for the next twenty years, no one in her right mind would do it and we'd have been extinct a long time ago. But, yes. I'm having second thoughts, too." We glided along a low flat. "We could still back out, couldn't we?"

"Not out of the purchase, but we could take the buildings down and return the fields to hay. That would be practically free compared to what we're talking about."

Pausing, he looked right at me.

"I suppose having kids was worth it. But, do you think you'll really like having a horse farm? You know, actually find it fun?"

The kid thing is a running joke between us. Married fourteen years before ambivalently taking the plunge, when parenting gets tough we ask each other: "Whose idea was it to have these no-neck monsters anyway?" He accuses me of not liking them, and I retort that I would love having them if I had a wife like he has. But his due-diligence into my staying power regarding farming reminded me that for a no-nonsense, tough-minded, relentlessly practical investment banker, deep down my husband is an aspiring romantic. The guy doesn't desire to ride, isn't crazy about animals, has an insanely busy life, but wanted to do this thing for me, knowing that already I was too emotionally invested to turn back. Over the past two weekends I had watched my kids play with a week-old foal, born to the last remaining boarder at El-Arabia, a mare too close to term to evict. The sweetest animal any of us had ever met, we were licked and nibbled all over by toothless filly gums and batted with long dark lashes framing oversized, curious eyes. We "ooohed" and "ahhhed" at Thea's attentive mothering of little Rosie, the pushing and probing, her teaching loving yet stern. We awed at the power, speed and knock-kneed majesty of this lanky, tottering new life, unable to tear ourselves away. Overcome with beatitude, I had recklessly promised Elliot and Jane their own foals to raise—a promise I whispered out of Scott's earshot.

I saw Scott's "fun" question as my chance, and I went for it.

"Absolutely I would have fun, no question there, but what an amazing experience. It would be wrong to kill a farm, and think how great it could be for the kids." I smiled, warming to my subject. "Jane will have horses instead of boyfriends. Elliot will be active and engaged rather than a teenage slug on the couch. We don't allow television, Nintendo or many computer games, the least we can do is buy them a horse farm." I gave Scott a wink, and he rolled his eyes in return.

Our conversations about money and our indulged children always go like this: he rides the brake, and I'm full speed on the gas. Usually we stay on the road. We pedaled our bikes faster, powered by the adrenaline of a major decision.

"I guess it comes down to the horse's ass rule."

"Aptly named," I said, "but how is it applied?"

"Do you wake up after it's all said and done and feel like a horse's ass?"

He wasn't kidding; I knew he used this internal restraint meter to make decisions.

"Well," I said, "if we're going to be in the horse business, perhaps being a horse's ass is an asset. But maybe we can cut some things...."

I said this but didn't really mean it, and we both knew it. If anything, when faced with a choice between pretty and prettier, or good and best, we mostly, sometimes foolishly, choose the upgrade in an attempt to get a jump on future needs. And it is easier to opt for the "best"; lesser options, even when wiser, require comparison, analysis and therefore time, the commodity Scott habitually lacks most. Luckily for the kids and me, he falls short of "workaholic" due to his efficiency at the office (he makes timely decisions and delegates), and generally he satisfies our demanding family requirements; he keeps that scale carefully balanced. But there is scant room for an ounce more. Still, we both wanted to crack this nut of a personally important farm project; he would tackle the business, and I the aesthetics, united in our innate desire to organize, restore, improve, make work, and, dangerously, perfect. We have checked this compulsion at the door when it came to our kids; regarding the farm, since we are not totally reckless, just the notion of trimming *something* got us over the hump of backing out.

We were born five days apart in May, both conceptions to four people just either side of twenty years of age, so I envision us both having been conceived under the same Saturday night, August moon. In 1959, our parents-to-be scrambled into timely marriages. That I was born in New Jersey and Scott in Michigan did not matter—we emerged soul mates. We think so much alike that our irregularly exercised communication sometimes results in marital discord. But generally our telepathy operates on the big things—lifestyle, how to raise our kids, politics, culture, friends, décor, food, art, movies, sports. We instinctively knew ourselves incapable of doing a half-assed job (even if we were horse's asses), so on our bikes we puffed, pumped, sweated and saw our way clear to approving everything on the estimate short of automatic watering systems for each stall and a fully heated barn.

Cutting the equine drinking fountains initially seemed crazy upon realization that each horse slurps down six to ten gallons of water a day. Multiplying this by thirty-eight horses, I envisioned stumbling stable hands yoked like oxen, one sloshing bucket to a side rather than the actuality (I discovered later) of long hoses pulled to each stall for refills. Moreover, the purists claim that an automated system A) makes it hard to gauge how much the horses are drinking, especially important when they are sick (regularly), and B) seizes up in un-insulated barns during the long New England winters. Plus, our horses were going to spend most of their days outdoors, and automatic watering systems for the paddocks were budgeted. It was a relief to excise this expensive idea as our habitual zeal to improve was already edging us from the Buick to the Cadillac of barns.

To her credit, Bobbi also persuaded us against the heating option. When I pictured the horses freezing their haunches off November through March, it sounded like a no-brainer. But I was considering my own comfort in the barn. I ushered my son through five hockey seasons and fully comprehended the misery of frozen hands, stump-cold feet and an ice-numb butt. Saving us from ourselves, Bobbi reported that as cozy as central heating is for us, it messes with horses' respiratory tracts and is unnecessary as long as they can get out of the wind. Their winter coats insulate them so well that they actually prefer to tough it out in the elements, and even a cold barn is sometimes too warm for their furnacy selves.

"It's more the heat of summer that you have to worry about with horses," she informed. "And there's always the tack room for us, the one well-heated spot in any barn."

I was thankful to be spared heating a holey, un-insulated structure, and that some of our pastures already had run-in sheds for the horses to take shelter as desired from sun, rain and bitter winds, if not wind shears that might part them from their shoes.

One topic left to consider was a name change for the farm. El-Arabia suited an operation dedicated to breeding Arabians, and given that El-Arabia was lately known as "that run-down place on Weatogue Road," we wanted to start fresh. We brainstormed selections: "Housatonic River Farm," "Canaan Valley Farm," "Rolling Meadows Farm," even "Jersey Girl Farm" with a wink and a nod to my southern New Jersey roots and the iconic Bruce Springsteen, a longtime favorite musician to Scott and me. I fondly remember an early E Street Band concert, in the mid 1970s in a Red Bank, New Jersey, movie theatre. Springsteen played four hours straight, and we all risked injury by dancing on the flipping up seats. Ahhh, those glory days... but ultimately "Jersey Girl" reminded Scott of a pendulous, sway-backed milk cow as much as me, so I took a pass on that glory.

My personal favorite was Elliane Farm, an awkward conjunction of my children's names Elliot and Jane. But consensus funneled us toward the place specific, the address being 33 Weatogue Road, and therefore practical "Weatogue Stables" (though more than one person has mispronounced it "way-to-go" stables). Bobbi indicated that "stables" suggests more down-market operations, but a neighbor had already claimed "Weatogue Farm." We briefly weighed "Weatogue Equestrian Center," but didn't feel that posh and in the end challenged ourselves to put some class back in "stables." "Stables" also nodded to our five years in London and so incorporated that aspect of our lives into what is, after all, a very English pastime. The "Weatogue" part of the name would help the hoards of people looking for the perfect boarding barn find us—wishful thinking couldn't hurt—and touches on local history, Weatogue being the Native American word for "Big Wigwam Place." Since our barn is the biggest "wigwam" of sorts around, situated in a stretch of valley where the Weatogue Indians gathered in large groups, it rang true. We love the road and respect our neighbors and liked the idea of cheerleading both. Finally, it is a name that future owners can retain once we relocate, broke and broken-hearted from years of horsekeeping, first to the poorhouse and then to the cemetery across town.

We had a decrepit farm, a cheerful manager, a game plan, a practical name and a lot of naïve excitement that oxygenated our still sparkling dream. We would work and build and ride and make horse-loving people happy. Our kids would grow up kind and well adjusted and not addicted to X-Box and Barbie. They would thrill to the outdoor life, responsibly care for beasts of burden, learn animal husbandry, and keep fit by shoveling shit. We were going to be farmers.

CHAPTER SIX

First, Death

·⊂══════⊃·

THE MAY MORNING DAWNED EXQUISITE against the dismal
forecast—one of the challenges of living among hills is that maver-
ick microcosmic effects buck prediction. But a perk of buying the horse
farm was another forty-five acres to walk on, and Scott and I are prolific amblers. For our first walk from our house to our new property, the
weather gods favored us. We began our ritual round across the freshly
cut alfalfa field and along the ancient tree line that demarcates our
property from our eastern neighbor's sixty-acre hayfield.

Crossing the narrow, wood-slatted, metal-railed footbridge, we
checked the culverts for fish and frogs and wound the trail through the
brushy woods, occasionally unhooking ourselves from the thorny Bar-
berry, a spreading "exotic" or non-native plant, that pricked through our
jean-clad thighs. Spring tinted the air, but the sluggish, muddy Housatonic still emanated a damp chill. We zipped our polar fleeces against
the forest shade and pocketed our hands. So far our walk mimicked
what it had been for eight years. But as we left the river, instead of heading back across the alfalfa field to our house, we exited the woods north-
ward onto the edge of the open pastures of what was El-Arabia, rechris-
tened Weatogue Stables. We paused, breathing in the privilege of open
space. On this very spot Scott and I had decided to purchase this property, concluding that a McMansion paved over this horse farm would
haunt us until we died.

As we crunched through last season's desiccated hay stubble with new growth peeping gamely through, we felt the satisfaction of preserving a farm in a time of their rapid extinction throughout Litchfield County. Though it benefited us and our neighbors personally and immediately, we also felt we were gifting future generations of Salisbury—open space for our children and their children. A sappy sentiment yes, but also true. Conservation easements would ensure our vision for this land, our little piece of immortality, control from beyond the grave.

Our boots tore through the more tangled, overgrown grassland in the middle of the field we anticipated coaxing back to a healthy carpet of green. We traced the dirt service road that curves past two ancient oak trees and around the eight fenced paddocks, saying hello to big brown Thea and her seven-week-old foal. Rosie sprinted and bucked, recklessly expending her youth in the sunny coolness. She gummed our fingers. Chipper bluebirds and stealthy swallows streaked impossible trajectories through the open outbuildings to rest and sing in the crannied rafters before returning to bug-catching over the manure-dotted paddocks. Reluctantly moving on, we paused again to greet the remaining four mares that Mrs. Johnson could not relocate in time for the closing three weeks previous. Not willing to let even these bedraggled, unbroken horses slide to auction, Bobbi agreed to find them homes. The mares stood ankle deep in mud but did not seem to mind, sensing spring's imminence. They recognized us now and coyly approached the fences for conversation. I breathed my hello into their nostrils, moist and velvety black. They snorted back and shook their matted manes. The sun's heat drew steam from their wet legs.

Heading to the barn, we spotted Bobbi, already tanned, sun-bleached blonder and comfortably poised atop a green John Deere front loader, picking up fallen limbs from the grassy entrance. She looked in her element, all smiles as usual. We talked some basic business about recent demolition progress and turned to the eviction of the few remaining mares and the once-celebrated stallion stud Stanislav.

"They should all be gone by the end of the week," Bobbi reported, proud that she had placed the four Arabians. "But I'm not sure about that one mare."

We looked toward the near paddock at the segregated skinny bay considering a drink from the black plastic bucket at her feet. She looked fine, like the rest, lazy from years of inattention. But as we gazed, on cue to Bobbi's words, the mare changed her aspect. She raised her head slightly, looking perplexed for a fraction of a second. She shuddered, twice, like she had caught a sudden chill, before sinking sideways over buckled legs to the ground. The collapse had the appearance of a staged faint, a too-tightly-bound, airless Victorian, sighing and lilting gracefully to the ground. The horse's head landed last, and even before she became completely still, up she scrambled, clumsily. She shook herself and again grew vaguely confused, like she could not remember having lain down, no easy effort for a horse.

"She's been falling down all week, just like that I suppose, though until now I've only witnessed her getting back up. Dr. Kay took some blood, but it must be a neurological problem, almost like epilepsy, because she rights herself and carries on like nothing happened."

The mare wandered away to a better patch of grass and grazed, seeming to accept her condition without anxiety. *Animals don't seem to worry,* I thought.

"She's awfully thin," I pointed out.

"Well, she's getting her share of the feed but can't keep weight on. She's not the low horse on the totem pole either—that fat mare is, believe it or not. Sometimes a sick horse is pushed out of the way and not allowed to eat, but she gets right in there."

"Can she be helped?"

"We'll try." Bobbi wrinkled her nose. "But I'm afraid we might have to euthanize her."

Sapped of carefree optimism, I fast forwarded to how much harder this will be when it is one of our own adored and long-cared-for pets.

This one didn't even have a name. Death is bad enough, but it is the preceding suffering, particularly by animals, that deeply disturbs me.

"The sooner the better, I suppose," I said quietly.

"We're just waiting for the test results to make sure there isn't anything we can do," Bobbi replied.

"Just don't tell Jane or Elliot," Scott said protectively.

Don't tell me, I thought.

"Or Roxanne," Scott added, as if he heard my brain whispering.

"What do you do with the body?" I imagined a large vehicle with straps and hoists. "Does the vet take it away like with dogs and cats?"

Bobbi winced. "No, you just dig a hole."

Our eyes rested once more on the mare's ribbed sides. I inwardly willed her to not convulse again. We moved on to happier topics before Bobbi climbed back aboard her tractor, and Scott and I continued our walk, along the road this time. It was our first brush with mortality at our new farm and probably not the last. The predicted cloud-cover overtook the confident blue of the sky. I pulled my coat collar close around my neck against the chill and leaned into Scott. Silently developing thicker skins, we bent our forms into the rising wind, toward lively, healthy children and the comfort of home.

CHAPTER SEVEN

Into the Woods

·⊂══════⫘·

WE TOOK THE PLUNGE: we owned a horse farm. Endless work, lots of money, sickness and death thrown in—how did we get into this mess, overburdened with needy acres, decrepit buildings, ailing and dependent animals?

For Scott, I knew this peculiar destiny related to the land—but how? Occasionally I nosed around Scott's past to uncover the seedling of his affinity for rural New England, but came up fallow. Nature poetry is not his cup of tea: he's more of a history and politics buff than a romanticist or a fictionalist. While I escape into Emerson and Thoreau and the Berkshire writers, he thrives in the competitive maze of Wall Street wrestling other capitalists. He is a poster boy for the great American story. Having immersed his youthful self in countless biographies of accomplished men from sports stars to steel magnates, from the age of twelve he planned to head east for school and a career in business. He worked hard at university, endured unglamorous summer jobs, and made two risky but ultimately brilliant career decisions: first, to leave corporate law for investment banking way back in the mid-eighties before the field became so popular and, second, to leave a ten-year, secure position at a prosperous large bank for a start-up boutique.

Scott was the fourth partner to join; eight years later there were forty-plus in a global operation listed on the New York Stock Exchange. Luck played its part as it does in many a bootstraps story: in his case the right place and time of being a white, educated, ambitious male born in the United States. He made the most of his opportunities, success met him halfway, and, at least from my perhaps protected perspective, he made the hard slog look relatively easy. I marvel at his skill and efficiency, and the security he has provided for our family, especially since money and I seem to part company as congenital fact. Making and hanging on to money is a talent like any other; Scott possesses it, I do not.

Scott had a Midwest suburban childhood, an urban college experience, a Jersey girl wife, a Wall Street job, a Big Apple life: yet, as soon as we paid off our loans and could afford it, he and I took to the country like spring salamanders to vernal pools. I know as a kid my husband spent hours catching frogs (and shooting them with a BB gun, he admitted) in the wetlands near his house, but he never revealed much nostalgia for his younger years in Michigan. His father took him deer hunting once, but Scott sat in the woods and read *The Grapes of Wrath*—in its entirety. No kills. But that is all I uncovered from my husband's veiled past: a foggy window to his nascent nature soul.

I hailed from the "Garden State," not the bucolically equine western part of the state, but the strip-malled, smelly, oil-drenched northeast and southern shore. As a kid, I remember regularly burying my nose into my grandmother's sweater on certain stretches of the New Jersey Turnpike and watching the stacks of the Budweiser factory pour smoke across the endless squat, laddered refinery tanks beyond. I recognized the landmarks in *The Sopranos* series' opening credits and knew people who could slip into those story lines with ease. According to my husband, I am an "animal nut," but my inclination is toward smallish, easily managed, clean, non-drooling, non-shedding, heavily-domesticated varieties. And Scott and I are not "handy," as individuals or as a couple. We bicker while simply hanging pictures. Our "suburbanity" and urbanity had not afforded us any traction in the wise and practical rusticity of the country. Even our six-year-old daughter admonished: "Dada, you don't look like the tractor type."

In our young married life we never thought we would even stay in this country, let alone settle in stodgy New England. Restless Anglophiles with the youthful spirit of exploration, one year after we purchased our first house in Salisbury, we knocked the dirt of the US of A from our shoes and moved to London for five years, from 1990–1995. Scott accepted a posting there, and we left with few thoughts of returning. Arriving on August 1st, the hottest day recorded in British history to that date, I panicked at the realization that air-conditioning did not exist in either houses or cars. Not comfortable outside the parameters of a 68–75 Fahrenheit degree window, I was all for flying home, pronto. All too soon I understood: we strode coolly damp and dimly lit through the next five years of British weather.

We enjoyed much travel, taking full advantage of a childless existence (fourteen married years) and the short plane rides to the Continent, but we never really fit in with the British and remained outsiders despite our officially stamped passports designating us permanent residents. I missed skyscrapers and food delivery, NYC street life and even rude, impatient salespeople, the twenty-four hour never-close pace, blue skies and white puffy clouds on frigid winter days, the blare of sunshine, the wilting summers, American enthusiasm and *naiveté*, a fat slice of greasy-good pizza, and the relaxed atmosphere of friends *eating out* rather than *dining in* at formal dinner parties planned weeks in advance. I hear London now sports a more American casualness, but I regret this slide toward globalization. My pet peeves largely made England, England, like antiquated paternalistic BBC telly and gun-less Bobbies on bicycles with nightsticks. Many of them carry guns now, and it saddens me.

I think Scott could have been happy in London indefinitely, but I chafed at a rootless exile, despite my happy years of literary study there. We left five years to the day we arrived, significantly changed and with England a part of us still. We made some good friends, mostly expatriates with lives similarly colored. My first-born's arrival six weeks before the move home meant we would not go back to American life as we knew it five years earlier: clever of us because return can be so disappointing. But that London cured our restlessness became the best souvenir of our sojourn; we found home. If I had not lived abroad, I would have gone to my grave yearning for greener pastures. I now believe in New York and Connecticut with solid confidence—not with defensive my-place-is-better-than-your-place bombast, but with steadfast, personal confidence of knowing my own heart's desires. It is not for everyone, but I chose the teeming, exhausting, nerve-wracking, frustrating, glorious New York City, tempered by the Puritan rocky soil and artistic pastoral beauty of New England, and never looked back.

Over the years we have dug into our repatriated territory with a vengeance. Our English sabbatical conditioned us to appreciate the Connecticut countryside: the weekend jaunts to Wales and rural England, the green, green, green misty valleys, the sheep-dotted hillsides, the walking trails encouraging trespass across private property, the ancient stone walls and hedgerows, the rustic pub convenient to refresh the wet, weary foot soldier. For Scott, this might have been the sum total of what turned him into a country boy and thus steered us toward Weatogue Stables. But for me, England's demure countryside was only a refresher course. When we returned to Connecticut, I embedded in the American forests because they invoked a past I had carefully vaulted. Sure, this Yankee terrain was breathtakingly beautiful. Yet underlying that, I fell in love with "the woods" because they reminded me of long ago people, places and times gone by. Repairing to our tree-insulated, rural home was to dip into my personal warehouse of memory and experience—an amplification of childhood beauty and wonder seared by the melancholy of loss and the hard-earned lessons of growing up.

I WAS A NORMAL KID, strong-willed and pushing at boundaries as unapologetic preadolescents do. Then just as I turned nine, my mother, Marilynne Marie, died.

I learned something that June day in 1968—bad things can happen to anyone, anytime, right out of the blue. I spent the next forty years waiting for the other shoe to drop, anticipating the next horrible thing about to happen; expecting the worst. The twisted goal, I suppose, was to cheat surprises and worry fate into submission. A "dyed in the wool pessimist" my husband insists, but I say I'm a fact-facer. I am also in a hurry: fully informed that life can be short, especially when beautiful, it is best to hit the ground running to get through all you can before your calamity finds you.

I struggle to remember happy times with my mother, times that I didn't annoy her. "Your mother loved you, but she took a hard line," my father said.

A therapist might say I have blocked good memories of my mother to blunt the loss. But I also learned how hard it is to be a parent, especially one with a short fuse, a trait I inherited from both sides. And, my mother was young herself—a parent at barely twenty and snuffed out by twenty-eight. When I reached that milestone age, it hit me, with the force of a punch, just how young it is both to be responsible as a parent and to die. From the perspective of nine, anything in the twenties seems geriatric, light years away. From the vantage point of forty-six, it is more shocking with each passing year. I have outlived my mother by nearly twenty years, and I still feel like a kid most of the time.

But I grasp the good memories when I reach, like her feeding me the chicken skin right from the soup pot as it boiled off the carcass. She would stand in her mini skirt, stockinged and heeled, with her "fall" hairpiece in a flip, towering over the stove, wooden spoon stirring. Craving fat, I also liked to eat butter, by itself, several sticks at a time if I could get it. In comparison the chicken skin seemed more legitimate as a stand-alone food, and I bounced, waiting as my mother stirred and caught the loosening skin. Bumpy, yellowy white and slimy, we called the pieces goose pimples. As she forked up each piece to cool, I'd turn up my head, just level to her hip and the blue/green flame under the pot, and open my mouth like a baby bird. She'd slip the wormlike nourishment in and go back into the pot, fishing for more.

M & M's were another delicacy. Mom adored them. She would eat them in bed, and though I longed for some, that she didn't always share made those brown flattened spheres all the more precious. I'd eyeball her holding them loosely in an airtight fist, snug and long enough to melt them on the inside. Then she'd eat each one slowly and deliberately, her tongue pressing the still hard candy shell against the backs of her teeth for the burst of warm, velvety chocolate: a delicate click, click: a sweet caviar. I didn't begrudge her selfishness: rather, I took the message that parents sometimes take to counteract all the giving, and that you are responsible for your own happiness.

Christmas rituals were important, and we followed the many she created to the letter. The real evergreen wore silver icicles—never garland. Spacing the decorations precisely, she draped the tinsel close inside by the trunk before my dad and I were permitted to dress the easier branch tips. More than two or three strands at a time threatened an unforgivable clump and a redo. My allotment always tangled, no matter how carefully she laid it, even and glittering, across my eager palm. With a steamy grip that wrinkled the strands, I endeavored to get it right. I marveled at her poise then, and even now, when I trim our family tree, I tame my inclination to rush.

A romantic, she also kept a special dress for me, used only Christmas morning: long and flowery from the waist down with a green velvet bodice and Victorian buttons that trailed down the back with short, puffy elasticized sleeves that matched the skirt. My femininity, still reverberating around my aging dermis, was born from this magical gown. I knew not to attack the presents until properly attired. I wore that dress through three or four Christmases, but at eight, the buttons refused to meet and the elastic cut into my strengthening upper arms. I willed myself smaller, desperately trying to shrink my burgeoning self. I feared I might outgrow my mother's affection.

Photos help me remember. My glamorous mother stretched nearly six feet tall and rail thin. Her hair ran the gamut—I saw her as a blonde, dirty blonde, redhead and brunette styled from a long straight flip to a short wavy bob. Mostly I remember soft auburn curls, layered to her chin. She spent long minutes inclined towards the bathroom mirror, myopically close enough to expertly apply eyeliner, mascara, foundation and rouge before popping her contacts in. I would squeeze myself between the sink and the wall, resting my chin on the cool mauve-pink porcelain, all eyes. Her creamy even teeth balanced a straight, strong Italian nose. My grandmother "Nana" passed on her excellent bone structure: Mom's face angled beautifully atop her statuesque frame. Athletic, she moved smoothly. My father maintains she played competitive basketball two weeks before giving birth to me, her only child.

Eventually topping out at five feet five, I slumped short and dumpy next to her and Nana. Mom tried to help me out through smocked dresses, elaborate buns twirling up my hair, and a flowery pin, but I persisted a pigeon-toed wreck and never did develop a sense of style. I slept in a metal brace supporting two old shoes with the toes cut out in a doctor's attempt to duck-foot me: a hideous contraption that tortured my body and mind. My beauty rehabilitation felt so hopeless that I fought it all, and my misery registered a sourpuss in every photo documenting the gussied up me. Shrinking in inadequacy in the shadow of these two swans, I clashed with Mom about clothes, about chores, about Dad, about everything.

My mother taught English to gifted junior high students, having gone back to complete her degree after my birth. I distinctly remember, at age four or five, attending her graduation from Kean College in New Jersey. Family and friends were extraordinarily proud since my dad truncated his college career. But her education gave her, what were then controversial, ideals. A passionate advocate of the Civil Rights movement, she regularly debated my father about black Americans' rights to get ahead in society, too often for household peace.

My parents spent most of their marriage in a house in Linden, New Jersey, that belonged to my father's mother Mary. About the time I was eight, my grandmother, prompted by her insecurity about money and her dying husband, wanted to move back in, essentially evicting us from a home that she had originally agreed to give to my father and aunt. My father begged her to reconsider because my mother was also gravely ill, having recently suffered a partial cerebral hemorrhage. Inoperable at the time, the doctors gave her six months to live, a diagnosis she was never told. But my grandmother stuck to her plan, and my father never fully forgave her. Making the most of a bad situation, my strong, six-feet four, soft-hearted Dad told my ailing mother to find a house she liked.

She fell for one on Parkway Drive in the nearby town of Clark. More upscale than Linden and with better schools for me, Clark's proximity to her school kept teaching an option once she, theoretically, recovered. Dad recognized the house as a nothing-but-work wreck, but my mother's enthusiasm for its rural aspirations on a winding road bordering a "forest" (a patch of woods and a stream) inspired him. He wanted my mother's last months to be joyful. We think they were. Later, he and I found some peace in her having kept a house of her own before she died.

So my father bartered his treasured boat for barn-red aluminum siding, and the house perked up. My ailing mother delicately hung wallpaper, organized cabinets and replanted the large yard that stretched out a new canvas for floral visions. A wooden privacy fence added to our feeling of insular, country living by blocking out the reality of suburban sprawl that engulfed eastern and central New Jersey. My father helped my mother shower and dress so she would not have to bend over and flow blood into her "healing" brain. He fretted and made excuses when she insisted on driving me someplace. I was told to help my mother recover by being good.

I was to have my own little oasis in our new house, too: the entire top floor as my bedroom. A roomy finished attic imitated a big girl apartment to my mind, though I baked in the summer up there under the roof. Draping cold washcloths over myself I'd toss and turn on those humid New Jersey summer nights until Dad finally slipped a noisy air-conditioner into the window. As a compensatory act after Mom died, he encouraged my friends and me to magic marker the white slanted walls and ceiling. My artistic father (his brother John was a commercial artist), drew life-size cartoon characters interspersed with my less accomplished scribbling. Roadrunner, a kindly looking vulture, Hagar the Horrible and Bugs Bunny chomping a carrot were among the roguish character angels that watched over me as I slept. My friends made their marks, and during my teen years we posted many hearts with boyfriends' names, and "Roxanne loves…" with a succession of romancers (real and imagined) crossed out. Of course my friends thought our graffiti exceptionally cool, but so did the people who bought our house five years later, because they didn't paint over it.

Our dining room was a sunny, glassed-in porch overlooking an in-ground steel pool and a backyard shaded with mature trees that required endless autumn raking sessions. Big watery blisters that I couldn't resist breaking lodged between my thumbs and index fingers but yielded hours of leaf pile somersaults. The grassy yard approached a perfect square, and my best friend Bette Jo, my cousin Mari Ann, my next door neighbor Joanne and I spent whole days spinning cartwheels, round-offs and walkovers as we daydreamed ourselves the next Cathy Rigby or Olga Korbut. My mother never swam in our much-anticipated, refurbished pool. We moved in November, and by June, just days away from our inaugural swim, she was gone.

Dad had many good friends from our large Catholic Czech/Polish community who helped him get by after my mother died. Becky, a broad, white-haired, always dark-suited, functional alcoholic knew Dad through my grandfather's gents' bar. When Dad took over Summer Street Tavern in Elizabeth, Becky, in his need, still came around. My father would be readying to open, around ten or eleven in the morning, and Becky would bring the best quality steaks from Barna the butcher that they would fry up for breakfast. Saturdays I'd twirl on the bar stool next to Becky and listen to the men talk. It wasn't particularly memorable conversation to a nine-year-old girl, but the smoke-deepened, world-weary hum and intermittent laughter soothed. A life-long bachelor, Becky resembled a tipsy Santa Claus—pudgy of body and jowly of face, with venous red cheeks flanking a corpuscular nose, rheumy hound dog eyes and a heart of gold. He'd often palm money into my hand and tell me to go get some candy. At my mother's funeral, crying profusely, he pressed $10,000 cash into Dad's bear-paw hand.

"Becky, what are you doin'?" Dad asked.

"Take it, take it," Becky insisted.

"Becky," he said through tears, "I don't need it."

"Just take it."

My father refused that money ultimately, but he never forgot Becky's myriad kindnesses to us, often in the form of steaks and change, that helped us through our grief.

So did the swaying "Aunt" Marys who prayed for us, collective surrogate mothers rocking us in a sea of care. Their numbers required tagging—Mary with the gold teeth, Mary with the club foot, Mary with the daughter Anka, Mary P., Mary G. They weren't necessarily closely related to us, but broadly tied through my father's parents and the "old country." We saw each other more or less regularly at Saint George's Byzantine Catholic Church and the Polish Home, where we danced the polka and ate pierogies, as well as at innumerable weddings and funerals that took place in the large hall above my grandfather's tavern.

I wonder how the priest, Father, later Monsignor Billy, kept the Marys straight. They were all bosomy, barrel-bodied women with tightly permed, dyed reddish hair and skinny varicose-veined legs bound in not quite flesh-colored support hose. Atop their thick necks perched wide, diabetic-flushed faces that wore the jolly look of a hard-earned better life etched over many a painful memory still echoing from across the ocean. They smiled, but their squinting, watchful eyes carried the sorrows of those left behind in homes with dirt floors and one scrappy chicken in the yard. Lovable worriers, they were always shaking their heads and gossip-whispering in Czech about the health, marriage and drinking status of the other Marys' husbands and their extended families.

In those happy months in our new home my mother played up the idyllic aspects of our arborous patch of grass, a mere speck in the endless stretch of densely packed suburb. She adored nature and flowers, having learned to seriously garden from her grandmother. As an impassioned student of English, French and American literature, my mother fully absorbed the idealized notion of the pastoral and fashioned her house across from the woods as her own Virgilian Arcadia. Perhaps our fixer-upper's tired appearance afforded extra charm in the way a woodsman's ramshackle cottage adds to the foreground of a landscape painting.

We only walked together through the woods across the street a few times, but it was enough to have secured a deep connection of nature and motherly love that still carries me. I treasure this and the two "wilderness" adventures we took together, to Maine and the Florida Everglades. Though I grew bored literally to tears through many carsick hours of driving through endless New England forest, the trees awed her. To reach Florida we drove down the coast, and the Spanish moss that covered the southern states' arbors fascinated her. For years I kept the moss she had collected in a yellowing envelope, until it was crushed into dust from periodic handling. Florida provided me memories of alligator wrestlers, and my mother in sunglasses, tank tops and knee-length shorts down-shifting her dark green '66 Corvair.

But my mother's affinity for, and my exposure to the rural were further indemnified by our family visits to Franklin and Lillian Hudson's makeshift cabin deep in the woods of northwestern New Jersey. This was the real deal. Uncle Franklin and Aunt Lid were friends of my mother's mother. Tall and distinguished, bespectacled Franklin resembled FDR before the polio. Always respectably attired in a hat, suit jacket and thin black tie, even at the cabin, I still picture him with a pipe and a book. An engineer and an intellectual, he was my mother's patron, paying her college fees. He shone the proudest at my mother's graduation.

Franklin was an old-fashioned husband, so Aunt Lid tensed up in that cowed spouse kind of way. Diminutive, with sparse white hair tightly pin-curled, Lillian's quick dark eyes receded in chalky, powdered skin. Her lipstick smudged deep red and her rouged cheeks referenced a robust Edith Piaf. Her voice pitched high and strained. I got the feeling she did not adore cabin life, but as it was buffered by a real house in Elizabeth, she played along. A genuine affection existed amongst us all, my rebellious father included, because he respected Franklin and, though at odds in lifestyle and manners, they shared a love of rifles, rare steaks, and my mother.

Arrivals at the cabin were always nocturnal: Mom, Dad and me half-lost in the kind of darkness that condenses the brain but quickens the heart with the possibility of adventure. Lacking electricity, our hosts would be waiting to wave us in with a heavy-duty flashlight. Dad always carried me on his shoulders up the hill, and Franklin, through the creaking of crickets on moonless nights, would trace the big and little dippers with his bright beam of light. I could never group the constellations, but I pretended to spot Orion's Belt and his hound, Sirius. The house was a double height grayish box with a steeply pitched roof and a tin-tube chimney pipe, set off the ground by stilts to escape the damp. Seven splintered wood stairs on the right side led to the kitchen that boasted a wood stove and a black-handled iron water pump, the shack's only nod toward modernity. Not insulated, it always chilled us a bit, even in the summer.

The kitchen led to a larger main room balanced by a sturdy dining table at one end and unmatched chairs, rockers and end tables scattered over worn braided rugs at the other. Hurricane lamps sat readily at hand against the dark. Along the front long wall stood the heart and soul of the house, an old player piano. Dozens of red and white boxes holding musty, flaking paper piano rolls layered the top of this chipped black warhorse and, as if words competed with the music, hundreds of books occupied shelves that lined the remaining wall space. It was understood that Franklin had read every one. Opposite the piano and adjacent to the kitchen were two tight rooms cordoned off by strung-up plain brown, floor length curtains. Each squeezed a double bed and served as the guest quarters. An upstairs room was reserved for Uncle Franklin and Aunt Lid, and I never ventured there.

My mother and I shared one of these cubicles, and I always shied at the sight of the flowered ceramic chamber pot peaking out from under the bed. My anxiety about it inevitably induced my urgency in the middle of the night. Try as I might, suffering my mother's frustration, I just couldn't whiz in that little pot, no matter how Victorian-prettified, so with our untied shoes ruffling our nightgowns and with flashlights in hand we'd trek to the outhouse. The grass tickled our ankles in the boisterous dark: blind and unsheltered, our vulnerability reverberated in the deep open space around and above us. Up the hill toward the edge of the woods squatted a miniature version of the boxy house, its door carved with a sickle moon. This stinky two-holer was all of rough planks, even the seats, and a bucket of lime with a scoop squatted beside. Beside the ever-present flies, it sported a flamboyant décor. Fertile womanhood plastered every inch of all four walls and the ceiling: overlapping magazine illustrations and photographs of pin up girls, partially clothed, occasionally tasseled, or completely naked. They waved their bottoms, pushed up their breasts and dared all of mankind to come and get some.

No wonder my feminist mother tried to avoid this room, but to me going pee in a hole in the ground became an escapade to be savored, even more so in the secret hours. Here I trained my handheld spotlight on bodies of all types, fancy women with laughing eyes and bleached blonde hair, pouting red lips, fluttery long, impossibly thick lashes; fat and thin bodies beribboned, bowed and tucked into frilly lingerie, fannies arching above seam-stockinged legs stretching from high heeled shoes. They winked and nodded, or so I imagined. My wide eyes glimpsed intimations of sex, at least the female half, and though my mother hurried me,

I took my time. When I was older and Mom was gone, I'd go by myself and delight in reviewing my favorites, wondering how classy Uncle Franklin could have done such a thing, a delightful paradox.

The Hudsons followed certain personal traditions. On warmer weather mornings we would stroll up the road to sponge off in the stream, returning to a poached egg and thick-cut bacon breakfast. My parents talked endlessly with Franklin and Lid, sitting on folding lawn chairs in the small clearing around the house while I'd explore the hornet's nest at the back corner roof-line and pretend to get lost in the woods. After lunch we would aim rifles and handguns at cans and bottles balanced along a fallen tree trunk. I was a pretty good shot, and Franklin and Dad sang my praises enough so that I felt one of the boys.

"Watch that 45 now, Bean, it's got quite a kick." The summer sun tanned me brown as a coffee bean, thus my long-standing nickname.

His massive arm reinforced my thin one. I'd brace myself, determined not to land girlishly backwards on my butt. My ears would ring for minutes, my consolation prize for reveling in such grown-up, illicit fun.

Plenty of bourbon moistened the dry heat, and at official cocktail time Aunt Lid produced the appetizer with a flourish—pink and white chunk crabmeat, an expensive canned luxury, tossed generously with mayonnaise and mounded delicately atop saltines. With long tree branches, Franklin and my father would be pushing around a massive, rubbery slab of beef in the stone grill pit half sunk into the ground. The open flames crackled the fat, and sparking smoke curled away into the treetops. Salted, peppered, and thick beyond reason, the steak cooked for hours, and even then, it remained too spicy, rare and animal-like for me.

After dinner, we would stargaze again before settling down around the player piano for a sing along. This was my favorite time, and my mother's, too. With the lyrics printed vertically along the edge of the music rolls, no one could beg off. Between the drink, the comfort of friends and the pressure of custom, everyone sang out, loud and melodious. Being the only child, and as yet unself-conscious, I belted with the best of them.

Always centrally included, Franklin enlisted me to pump the pedals, a job necessitating my full body weight angled toward a vigorous rhythm, and I made my song selections in turn with the rest. Later, when I was ten, and after my mother died, Dad bought and renovated a player piano for me for Christmas. Painted a lacquered, cherry red, it wore a brass plate that read: *Made exclusively for Roxanne, Merry Christmas, December 1969.* An inspired gift, my habitually grand-gesturing father gave me something my mother and I shared to help me remember.

Sing-a-longs continued to stud our family history, through the years of my stepmother and my husband and into my life with my own two children. While my bright red player is long gone, I eventually found and restored a flame stitch mahogany Steinway, made in 1907 when the quality Pianola was king. My son Elliot sings along with the words at ease, and delights in all of my old favorites.

> *She's hard-hearted Hannah, the vamp of Savannah, the meanest gal in town. Talk of your cold, refrigerating Mama; brother, she's the polar bear's pajamas. To tease 'em and thrill 'em, to torture and kill 'em, is her delight they say. I saw her at the river with a great big pan, there was Hannah pouring water on a drowning man, she's hard-hearted Hannah, the vamp of Savannah, GA.*

We sing *You Are My Sunshine, Sunrise/Sunset, Bye-Bye Blackbird* and *Take Me Out To The Ballgame*, and dance to *Ballin' The Jack* and *The Hokey Pokey*. My Jane dresses up as a princess and flits all feathers and sequins and plastic high heels in and around the sound, getting us all up on our feet. "Dance, Mommy, *Dance!*" It's corny but fun, and its sweet melancholy connects me to my mother and my children, simultaneously accessing the past, present and future. Even my husband, a player piano *ingénue*, gets the spirit, and we bellow our best, as a duo, to perfect the challenging range of *Danny Boy*.

As a finale to each Hudson farm visit, with serious care we would sign the guest book. A mere signature would not do: Franklin expected a colorful record of all we did, saw and ate, and amongst this erudite crowd I felt the pressure of eloquence. Our efforts were richly rewarded: we always skimmed over past entries, noting my handwriting and grammar improvements over the years, and relived visits forgotten. I would like to reread that guest book now, but Franklin and Lillian are long gone, and I've lost touch with their children and their keepsakes. After my mother died, my dad, my stepmother Irene and I would revisit the Hudsons' place and try to enjoy our familiar round of activities. Mostly we managed, but my mother's ghost permeated the cabin, the chamber pot, the piano bench, the very air. And, childishly lacking tact and consideration, I always requested her favorite songs on the piano.

"He walks with me and he talks with me, and tells me I am his own. And the joy we share as we're standing there none other has ever known," and *"Lav-en-der Blue, Dilly Dilly, Lav-en-der Green, you'll be my king Dilly Dilly, I'll be your queen...."*

We'd still sing, half-heartedly, the adults humming while they wiped their eyes. I took perverse pleasure in summoning her memory, wounding them with every note tearfully sung in a vain attempt to help myself.

OUR NEW HOUSE IN CLARK was far afield from the Hudson farm in distance and flavor, but the woods across the street at least hinted at that country retreat we savored. The next-door neighbor girl and I spent endless hours in its tangle of trees and vines building forts, racing along the paths and splashing in the slow stream that fed the broadening river down at the falls. Once we tried to erect a tree house. Our attempt to dislodge a heavy trunk from its wedged position sounded good in theory.

"Push it off and run," Joanne instructed pointing left.

I ran straight and took it square on the top of my head. Not wanting grown-up trouble we went home and quietly applied ice. I prayed I wouldn't die in the night from a concussion, or a cerebral hemorrhage, a term I'd heard my father whisper.

The woods sheltered an abundance of not so wild life, mainly frogs, squirrels, raccoons and skunks. It was enough to tweak our imaginations about a suburban frontier and even my father caught the pioneer spirit. He found some fresh road kill one day, hit by a car but not demolished.

"Bean, let's skin a skunk." He wielded a kitchen knife.

"What?" I stopped popping wheelies in the driveway.

He walked off. I dropped my bike, all charged up about a real *National Geographic*-type adventure. I regularly poured over that magazine's photographs, but the looking always left me hankering for a piece of the drama captured on those pages.

Skin that beast we did, or *he* did—I watched mesmerized—taking special care not to break the scent gland. Toting the limp black-and-white fur we left the scene of the massacre.

Sniff, sniff.... "Do you smell something?"

Dad had stepped on the edge of the sack kicking the guts into the brush. We threw his shoes away, but it was worth at least that to my mind. We nailed our prized skin across the tree trunk in the front yard. Over weeks the fur fell out in patches and the sun baked the hide into a homemade chamois Dad planned to wash the car with, but some other plundering creature chewed holes in it.

Our new environment trained me to novel physical and psychical experiences spun by my mother's choice of house and her sensibilities toward nature. This pseudo-country life, along with player pianos and literature braided a connection between us that withstood parting. Parented afterward by my wonderful stepmother for thirty-four years, I am still more my mother than anyone else. I understand the tenacity of early imprinting raising my own children, how much of their personalities and inclinations, for better and worse, would come from me even if I died tomorrow. I cannot remember day-to-day interaction with my mother, cannot hear her voice, but I feel her influence and instinctively know that I am like her, even if Dad didn't tell me.

"You are more and more like Marilynne every day. Jesus Christ,

Roxanne, it spooks me sometimes. I swear to God, you look like her, you talk like her. Your smile is hers."

SHE DIED IN JUNE, after her cherished tulips nodded their heads and dropped their petals. She and Dad were dressing for her tenth high school reunion. I bounced between the bathroom and bedroom doors excited by these two giants' romantic, sophisticated night out. My mother knew she still had her looks and anticipated the ritual preening among classmates. A Cinderella released from the page, she was transformed before my very eyes for the ball. Hair high and curled, eyeliner, mascara, powder and lipstick expertly applied, enhanced her face concentrating in the mirror, and a long green taffeta dress accentuated her small waist. We were all squeezed in our tiny bathroom when she cried out once and collapsed. My trim, handsome father, who had, according to the doctors' estimates, been anticipating this moment for six cruel months, caught her, and laid her across the bed, now Snow White.

Was I ordered outside or did I run from fate? I shuffled in the grass alongside the driveway, just waiting. I doubted anything too awful could happen to someone so powerful: mothers were always in control. But they whisked her into the ambulance and away, with her full skirt rustling, the siren's dirge crying into the distance, and the fresh green trees swishing in her wake. She died the next day of a "catastrophic cerebral hemorrhage." I waded through the chaos of days and days of everyone's tears. I attended the wake. I liked the fuss everyone made over me. My father blanketed her casket and the viewing room with hundreds of her favorite gardenias.

From then on, this tragedy branded Dad and me, and the Marys forlornly shook their heads in our direction, a miming Greek chorus. I swallowed all pity by refusing to be pitiful. Still I felt marked, tattooed, and strength seemed my only life raft. In my confused attempt to spare Dad more pain, and though I forced tears when he took me across the street into the woods to tell me, I never cried about it again. At nine, I was too old to act the baby, and too young to be grown-up, but I opted for the adult route. I packed up my heart and became the woman of the house, ironing, cleaning, cooking, organizing—at least in my own mind—and stoically muscled through to bolster Dad. We carried on, in fits and starts, and he and I made good lives for ourselves, first together and then apart. We try not to dwell on the past, though that effort keeps it present, and we have much to be thankful for. But nearly forty years later, we both live on high alert, bracing ourselves against the next catastrophe.

When I had my own children, I realized that a nine-year-old boy still has a high-pitched little girl voice, still needs to be tucked into bed at night and wants his head held when sick. But for me the bell went off too early, and I raced toward a less-tender adulthood, indoctrinated to life's blows. And once that first burst is made, there is no gathering that momentum back into the starting gate, stepmother or no. When my mother died I was handed a bag of grief. If I had been a few years younger, I'd have held it for awhile and set it down, forgetting it. Had I been older, twelve or thirteen, I'd probably have clutched it a while longer and then slowly would have unpacked it, placing memories here and there, spreading bits of her around to release the pain, emptying the bag. At barely nine however, I held that full bag, tending it carefully, and never let it go. Unlike the Spanish moss, my grief never disintegrated. What a loss my mother was to me and our little world.

But she had awakened me to the magic of the woods. My rural affinities connect me to her and reach deep emotionally and back chronologically to times infused with essential elements of childhood, adventures and loss. My home in, and appreciation of, more authentically rural northwest Connecticut is built upon my mother's securely laid nature foundation. Just that the "wild" was important to her, that she was deeply affected, was enough. A romantic at heart, she valued nature and I took notice.

Once she died I engaged the country as a tool to remember until the pain dulled and nature grew pleasurable in its own right. I share "wild" adventures with my own children, both by subtle example and outright manipulation. I make sure they get outside: in Connecticut we routinely brave ticks and bears to traipse through the woods around our house, kicking through the stream in our Wellies, building forts, crashing through the undergrowth collecting beetles, frogs and spotted salamanders, theorizing over rotted animal carcasses, toting home skulls and femurs, startling deer, picking wild berries, and not forgetting to sit and hear the wind rustling the trees' canopy, the crack and thud of a falling branch, the water smoothing river stones, the bark of a crow, the woods' collective non-silence. Rather than grow apart from my mother all the years I approached and passed her age, I understood her better.

CHAPTER EIGHT

A Horse Is a Horse, of Course, of Course

·⟢━━━━⟣·

THE NEGLECTED BARN inhaled a huge breath, like a surfacing whale too long submerged. Everyone "heard" it, felt it, commented on it when cracked plastic windows were pried off, stuck doors swung open and cleansing air allowed to circulate. Builder Gary and his crew power washed decades of dirt and spider mastery away. A new roof sported ten skylights that angled beams of sunshine and playful shadows to awaken the dark cavern. It is amazing, as I've learned from years of yoga pranayama, what simple breath can do. Merry in transformation, all spookiness dissipated. The fresh air peeled away years of sickliness from our long-secluded invalid: the patient was still wheelchair-bound, but with mobility only weeks away. Even the homes Bobbi found for the last unbroken, hard-to-place horses proved successful. One mare was already pregnant, and the old stallion, Stanislav, rehabilitated into a happy, docile guy upon being freed from his prison and turned out into pasture for the first time in years. Four reprieves.

"I was the most worried about Stan because everyone seemed afraid of him. I just wanted to get him out of that dark stall and see what he'd do," Bobbi told me.

"But the guys said he strikes," I said, unable to imagine who would approach a caged, desperate stallion known to rear on his hind legs and give a one-two punch with bare front hooves.

"Well, at least I knew what to expect. Plus he's so small compared to what I'm used to."

Her comparison was Toby, seventeen hands to Stan's Arabianesque fifteen. Still, her bravery impressed me.

"So, how did you manage to find someone to take him?"

"Once I got him turned out, he was a pussycat. The poor boy just needed to get some fresh air, run around and be a horse again. He hasn't been any trouble since, and his new owners are just in love with him and want to breed him again. He really is a fine Arabian."

With that, the last tenant of El-Arabia left and a hive of workers went to work the very hour the closing papers were signed. Over weeks, their number swarmed. More wood came out of the barn than was left in, and Scott and I joked about memorializing the one remaining original two-by-four in the glass trophy case for posterity's sake. The excavator, Kenny, got busy rescaling the land to address the lack of drainage, but piles of soil redistributed seemingly without rhyme or reason.

"It looks like he's having a lot of fun moving that dirt around," I said.

"Do you think he actually has a plan?" Scott asked, annoyed.

"Who knows?" I watched Kenny, burly in a tank top, drive his front loader into a brown hillock, lift the bucket and speed off. "He looks like a grown-up version of Elliot playing in the sand with his building machines. But you have to admit it does look like fun."

Scott shrugged. "Yeah, well, I guess we'll just have to trust him."

"It's got to be costing a fortune," I added, counting the bulldozers and dump trucks attacking other mysterious jobs.

The destruction that preceded the construction shocked us. This near-tear-down would redefine the term "only cosmetic." But we could only go along, and focus on the big picture. The good news was that the assembled team was friendly and dedicated, and that this lump of a barn might actually surprise us aesthetically. Gary's suggested touches, like curved cupolas on the roof peaks in place of the old boxy ones and cross-trim on the doors, held promise. But right then, spring was nothing but brown muck and revving machinery. I apologized repeatedly to our neighbors for the ruckus. They were unfailingly gracious, appreciative and patient, unlike ourselves. Our thirst for our envisioned beautiful green farm dotted with horses wouldn't be satiated any time soon. We felt years away from our tarnishing dream.

Bobbi must have sensed our project fatigue. About a week after the kids and I moved up to Connecticut for the summer at the end of June, I got the call.

"I think I may have found you a horse," Bobbi said.

"Oh?"

"He's down in Woodbury: a chestnut Quarter Horse, just your size. He's eleven years old, old enough to have the kid out of him and some manners, but young enough to be sound with a good many years left. He's lovely on paper, but that doesn't necessarily mean he's right. We'd have to take a look. How about Thursday, we take a ride?"

"Am I ready for this?"

"You're ready. Anyway, we have to start somewhere, and we probably won't buy the first horse we see."

You don't know me, I thought to myself.

"How much is he?" I asked, genuinely curious. She could have told me anything from a hundred dollars to a hundred thousand.

"Fifteen."

"Hundred?"

"Thousand."

"Oh."

THE DAY BROKE COLD AND WET. Bobbi called early.

"Are you still game?"

"Sure," I said, not really meaning it. I pictured slipping and sliding atop a horse that hated me already for getting him soaked. *How do they not fall in the mud,* I wondered? Already stiff with fear, I tried to sound vaguely intelligent.

"Would it be a fair trial?"

"Well, let's put it this way: if he's nasty in the rain, we don't want him."

"Okay. Let's go for it," I said, hoping we'd see any "nasty" before I got on.

On vacation that week, Scott tagged along. We chattered all the way about the farm and our plans. We critiqued horse farm signs since we were deciding color, size and style for our own. Eventually we pulled up to a low pasture studded with a naturalistic jump course. Despite the fog and spitting rain it looked inviting, and we wound the long driveway to a mushy parking area surrounded by three red barns with worn white trim. Stacey the trainer met us, and we sloshed over to the farthest set of stalls. I knew what Scott was thinking: twenty-four years of marriage afforded us symmetry of mind. Sure enough, later in the car he immediately criticized the site.

"We have to be sure to put down some kind of stone to avoid a mud bath of a parking area," Scott said, kicking his shoes against the running board.

I laughed. "I knew that would be the first thing you would comment on."

"What? It's a mess there," he defensively replied.

"I agree. It is a pretty setting though, with that big hill up in back."

"Yeah, but the barns look run down. And what's with all that old equipment lying around?" My stickler husband couldn't let it go.

Bobbi chimed right in, "Yeah, it is quite sloppy, and unnecessarily so. But the horses are well-kept and appear happy."

Ah, a diplomat, I registered happily. I supposed it best that Bobbi recognize our characteristic meticulousness right up front. Scott and I are not savers: we mercilessly pitch stuff when many a sentimental Gus would give pause. Organizing makes us happy. I sometimes aim to achieve a more casual approach in our day to day living, but we are who we are. Bobbi seemed to fit right in, and I pitied any untidy employee who happened to find his or her way in amongst us neatniks.

"Steal the Show," barn name "Bandicoot," gave us a good smell as Sandra, his thirteen-year-old owner, stepped confidently in the stall to groom him. I searched my mental dictionary to define a Bandicoot—a type of monkey, maybe? *What kind of name is Bandicoot for a horse, anyway?* Later, my OED set me straight: "A large, destructive southern Asian rat."

A coltish, bubbly teenager, Sandra genuinely loved "Bandi." The first thing I noticed was his orangey-brown color, not my favorite hue. But he sported white socks on his hind feet, a white blaze on his face and dark sultry eyes. His mane sprung short and full and his tail long, and both burnished brassy with highlights. His ears pinned back as Sandra combed him, a habit she brushed aside as his customary response to grooming, and temporarily worsened by his unappealing neighbor in the adjoining stall. Now, I like my animals warm and fuzzy and extremely affectionate, so this wasn't going well. Not really knowing how to behave around a horse or what questions to ask, I listened to Bobbi question his feed regimen, daily habits and tack arrangements while subtly probing about his temperament.

"Sandra has been riding him since she was six," Stacey said.

"He is soooo sweet," Sandra added.

"Bandi taught her how to ride. He had one other owner besides Sandra who bought him directly from a breeder whose child learned on him. He is really great with kids and excellent for new riders, being both safe and willing," Stacey said as she handed Sandra a bridle. "I'd trust anyone on him."

Sandra was selling because she needed a more athletic horse that could jump higher than Bandi's limit of three feet six. She also had had him sold once before, but backed out at the last minute, unable to part with him. If true, that counted for a lot in my book. I understand the love of a good animal, maybe even more than I do the human kind. In theory, he seemed perfect: safe and calm, but with enough go and jumping ability to allow me plenty of room to have fun and advance. And, she claimed he was steady on the trails.

Bandi tacked up agreeably, and we climbed the steep hill to the outdoor riding ring. Sandra mounted and effortlessly walked around, left first, then right, hugging the fence and turning with ease. She trotted, cantered and jumped perfectly as far as I could tell. He looked lovely with his legs curling under him and tail swishing at the trot. Perky despite the rain, he followed her commands to the letter.

Bobbi asked, "Do you want to go first or should I?"

"I'll go," I said, calmly.

Truth be told, I was anxious as hell and wanted to get it over with. But Bandi looked so easy with Sandra, I grew confident.

I walked. At the trot I bounced around barely in control. I certainly couldn't steer, and I zigzagged in and out from the rail. Bobbing and weaving, I crossed the ring and bumbled to a halt by the group. At least I was billed an amateur.

"Do you want to try cantering?" Bobbi asked.

"No, thanks. I'll leave that to you."

It turned out Bobbi was nervous too. I had never seen her ride. Our relationship was in its infancy. My mistakes and inability were to be expected; a discombobulation on her part, in front of her new boss, would be embarrassing all around. It occurred to me I should have watched her ride before hiring her, not that I would have had a clue how to assess her skills.

To our mutual relief, she rode beautifully and jumped this unknown horse as the veteran pair they weren't. Bandi endured us strangers, and the weather, with poise.

We trudged back to the barn, all of us wet through, and fed Bandi treats as Sandra brushed him dry. He ate eagerly, but gently careful with his teeth. I liked this, thinking of Jane's petite fingers. Wet, his orange tints shifted into a burnt copper coat that was growing on me, and he calmed as I patted his sides and rump. I reminded myself that personality trumps beauty, and the more I looked, he struck me as really very handsome—well proportioned and evenly shaded. Even Scott surprised me by saying then, and many times since: "He's a good looking animal."

In the car I confessed my inability to keep time with Bandi's bouncy trot, as if Bobbi didn't notice.

"He does have a large, swinging trot, but he also has a slower one that you would learn to engage. But a big trot is generally desirable, especially for dressage, and you will gain a good seat with time and muscle control," she said. "But you have to be comfortable."

I figured my skills would improve eventually, although controlling a trot loomed as distant from my skill set as my belting out tunes on Broadway. But I wanted to think long term, especially in terms of a partner that could be mine another twenty years.

"How is his canter?" I asked.

"Very nice: much smoother than the trot. It is exceptional really. But every horse is different, and you haven't ridden many yet."

I pictured future dates with horses in a variety of colors and builds. "What do you think of him as a whole package?"

She paused, lumbering her truck onto yet another back road. "He might be a really good horse for you, though I would want to try him again and take a trail ride to test him under those conditions. He's got possibility and can grow with you. That he's a willing jumper is good, and Stacey questioned whether we'd take him to shows and jump him occasionally because he really likes that. They seem to care about this horse."

"I may never jump," I reminded her.

"Oh, I think you will, and even if you don't, I would keep him in tune and interested. I love going to hunter pace shows. We'd have a lot of fun. And someday you might too. But, this is the first horse we looked at. There is no need to buy him, even if he is right."

"How often do good horses come up?"

"Depends. Sometimes there are plenty to choose from; other times you wait a while. You never really know."

PATIENCE IS NOT MY VIRTUE. Horse shopping is time-intensive, and I prefer to get on with life. The next day I called Bobbi.

"Why don't you take another look at Bandi? If he seems right I think we should just go for it."

"Okay. I'll talk to Stacey, and see if we can also have a week's trial to get a better feel for him."

The following Tuesday, the 5th of July, Bobbi called to congratulate me. The test ran perfectly: I owned a horse, at least provisionally. He would arrive Monday, the 11th. We would park him at Riga Meadow, a facility across town, until our place was ready, with a little luck by August. Dr. Kay would "vet" him, and we'd try him for a couple of days to make sure.

"Okay" was all I could say, and hung up. I swallowed hard. I was a kid again—thrilled at owning a horse, like I won the sweepstakes of the animal world. But soon enough the adult resurfaced to shout "RESPONSIBILITY" and the speed of the acquisition unhinged me. The simple transaction of buying a horse seemed huge, but in retrospect, what baby steps they were in a brand new world!

CHAPTER NINE

The Trifecta

·◁━━━━━▷·

THE MONDAY BANDI ARRIVED did not go quite as I had envisioned. My parents had flown in from Florida the night before, and by the time I crawled into bed it was 10:30 p.m., late for me. Alone since Scott had headed back to the city for the work week, I read for more than my usual five minutes and didn't crash until nearly midnight. At 1:00 a.m., the phone rang.

"Hello?" I was groggy, but still braced for disaster.

"Roxanne, it's Marie," my kids' babysitter enunciated slowly. "I have to tell you that Mrs. Kilner's house is on fire, and it's fully involved. I'm on my way."

As my brain parted dream fog, Marie repeated herself, only louder and even more slowly, like I was hard of hearing, or a two-year-old.

"Okay. I'll be here if you need anything." I tried to sound ready to help.

"Fully involved, fully involved" looped in my head like Neil Diamond's *Sweet Caroline* once it's stuck. I couldn't fully decode Marie's professional lingo, so I shuffled around my bed to peer through the wooden blinds. Ursula Kilner's two-hundred-and-fifty-year-old schoolhouse had grown over the years into a sprawling maze called Bird Bottom Farm. The house is hidden from our view all year by a line of property-dividing brush and trees, but flames shooting above the seventy-foot pines, oaks and maples slapped me into sharp focus. A sunset orange lit the midnight sky and the flames towered high enough to cast menacing shadows across my lawn. My ears tuned in to the crack and pop of burning wood through my tightly closed up house, penetrating the hum of the AC. My heart thumping, I jumped into some clothes and ran out the door.

By the time I reached my driveway, Bobbi's husband Chip was there, frantically donning his uncooperative fire suit, his face sleep-creased and bug-eyed. Living down the street, he was the first on the scene. I remembered him telling me about the rigorous ladder test he had been training for. I wondered if he knew what to do. His voice was more gravelly than usual.

"You don't mind that I'm in your driveway, I hope. I must be one of the first ones here." He sprinted down the road juggling his gear.

What to do? Adrenaline revved my body but my head told me to stay out of the way. I walked the street toward Ursula's house. Help was arriving fast, and I let them know my home and property were available for anything needed. "Fully involved" became fully illuminated: a ravenous fire and good-bye house. I later heard that the term designates an inferno they hope only to contain. The structure is already presumed a total loss. *How did this happen so fast,* I wondered?

The familiar faces dashing around oddly comforted me. We had been in this small town long and deep enough to have integrated in a way many weekenders do not. We know a lot of local people, and many think we live here full-time, or at least some pretend we do.

After Chip, I next spotted Jacquie, the first woman firefighter on the Salisbury volunteer force. She is always in control with knowledge and a no nonsense authority that you sense goes even deeper than all you see on the surface. People like Jacquie you instinctively trust. Then there was the ubiquitous Bullet. My husband and I often marveled at how quickly he presented himself at every auto accident, fire, downed tree limb, or even to rescue a pet cat stuck between the walls of our friends' newly renovated house (he axed the sheetrock in two places and in return "persuaded" the family to patronize the firefighters' pancake breakfast the next morning). A dense hulk of a man with a flowing beard and squirrelly hair, he waves his trunk-thick arms like mad to direct traffic, inducing guilt for just *thinking* about rubber-necking. You don't dare do it; his bulgy glare will shame you out of even the quickest sideways gawk such that you tend to speed up through his detours. Yet, I suspect he's a softie when not in disaster mode. He plays Santa for the town's needs at Christmas including the Rockwellian tree lighting, complete with a town band-led, candlelit carol sing on the green in front of The White Hart, a long-time village favorite event. I once asked Marie how he got tagged "Bullet."

"I know it's hard to believe, but supposedly when he was a kid, he was really fast."

He does move his arms pretty quick for a big man, so I can vaguely conjure a younger, lither Bullet. Later in the summer he was forced to cut back his duties courtesy of a struggling heart and suffered a strict diet. Many townspeople kept an eye on him. His son married at The White Hart the same summer and looks just like him. I had heard it was a boisterous affair; no doubt Bullet's traffic arms kept order and a record pace at the buffet line.

I found Marie with my neighbor. I approached Ursula Kilner at ease in an aluminum lawn chair in the aisle of road watching her house burn. Her once-white hat sat low and crooked on her head and her shrunken body rested as lightly and still as a pinned insect. A cane and her pocketbook lay across her lap. Moving only her lips, she cracked jokes while two EMTs monitored her vital signs. Ursula was not the least bit fazed, but then she is a tough old bird. This frail but feisty seventy-eight-year-old Daughter of the American Revolution had lived alone since her husband of forty years died ten years ago. A collector and a penny pincher, she had frugally wedged stuff into the nooks and crannies of her red-boarded, serpentined "Bird Bottom" farmhouse for decades. She once lugged home a decrepit piano from the town dump believing the ivories worth cold hard cash. Unfortunately the keys proved plastic and the wooden carcass has been rotting in her front yard many years. Childless with only a few distant relatives, over time she parented fifteen rescued greyhounds and thirty-three stray cats as her family.

Her two remaining dogs escaped and were sheltered in her car that firefighters relocated to our field across the street. Our caretaker George got out too. He lived in an apartment over Ursula's garage and managed her property and Ursula too, by default. They both complained bitterly about each other at every opportunity, but comprised, in their own weird way, a family unit.

I volunteered to check on the two dogs. Albeit confused, they mostly relaxed on the back seat. Eventually the local animal hospital vet arrived, checked them for smoke inhalation and removed them to their boarding facility a few miles away in Falls Village. No one knew about the cats. I returned to my house to make sure my parents and kids were sleeping through the commotion. What I saw unnerved me. Large burning embers were raining down over my yard and across my wood shingle roof. I kept alert to the singeing of my own flesh, batting cinders away. The amplified snapping of incineration made me reconsider our comfort-giving fireplace blazes. Spontaneous combustion of my house, myself even, felt possible with the heat blowing onto my face. I wondered if I should alert the firefighters, but they were all completely occupied, and it was, thankfully, a very humid night. I did not see anything catching, but I thought how quickly Ursula's house engulfed and it petrified me. I imagined another "fully involved" fire with my family asleep inside.

I decided to wake Dad. He was barely coherent having taken a sleeping pill. But he and Mom eventually crept downstairs and suggested we water the roof, at least where we could reach. He wrangled the not-quite-long-enough garden hose while I jogged back to check on things at Ursula's. Blackened firefighters, shed of their suffocating suits, lay sweating and exhausted on tarps absorbing oxygen administered by EMTs. They were guarded from overexertion by clearly defined rules of engagement, and I witnessed one firefighter debating his minder for the nod to get back to work.

Chip was one forced to rest. Two even slept, fatigue trumping adrenaline. The rest, taking turns, ringed the structure on the ground and angled high on wedged ladders, all aiming hoses into windows toward sucking flames; thus tiered, these slick, black mermen spewed water to arc a grotesque fountain, their yellow chest reflectors glinting light from the flying droplets. For all that, I was witnessing a lost cause. Already the roof had burned away, and the flames controlled every inch of what had been a red-sided, white-trimmed nest of domesticity woven through with memories—most recently two lives lived, celebrated and treasured. I mourned how quickly a life-long collection of comfort, a home as opposed to a house, could, literally, go up in smoke: the photo of Ursula's husband, Glen, by the pond with the dogs jumping up to a treat he held aloft; crumbling letters and yellowed postcards in collapsing shoeboxes; a favorite, well-seasoned cast-iron skillet; stashed addresses of old friends; a moth-sealed, creamy lace wedding dress. I imagined Ursula's future years of suddenly remembering, at odd times spurred by a casual sight, sound or smell, another precious keepsake she once had owned and had forgotten about until that moment, now permanently gone: a pansy-embroidered handkerchief of her mother's, the bin of Glen's old wristwatches and their sprung springs, the cockeyed door-frame in the pantry, the sweet lilac bush that crowded the porch rocker. Then I heard some firefighters shout that they had run out of water.

Only townspeople housed near the village center drink from centralized water and empty into sewers. The rest of us dig wells and install septic systems. Ursula's property borders a small pond filled periodically by runoff heading to the Housatonic River from the higher hills in the hundreds of wooded acres behind. Being summer, the pond and its feeder streams were bone dry. My indoor swimming pool held potential, but the barn that held it—situated up the hill in the woods, aesthetically out of sight—was deemed inaccessible. *How can they be out of water*, I wondered? There was no shortage of equipment or companies responding. Indeed, the newspaper would cite that thirteen fire stations helped out, one of the largest responses in the town's history. But there is rarely enough trucked-in water for thirsty fires like these. Several trucks eventually headed half a mile down the road to Dutcher's bridge where eighteenth-century pioneer Dutcher ferried travelers across the Housatonic. Now, under the overly constructed concrete and steel span that encourages speed and accidents, the firemen found a suitably inclined bank allowing the tanks to suck up river water.

I checked on Ursula again.

"Should we move you to my house, Ursula? You can't be too comfortable in that chair." I looked to the EMTs for guidance.

"That's not a bad idea," she said, strangely chipper. "There's not much left to see here."

Jacquie nodded her approval.

"Do you think you can make it up our hill?"

"Of course; I'm not *that* old, yet."

Slowly we guided her bent form along the road, up the gravel drive and through my kitchen door. The slamming screen snapped the quiet while I flipped the lights. Ursula practically disappeared in the comfy swivel rocker and sipped some water. My parents gathered and we listened to her stories about her abusive parents, her Lyme disease and her distrust of all politicians local and federal. She appreciated an audience. Her lighthearted excitement disconcerted, but we attributed it to shock. George, who later told us he had gotten Ursula and the dogs out of the house—and Ursula more than once since she had to collect her handbag first, her hat second, and tried to go to the bathroom, third—was having trouble breathing and had been whisked away to Sharon Hospital for treatment. At 3:30 a.m. my dad, who was not in the best of health, went back to bed. I sent Mom with him and called the hospital.

"George, how are you?"

"I'm okay (pause) but my lungs (pause) hurt (pause) bad," he wheezed through oxygen apparatus.

"Ursula is with me and we're worried about you. Do you need anything?"

"No but (pause) I might (pause) need a (pause) ride home."

"Sure George. You just call me when they say you're ready to go. But don't rush it; let them make sure you're okay."

I remembered last summer George retrieved me from the same hospital after my bike accident. After several hours of waiting in the ER, and several more having gravel dug out of my left palm and my road rash scrubbed with a plastic nail brush, I felt eternally grateful when he arrived five minutes after I called him, and it is at least a twenty minute ride. George had been a loyal caretaker for our property for five years. Living next door meant he was always around in an emergency, and he proved able at most tasks, large and small. His specialty being the grass, he is just as nutty as my husband about grooming it to putting green quality, a challenge given that I vigilantly guard against fertilizers and pesticides. Thick, deeply rooted grass that crowds out weeds is his mantra, and he takes great pride in recounting how many passersby stop to inquire after his secret recipe. He is also happy to do anything, from cleaning and maintaining our two car-seated, kid food-crumbed autos, to clearing our wooded walking trails, to keeping our birdlife singing with full feeders and Crisco suet cocktails, to just being around to police the revolving wheel of workmen needed to keep our old house functioning. A quirky combination of odd and domestic, he can wrap a present better than a Macy's pro (in desperation I had enlisted him several Christmas Eves), and he went to the trouble of ordering a fade-resistant Old Glory specially run up the Capitol's flag pole for Elliot's eighth birthday.

He talks a blue streak however, to all comers, and I debate whether he has a tendency to spin yarns or is just destined, Forest Gump-style, to have so many crazy things happen to him. Some people think him a bit off, even untrustworthy, but then many people are eccentric, both in the country and the city. I am convinced he pegs us the oddballs, and I can't argue: why would anyone have such labor intensive infrastructure and not live in it regularly? And care so much about a smudgy car windshield or the spring-fattened birds going hungry during the week when we are not even there? A fraught, oft-bemused relationship between proprietor and caretaker is a strong current and we go with the flow: we are too lazy to look for someone with a stellar resume, so we give ours the benefit of doubt as well as keep our distance, maintain a sharp eye, occasionally wonder if we're being taken to the cleaners, and accept him with a grain of salt. If George interrupts our Saturday breakfasts with a long, unbelievable story or a gossipy complaint about Ursula, well that's the price we'll pay for a house that works and grounds that wow us.

I figured the hospital would keep George for the night, but he sounded in good hands, and I relayed this bit of good news to Ursula. Then I ran back to her house for a report on the firefighting. No change. When I returned, she was gone. *What the hell?* A quick search found her in the guest room, asleep on the bed. Apparently she knew her way around the house and her back hurt, so she helped herself. I saw her shepherd's crook of a fragile body curled over on its side, with her sparse grey locks threading from her grimy boater. In her sleep her hands gripped her cane and pocketbook, likely her only remaining possessions. Her ancient, stuffed wallet was open; cards, cash and bits of cracked, stained paper escaped across the blue damask coverlet. She had been searching for the name of her nutritionist, "the only one willing to help with her Lyme disease," though George claimed she refused the antibiotics prescribed by her succession of doctors. Crotchety, stubborn and sometimes mean-spirited, nevertheless my heart went out to her. *Not fair*, I thought, and I wondered what would become of her.

By weird coincidence, Ursula's great-nephew from Illinois arrived the day before the fire for his annual visit. Over the years, Ross had urged Ursula to move in with him and his family, but she would not budge. The man's a saint for begging. During the blaze, based on Ursula's vague description of a place called "'Lantern' something or other" we tracked him down at a motel in Great Barrington, Massachusetts, but it took him over an hour to arrive, what with driving twenty miles and walking one more in the dark around the trucks and equipment that blocked the road. A cued ghost on the stroke of 4:00 a.m., he appeared just in time to disentangle Ursula from a well-meaning but inept facilitator to the homeless, supposedly connected with the Red Cross.

Waking her, Red Cross man had said: "Ursula, it's not too early to begin thinking of where you'll go in the next chapter of your life."

"What do you mean?" Ursula leveled him a squint that made me glad she didn't have her rifle.

"Have you thought about assisted liv—"

"I will NOT go to any of those places," Ursula snapped, propped on her elbow, shaking her fist. "They try to kill you in there, and the food is just horrible. I'm never going back there!" She gathered her handbag's contents in preparation for flight.

"But you need someone to take care of you. I know how these things go. I had a fire once myself, and I learned valuable life lessons. You've lost everything. You can't begin to know what's involved here."

"I can take care of myself! I have done so for sixty years. I told you, I'm never going to a home. I won't do it. I'd rather die." She reached for her stick to beat the idea out of him. "Leave me alone!"

At first I stayed mum because what do I know about assisting in a trauma? But this was ridiculous.

"Maybe she doesn't have to make a life plan while her house is still ablaze. And, it's four o'clock in the morning," I said.

I had heard from George that Ursula was hardly destitute: apparently she was the kind of old lady that saves used twine but has files full of AT&T stock certificates issued decades ago. When Ross arrived, the mysterious trauma junkie had already exited, but not without reiterating to me, on my own dark doorstep, his plan for Ursula and his own life's "revelations." Later I found out that Jacquie was our local Red Cross affiliate, and she had never heard of this mystery guest. Who did I have in my house: an insomniac nut with a police radio and a compulsion to meddle? Strange things do go bump in the night.

I gave Ross and Ursula some privacy at the kitchen table, but resisted the lure of bed. I wandered the halls aimlessly—a strange feeling, not knowing where to put myself in my own home. Marie reappeared to check in and confirmed the obvious: Bird Bottom would be a total loss. Helpless, we bandied platitudes about two hundred and fifty years of history down the drain and how the important thing was that everyone escaped safely. We expressed optimism about the cats, notoriously wily survivors.

Pat the fire marshal arrived. He gently questioned Ursula and shifted to a lengthy discussion with Ross. By the time Ross escorted Ursula through my front door to go back to his motel, dull light inched across the horizon. My kids never heard a thing. This was good and bad—they would be well rested, but raring to go in about forty-five minutes. It was 5:15 a.m.

I climbed into bed, my body so grateful to be horizontal. I dialed Scott knowing he'd be rising for his gym workout back in NYC. I was done-in but wound up: like a kid with a secret to spill and punch-drunk with exhausted excitement. Scott answered, a little anxious at the early call.

"Hello?"

"You won't believe what happened," I said with disingenuous calm. "Ursula's house burned down."

"What? What do you mean?"

"Totally demolished, and it's still burning."

I satisfied his questions, as best as I was able, realizing the difficulty of his grasping such a changed landscape in the ten hours since he had driven off. I fell lightly asleep for half an hour until my kids woke me for breakfast and camp. As usual. Just another day. Except that a burned-out bonfire smell of smoke hung thick in the humid air. The road remained closed off throughout the day, following firefighting stake-out procedures against flare-ups. Despite all that dousing water, the site burned for another twelve hours and smoldered for two days more.

I wandered my eight acres of yard examining notepad-sized, carbon-black pieces of burnt paper. Mostly book pages, the high heat charcoaled them such that I could still read the even blacker words, like they were printed from the devil's own underworld press. Ursula curated an important, personal library of old books at Bird Bottom, mostly about local history and the genealogy she studied. Overnight these phoenixed treasures floated down, summer leaves of incinerated stories across our green grass and away into the woods. I knelt to collect them, soiling my fingers, but soon gave up, allowing the trees to reclaim their kind's earlier sacrifices. I kicked aside foil wine caps and singed labels from kitchen staples, Pillsbury and Bisquick. Smoke still billowed into the sky.

The kids took the news with vague interest. Healthily self-absorbed they went about their morning routines. I returned from camp drop-offs and was met at my door by our housekeeper Maria.

"George is pacing around outside," she said. "He looks terrible. I wasn't sure what to do."

We found him in the driveway, a wreck: his face was flushed, creased and drawn all at once, and his eyes receded red and watery. In a croaking whisper that grated my ears, he cried through his story.

"George, what are you doing here? I thought you were in the hospital."

"I walked. I'm looking for my car."

Ross had taken Ursula to his motel in George's car since his was inaccessibly down the closed road. The alternate route spared Ursula a last view of her burning house. She never did return, refusing adamantly even to scavenge important keepsakes. In my mind's eye she looked even more desiccated, almost transparent against the backdrop of a motel room. With all physical evidence of her life erased, she floated, an unanchored ghost. George, however, stood solid and desperate.

"You *walked*? From where?"

"The hospital."

"What? Why didn't you call me? I told you I'd come get you!"

The hospital is at least fifteen miles away. I was also shocked they would let him leave in the condition he appeared to be in.

"I only have hundred dollar bills. They wouldn't give me change and wouldn't let me use the phone," he whimpered.

"Did they release you? Are you okay?

Silence.

I intuited he had snuck out.

"They were so mean in there. So I walked home in my bare feet and shorts."

He was still crying, and his voice deteriorated. But he needed to talk.

"You walked bare-footed?"

Incredulous, Maria and I looked at each other and down at his feet, in shoes.

"I got these from the garage just now.... But I couldn't believe it. No one would pick me up," he complained, outraged. "I tried to get a cup of coffee in the gas station, but they locked the door and wouldn't let me in."

George was in shock and paranoid to boot. So I tried a little humor with the truth.

"George, no offense, but you look like a mass murderer even now. With no shoes or shirt, how could they guess you were a victim of a fire? You look like you've been on a three-day bender."

He laughed through his tears.

"I wouldn't have picked you up, and I know you."

He laughed a little harder and coughed.

"Why don't you come in and have something to eat. And I don't think smoking is a good idea."

We all looked at the lit cigarette he cupped in his hand. He had told me he quit last year. I witnessed him get heavier and then thinner again, so I figured he had relapsed.

"No, no, I can't eat, and I have to go next door to see what's happening."

"Are you sure? Do you need some money?"

"I got plenty of money." He pulled out a stack of hundred dollar bills.

"Well, let me give you something smaller, so you can get a cup of coffee when you want one."

He took my proffered twenties with gratitude. "I lost all my money in the fire. This is all I was able to grab."

"What do you mean? Don't you keep your money in the bank?" I asked with the sinking feeling that he would be exactly the person to stash cash around the house.

"I used to hide some money in my bedroom, but they say not to keep it there, so I had most of it in the hallway. The fire was bad there." He started to cry again.

There was nothing to say.

We stared at the ground.

He shuffled down the road.

It was a pearl of a day with the same cornflower blue cloudless sky that back-dropped the Twin Towers assault: oblivious nature rubbing its overbearing resilience into the wounds of our puny disasters, or so it seemed. But, like an astringent treatment in the midst of tragedy, quotidian life ticked on, then and now. All morning *that* 11th day I watched the towers burn from our uptown, thirty-seventh floor apartment. At mid-day my dog still needed to be walked despite tragedy. As Velvet and I headed south on 1st Avenue, our regular route, the day still shone brilliantly, and my dog sniffed the same tree-protecting pachysandra beds, peeling hydrants and rusted signposts, and peed and shat on the curb. "Go hurry up, Velvet, go hurry up," I urged as usual. Like every other day, I collected her waste in a blue plastic bag and tossed it in the nearest trash bin.

"Good girl, Velvie, *good* girl."

If not for the flow of dusty, dazed people shuffling almost exclusively north positioning me against the current like a spawning salmon and the black grey smoke ballooning eastward across the distant southern skyline, I would simply have taken the day for granted: a lovely late summer boon. *This* beautiful day, July 11th, Ursula's home, and all she had, was gone, but my horse was on his way nonetheless.

Back inside, I briefed my weary parents and realized the time. I had completely forgotten about Bandi's arrival. Though my heart was not in it, I was glad for the diversion. Mom, Dad and I pulled up to the barns at Riga Meadow just as Bobbi drove in with Bandi trailered behind her pick-up. She was excited because he travelled with no trouble—always a relief with such unpredictable and unwieldy cargo. Bobbi had shared many examples of the mishaps her horses managed while standing in a metal box behind her truck, many miles from help and home.

Though Bandi should have been the man of the moment, I first inquired after Bobbi's husband who I last glimpsed re-equipping to get back to the fire fight.

"How's Chip?"

"Oh, he hasn't come home yet."

It was 11:00 a.m. I tried to fill Bobbi in on the fire as I reached in to pat Bandi, but she was preoccupied with my new horse. Fumbling the trailer door latch, she carried on, unconcerned about the event her husband and I had shared, habituated, I figured, to sleeping through his midnight emergencies.

"Here's your boy," she said cheerily. "He did just fine on the ride."

Indeed. Serene as a yogi he stood munching away at some hay in a string bag tied at mouth level. She backed him out and down the ramp slowly and he shone reddish brown in the sunlight. Despite my sleep-deprived funk, I remembered the camera, and Mom snapped a few photos. I had a new male, or half-male, in my life, my first eunuch I suppose, and joy eclipsed my exhaustion. A beautiful horse, my very own: our future partnership of show ribbons and glorious trail rides streamed out before us. Over the next hour we settled him into his new quarters, and in the physicality of the tasks I forgot about Ursula and the fire, indulging the moment.

Late in the afternoon I felt smoked over from the fire and lack of sleep. With plenty of the day still to go I retrieved my kids from camp. Elliot had a Little League game at 6:00 p.m. across the state line in Millerton, New York. Excited that his Pop (my dad) would see him play, we settled in for a hot, slow-paced time. Baseball played by ten-year-olds is like watching paint dry. These kids pitch overhand, hard, but with dicey accuracy. Satisfying hits are rare, and stealing home on wild pitches is common. Singles regularly score as home runs based on overthrows that roll to the back fences. Elliot's good eye ensures that he walks a lot—even though all the parents yell "swing away" just to get some action going.

Halfway through the game, small-talking to some of the parents in the bleachers, I relaxed while a bored Jane balanced and banged along the metal bleachers. I let my mother bear the burden of watchful care and took advantage of the respite, figuring the roar of the crowd would alert me to any developments on the field. The crack of a bat alerted me to see Elliot drop the ball thrown to him at third base for an out. He scrambled after it and made a decent throw to home plate to get the same runner, but it was too late: a run scored.

"Roxanne, Elliot's hurt."

I looked back to third. Elliot was down on his knees, flapping his hands furiously in front of his face. I raced over, hearing "bloody nose" spoken by parents as I passed. *Thank God*, I thought to myself, *only a bloody nose*. By the time I got there, he was crying, almost hysterically, and covered in blood. I knelt and took over the coach's hold on the bridge of Elliot's nose with one hand as I held a rapidly soaking tissue to his nostrils with the other.

"Put your face forward Ellie, so you don't swallow the blood," I counseled, falsely calm. The old custom of tilting the head back thankfully has been debunked—I still remember that disgusting feeling of blood pouring down my own kid throat.

"Elliot, don't worry, honey. I've had plenty of bloody noses and they look a lot worse than they are," I soothed.

I waited several seconds and lifted the wad of tissue a centimeter away from his nose, talking all the while. The blood gushed forth. I replaced my hand. Helpfully, people were gathering up tissue and towel reinforcements.

"If you calm down, it will stop sooner," I told him, fighting to maintain my own composure.

Though I have run many alarming nosebleeds that eventually ceased on their own, one did send me to the hospital where I endured an unpleasant gauze packing and eventual cauterization. Although rarely life threatening, so much blood from the head invariably begs the question "will it stop?" And this was my beloved child, scared stiff and hemorrhaging. I felt panic circling rationality in my brain.

"But it's not stopping!"

"It will soon, I promise. Look it's slowing up."

I inched the towel away, but it still geysered. I lied and told Elliot it ebbed some. I glimpsed the head coach looking worried as he worked away on Elliot's redder than orange glove with some wet wipes. He needed an occupation, and his busyness distracted Elliot. My son's shirt streaked red down the front. He held his dripping hands out *a la* Frankenstein while blood pooled on the grass. My stomach lurched and a buzzing sounded behind my eyes. *No, don't wilt now.* I lowered my head to steady my blood pressure and pass the nausea. It was eight o'clock at night, and I had been up since one, working on an hour and a half of sleep. I bolstered myself, breathed deep, and re-adjusted my squeeze lower down on his nostrils. My faintness faded as the coaches and parents recounted how the ball flew off the tip of Elliot's glove, clonking his nose before rolling away.

"How about that, El? You made the play after you were hurt."

"But I didn't make the out."

"But it was a good throw."

Another three minutes passed, with intermittent checking. Just as I suggested a trip to the emergency room, the red tide receded. The game had resumed earlier, but the coaches suggested we sit on the bench for a while to be sure he was okay and then take him home.

Elliot perked up once the blood stopped and watched another of his friends get clocked in the back by a pitch.

"I have to go see if Jason's alright," he shouted, and took off toward home plate.

Soon, he had trotted back to me begging permission to hit. I questioned the coaches, who shrugged their shoulders and nodded, and though every bone in my aching body urged retreat, I waved him on: "Go." I aligned my decision with the folk wisdom of falling off a horse—if you don't get right back on you may never ride again. Elliot is a thinker like me, so I worried he would over-ruminate given time and inaction. He loved baseball. Playing rather than fretting was probably best, as long as his nose didn't unclot. I watched him approach the plate. He bent to it without any trepidation and whacked a double, hitting in a run that turned out to be the winner. *Alright, Elliot,* I exclaimed under my breath. Later in the game, he climbed the mound. He had never pitched before, except with Scott in the backyard. He performed more than credibly, and I beamed proud rays toward my warrior son. What a day.

At the following week's game, Elliot did end up at the emergency room. He took a solid hit in the kidney with a forty mile an hour late throw as he righted himself from a successful slide into home plate. Though he tried to shake it off, the pain escalated rendering him doubled over and howling. He is not particularly sensitive to pain, and doesn't dramatize, so after conferring with a doc parent, we sped off to Sharon Hospital for an x-ray. By the time we arrived, poor Elliot's writhing and begging for help prompted some pretty quick action in the ER. A morphine drip worked wonders. All tests proved negative, and he woke up right as rain the next morning. We figured a muscle spasm was to blame, since anything else would have left him sore at the very least.

It was torture witnessing Elliot in severe pain begging for relief I was unable to supply. I morphed into a panicked animal, screaming at people who couldn't possibly move quickly enough. This time, thankfully, I had Scott with me and more sleep. But between Elliot's two injuries, I had earned some grey hairs and was reminded how draining parenting can be. Do I have the energy to squeeze in new projects like horses and a farm and the danger they entailed? The hazards of baseball, let alone his winter sport of ice hockey, seemed enough excitement.

As for Ursula's house, it was a complete loss, with the exception of George's more recently added, unfinished apartment above the garage, though even that was smoked and wet. The fire department camped out two more days to keep watch. The source possibly sparked from the forty-year-old attic fan that Ursula swore was turned off. We put George up at The White Hart for a few weeks since his remaining section lacked electricity and water. I took the kids to the site to show them what fire can do, and the charred remains surrounding the hole that was the basement made us cringe for Ursula. Very little could be salvaged, and in the humid summer heat, mold soon crept lava-thick across it all. George informed us of the nightly rat troops, and our own sightings around our house prompted a call to our vermin buster, Jim, who put down poison, and to the county sanitarian to speed up the inevitable demolition. But bureaucracy moves at a glacial pace. Even though she had more than adequate insurance and a helpful agent, Ursula inched through the necessary decisions.

In late September the rubble finally was cleared away. George reverted to living in his car for months, unwilling to give up on his damaged home, and felt compelled to stand guard against varmints and voyeurs. He posted too many KEEP OUT/NO TRESSPASSING signs, inviting attention. Because of a fall that broke her neck, Ursula spent time in hospital and then in a nursing home, the very fate she had feared. But she adamantly refused to move to Illinois with Ross, and, still in possession of her Yankee iron will, planned to rebuild. I hoped she would live long enough to see it through.

CHAPTER TEN

A Colt and a Filly

IN ACCORDANCE WITH THE HYPERBOLIC PHRASE, I would "kill for" my children, Elliot and Jane, as they are my own flesh and blood. I fully believe I could lift a vehicle off my kid as described in those emergency tales of superhuman strength. When Jane asks how much I love her, I honestly submit a superlunary answer.

"I love you and Elliot more than anyone or anything in the entire universe."

"Even more than Daddy and Velvet?" she asked.

"Yes, even more than the two of them put together."

"Hey," Scott said, "I'm sitting right here."

"Someone I created takes precedence over someone I married." I rolled my eyes at him like "*duh.*"

"Where do I rank against the pets?"

"Velvet or Bandi?" I frowned, thinking it over.

And I am not even especially maternal, not naturally the giving type. One by one our friends began spawning with gusto claiming that "your life isn't complete without kids; it's what *makes* a family." Ambivalently, after fourteen years of marriage, we took the plunge, had one, barely made it through the baby stage and then, according to rules of genetic conspiracy, five years later we forgot the mastitis and sleepless months and had another, and persuaded everyone we knew to do the same to convince ourselves we had done the right thing. There is no u-turn, nor

any upside in admitting that life as we had known it—long Sunday mornings with the *New York Times*, sex without the door barricaded, some hours of the week with nothing to do, a leisurely, narcissistic self-indulgence—ceases to exist, and the needy, adorable little people, whom you love more than anyone you have ever known including—and this is big—*yourself*, are yours for life. And though other parents do not like to admit it, and with rare exceptions, we really only deeply love our own: everyone else's just don't compare. It's primal.

While Scott and I will do absolutely anything for them, it doesn't mean that self-sacrifice is returned. By nature, children experiment, and we are the laboratories. Just when we think we've got their fastball sorted out, they throw us a curve: Elliot yells "Damn it" in the middle of a crowded store when they are out of cupcakes; both kids get ornery and bored while sitting among enough toys and books to stock a day care center; Jane throws her first and only tantrum during an all-important elementary school interview (the bright-eyed admissions director turned sullen at my protestations of "that's a first, we've never seen that before," and replied "Of course," while scribbling Xs and !!!s across our file); one regresses and wets the bed again just when I had disposed of the waterproof mattress pad, and, well, you get the picture.

Scott and I are decent parents, maybe even better than average. But we have our weak spots. For Scott, it's the car. When both kids jabber at once to a tired Pa who just finished a hard week's work, trying to get his attention—that is, each trying to get all the attention, pitching the decibels louder and louder, and Scott is trying to maneuver a Suburban around the craters on the Willis Avenue bridge at rush hour, and 1010 WINS is blaring a twenty-minute backup on the Bruckner Boulevard onto which we have just turned, well, think pressure cooker and Linda Blair. I smile smugly when Scott loses it because it is so rare. Volatility is more my trademark with mealtimes, particularly family dinners, my Achilles heel. An example:

"Jane, please tell Elliot dinner is ready."

Scott is already doing his best to tilt this dinner toward success. Flattering Jane with a job gives her some ownership and a vested interest in cooperation.

"OK, Daddy," she chirps, and runs in tight, excited steps to the playroom.

"Aayot [her mutilation of Elliot], come eat dinner."

Immediately she races back.

"He's not coming."

"Yes I am, Jane, give me a minute. Sheesh," Elliot yells, slamming his laptop shut.

He bounds in and slumps into his chair. We assemble around the table, and the kids assess their plates. Neither child is happy with the appetizing marinated chicken and broccoli that Scott has given up time with his Sunday newspapers to lovingly prepare. Tonight, like all nights, they would have preferred pasta with "Farmer John cheese" as Jane persists in calling parmesan. But, to his credit, Elliot rallies.

"Rub-a-dub-dub, thanks for the grub."

Scott and I cautiously exchange glances. Our hopes rise. Maybe tonight will be that rare experience of cute word-play and meaningful conversation, where we manage to keep some control and perhaps impart a tiny bit of wisdom, so that even if we cannot quite label the meal pleasurable, we can tag it a "learning experience."

"Mommy, when will I get booties?" Jane says, suddenly looking very concerned.

Elliot chokes, spits some chewed greens onto the lazy Susan and howls because he knows that Jane means "boobies," her twice-mangled euphemism for breasts. She has been asking this question a lot lately, and Elliot, embarrassed about all things sexual, finds it hysterical every time. I'm just grateful when the "booties" question comes out at home rather than in an elevator, or in church. Maintaining an even keel, I reply:

"Elliot, don't be a barbarian. Please eat over your plate and use your fork. I've told you Janie, you'll grow breasts when you're a teenager, but only if you eat your dinner."

"What's a teen-angle again?

"A teen*ager* is someone thirteen, fourteen, fifteen, sixteen, seventeen, eighteen, or nineteen years old—all the numbers that end in 'teen.' Please take a bite of chicken. Daddy made it special for you and it's really yummy."

"What's for dessert?" Jane wants to know.

Elliot snorts again, sending milk out of his nose.

"EEWWW, GROSS," Jane declares.

Dessert is a loaded topic. Because Scott and I have fallen into the trap of bribing Jane with dessert to prompt her to eat her dinner, a practice that the childcare gurus declare the ultimate no-no, it raises our hackles. Every day we say we have to call a halt to the practice, but there is usually some mitigating circumstance that saps our will. It doesn't help that Elliot eats well: rather, it makes us feel like we've run out of steam with child number two. Elliot takes great pride in his attention to vegetables and his restraint regarding dessert, if only as a way to distinguish himself from his little sister, who, as he has announced on numerous occasions, was "the worst thing that ever happened to me when I was five." Internally, Scott and I are beating our selves up about our inadequate parenting in regard to food and projecting ahead to inevitable eating disorders, and then my thoughts shift to Cain and Abel, but little Freudian Jane has already moved on:

"Will I get a penis when I'm a teen-angel?"

Elliot bursts out: "Of course not, Jane—you're a girl. You have a *vagina.* Sheesh!"

"Sheesh!" Jane shouts louder, and rolls her eyes at her brother.

A volley of "sheeshes" ensues.

I consider myself lucky that body parts are only discussed. My good friend's daughter once showed her vagina to her grandfather at the dinner table.

Scott comes to the rescue with the double-whammy of a conversation stopper:

"HEY! Elliot. Tell me one good thing that happened in school today. Jane, eat a carrot."

Dead silence, with the exception of scraping forks sculpting food pyramids.

That's inventive, I think to my own unimaginative, sulking self.

"Well?" Scott persists.

"Lunch and recess," Elliot sullenly replies.

"That's two. Did you finish reading *Skinnybones?* Jane: pick up a carrot, put it in your mouth, chew it and swallow it or Daddy will be very angry with you." He looks back at Elliot, who, feeling the pressure, replies,

"Of course I finished *Skinnybones*. It was so dumb."

Elliot re-slumps and probes a piece of chicken only to smear it around in a dollop of ketchup. Simultaneously, he rolls his eyes at no one and Scott rolls his eyes at me. Looking for support, he forces a smile, and I icily return a grimace. Mouth full of carrot, Jane pipes in:

"Daddy, you have a big butt."

Elliot snorts out some more food, and Scott knows instinctively that this will push me over the edge into my "I hate eating with the kids mode," about which we both know I will later suffer guilt because, as the same aforementioned child-rearing experts have said, it is crucial to their pint-sized psyches to share quality mealtimes. Right now, I would rather be having a root canal with some good nitrous. This thought sours me more, but I feel I should defend my maligned husband.

"Jane. That is not a nice thing to say. And Daddy does not have a 'large bottom'. People come in all different shapes and sizes and it's what's inside that matters."

The content of my saccharine speech falls as flat as my delivery. To quote a Dr. Seuss character: "I said and said and said these words, I said them but I lied them."

Losing ground, I cave and pull out old faithful.

"Besides, Jane, you are not eating your dinner. Please eat a piece of chicken. When you eat well, you can have an Oreo for dessert."

"I'm eating a carrot." Jane opens her mouth wide to display chewed carrot, but it is not lost on any of us that though Jane has artfully rearranged her plate, she is still working on her first bite of the meal. The rest of us, meanwhile, have set a record pace in order to end our misery. Elliot, impatient for some Oreos, can't restrain himself any longer.

"Jane, you are so slow. And, you have the worst eating habits. All you ever eat is candy and ice cream and snack all day long. You're gonna' be fat."

Jane crumbles. Shoulders sagging, she hangs her large head in shame. Her straight brown hair covers most of her face, and hot tears drip onto her untouched chicken.

"Good move, El," I say.

"But it's true," he protests, genuinely hurt.

"Jane has to learn to pace herself just like you did when you were four. Please say you're sorry to Jane, and Jane, please have a bite of chicken." I catch her just before her "woe is me" point of no return.

There is a thoughtful pause in which we are all humbled. Elliot rescues us.

"Sorry, Janie."

"It's okay, Aayot."

I REALIZE THAT A KID BEHAVING BADLY IS EXPECTED and necessary for proper development. And it is often funny in retrospect. But there are the times when parents behave atrociously and can broker no excuse. Many of us have cringe-worthy experiences we wish we could take back or at least forget. They never invoke nostalgia and torture us forever. My lack of skill on one particular day shocks me still.

I had had too much tea, caffeine being both necessary and the enemy. On the one hand, I'm naturally tightly wound, and stimulants are the last thing I need. On the other, to play with my kids on weekend mornings instead of sleeping late while they watch videos, I need a little boost.

So, this Saturday morning in February, in Salisbury the cruelest month, I was over-caffeinated and bushed from a long week.

"Okay, this is the plan," my husband brightly declared over the Snap, Crackle, Pop! of Rice Krispies. "Elliot: you need to be at the rink early for Coach John's pre-game strategy, so we'll head off first. Mom and Jane: you two can follow in time for the game."

"Okay," Elliot and I shouted in unison.

Jane looked at her feet, jutting out her lower lip.

Scott and I were excited about the tournament this year. Elliot's hockey team's win/loss for the season was a respectable eight and eight, much improved from last year's record which Elliot accurately termed "undefeated defeated."

We said our goodbyes and good lucks.

"OK, Jane," I said cheerfully, "let's tidy up the kitchen, brush your teeth and catch up with the boys."

Thinking ahead, I had already brought Jane's toothbrush downstairs since my kids both complain about having to go back up after breakfast.

"But, I don't wanna' go," Jane whined.

"Why not? It'll be fun, and Ellie's counting on us to root for him. We need your loud cheering."

"But I don't like hockey. It's cold."

She was damn straight about that, but I reminded her, "You can play in the warm room with all the other sisters and brothers."

"No. I'm not going!"

"Well, let's just brush teeth and see how we feel. How about a lollipop once we get there?" I maneuvered her backward-dragging, surprisingly sturdy thirty-five pounds into the powder room.

Through tears Jane stepped onto the footstool next to the sink, getting madder by the second.

"Opennnn uuuup," I sang, trying to keep the mood light, her funk at bay.

She locked her jaw and lips and wagged her head slowly from side to side. I encouraged, but she gave me the "dare stare." I yelled at her to open up. Time was of the essence: these hockey games go fast and I wanted to see my son play. The games were finally exciting after four long seasons of slow motion skating during which Scott and I faithfully froze our butts off very early weekend mornings from November through March.

The tea, tension and weariness kicked in.

"Alright, Jane; I'm leaving without you."

I stormed out of the bathroom and opened and slammed the front door without going out. I was out of control, flushed and angry. I was the nine-year-old my mother left, part of me still stuck in that time and place.

Being four years old, Jane missed that I lacked shoes and a coat. I quick-turned upstairs to my bedroom to wait, unconscionably planning to hide when she came looking. Soon she was screaming, the full combo platter of hurt, hysterics, rage and fear.

"MOMMY, MOMMY, MOMMY!

I heard her feet thundering the hardwood floors. My heart raced, but I was red hot enough that I continued to ignore her. It surprised me that she didn't look upstairs, but then again, she thought I had left. I waited, maybe three minutes. In that sudden flash of mother's intuition, I felt the eerie emptiness of too quiet. In a cold panic, I flew through the rooms.

"Jane! Jane! Here I am!"

I almost fell down the stairs, taking them three at a time, using the banister to propel me faster.

"Jane! Jane! Mommy's here! Jane!" I shouted, desperate.

In the kitchen, a raw fear directed my glance out the window only to catch a last glimpse of Jane as she disappeared around the bend. She had crossed our country road, where traffic is intermittent but rural fast, and just where the hill creates a nasty blind spot. Small and low, she was marching along the snow-dusted edge of the road, against traffic as we do on our family hikes. She had no coat, and her shoeless feet were clad in white GAP socks with the non-skid bottoms.

I tore outside, listening hard for traffic so I did not have to stop and look, praying madly: *Don't let a car come, don't let a car come.* I waited to call out to her, not wanting to lure her back across the road. Catching up, I knelt and took her in my arms.

"Janie, Janie! Where are you going?

"I'm going to find you and see the boys play hockey." She was still crying, but less because she was on a mission and in the right direction, too.

"Oh, Jane! Did you look both ways?"

I needed to know this was a "Yes" or I would die. Not that it really mattered, because when little kids look, they rotate their heads dramatically and say clear, whether it is or not.

I scooped her up, ran inside, and held her tight on my lap on the hall stairs. The clock chimed Scrooge's warning of a horrible future if I did not shape up. I hugged and kissed her repeatedly like a Catholic penance, and in my head thanked God over and over that she was safe. I took her puffy, beautiful face in my hands.

"Jane. Look at me. Mommy did a bad thing. I would never leave you here alone, ever. I was mad and I tricked you. It was wrong, and I'm very, very sorry. I'll never trick you again, I promise. You have to promise Mommy that you'll never go outside again by yourself, no matter what, and never, *ever,* go in the road."

"OK Mommy, I promise."

We drove to the hockey game. Her mood improved remarkably, her ego fed by my prostrations and seeing her mother make, and admit to, a whopper of a mistake. While she recovered, I brooded. Reduced to more of a wreck with time, I despaired clandestinely for two days every time I thought about it, which was perpetual. *Why can't I be one of those maternal mothers who gives everything necessary and has endless patience?* I wanted to cry for relief, but some acts are beyond catharsis.

The next night Scott and I went on our weekly dinner date. Over a stiff martini I started to shake.

"Roxanne, what's wrong?"

"I don't think I can tell you."

"Well you have to tell me now."

I blurted out the whole despicable story, right down to the GAP socks, trying to justify my end of it by weakly emphasizing Jane's uncooperativeness and the tea, tension and weariness. But we both knew it for brutality, plain and simple, and that my childish self had gotten the better of me.

To his credit, Scott did not flip out. Worse, tears formed in his eyes. A few of mine fell into my drink. I gulped all to dull the sting.

"Oh, don't cry. She's okay. We're not perfect, and they can really get you angry sometimes." He took my hand. "Really."

"Thank God she's alright. But you know how fast those cars go, and they can't even see *us* over that hill, and she's so little. What if...." I couldn't finish.

"But it didn't, right? We're lucky no car came. It's okay. I'm glad you told me.... I don't know that I would have told you."

He paused.

"One time, I told Jane to go out front and wait by the car, and when I came out she was very close to the road. I couldn't tell you."

"*Close* to the road," I whispered angrily, "that's nothing! She *crossed* the road! I'll never get over this, ever. I'm afraid to go to sleep tonight— I know I'll have nightmares and then the worst will happen. How can I live here and see that hill all the time?"

He eventually calmed me and getting it out helped some, though Scott's story of his own mistake paled in comparison.

This happened almost two years ago. Is it true that what doesn't kill you makes you stronger? I'd like to think that mistreatment of one's own children happens at least once to every otherwise good parent, but maybe this is wishful thinking. My stomach lurches when I think about it. Every time. I wonder if it will ever recede in my mind's eye—that clarity of little Jane, at four, crossing the road in her baby socks, and a car flying over the top of the hill.

KIDS EVENTUALLY FORCED ME TO GROW UP and stop indulging the child lingering in my forty-six-year-old skin. Well, most of the time. The refocus from a narcissistic me, me, me to "it's all about them, stupid" was a seismic aftershock of recognition if not a full tectonic shift in practice. It's damn hard to balance their needs—more of me all the time—with my preferred occupations of the adult variety. So, I carefully avoid crossing the line where complete self-sacrifice will render me a resentful monster. Call me selfish.

I hoped the farm could address all of our needs. Responsible animal care could conjoin parental obligations of high-quality, weekend family time and my own unrealized fantasies of adventure. A practical plan: together we could learn farming, and what animal-loving kid could resist a private petting zoo? I envisioned the four of us taking a late afternoon stroll around the new farm, relaxing together as a family, performing tasks that intrigue, and do not bore, any of us. I assumed that they, and Scott, would happily tag along through my clever tactic of manifesting my dream for all of us.

Humph.

Scott, Elliot and Jane craft their own agendas that seldom conform to mine. Every time I suggested a walk to check out the farm, which I grant was often, everyone begged off. A lackluster "we just went yesterday" or "can't we go later?" deflated my plumping eagerness. *Huh?* I couldn't wait to see the fresh wood going up in the stalls, the custom-made stall doors that slide at the touch of a finger, the bright lighting powered by new wiring, the brown paint job with the cream trim on the cross hatchings, the additional view-enhancing windows in the tack room (my idea), the safety railings on the loft, the finishing trim along the hall ceilings. Not to mention the outside developments—the newly sawn light brown wood against the salvaged old blue/grey planks on the outbuildings, the carefully measured and leveled riding ring, the expansion of the fields with the old fencing dismantled, the wood-fresh, patient piles of replacement posts and boards, the buttressing skeleton of the round gazebo, stripped of its sidewalls and shot through with sunbeams, the water line trenches dug deep into moist black earth en route to the automatic paddock waterers, the mountains of soil transported to shift the wet spots.

I could not get enough of just getting a feel for the place. When I could, I'd sneak off to the farm at the end of the day. I would wander around alone, pace through the quiet of the fields, guiltily watch the birds and deer reclaim their abused land, and absorb the hollow of the barn absent of creatures and purpose. As a business, its "personality" was undeveloped. All was hopeful possibility, potential: the dedication page of our book or the preface. Yet volumes were already written on this land: those of Mrs. Johnson, the Dutch settlers now resting in the small cemetery, and the Weatogue tribes. Old barns and cultivated fields hold secrets: buried histories of work and process, life and death. Ours will eventually join them, living first through the new skin of crops re-tended and animals once again sheltered, only to someday pass into silent, subtle signs, like Mrs. Johnson's to me: the patterned trails grooved by horses' hooves, the mare and foal weathervane atop the gazebo, the uncommonly flat footprint of a vanished outbuilding's foundation. Many years hence our own forgotten souvenirs may include a half-rooted, rusted weathervane with specs of gilt stubborn in the carved recesses of the dressage horse's tail and mane, a brass harness buckle long-rested in some tall grass of an abandoned paddock, or, among the cobwebbed rafters, a thickly dusted Weatogue Stables ribbon of faded blue that crumbles upon lifting.

But if my family lacked appreciation for our new venture and its place in history, at least two of my brood eagerly anticipated the riding. Elliot especially "got" that part, at least. And it was pure—free of the material aspect, be it barn-building or trophies. He harbored no ambition to show, compete, over-analyze or perfect his skills, and barn aesthetics were inconsequential. His ability to be "in the moment" on horseback was a beautiful thing. Or, was I glamorizing things?

"Are you ever afraid, Elliot?" I asked.

"No."

"Do you find it hard to post and trot?"

"No."

"What do you like about it?"

"I don't know. It's just fun."

"Would you like to do it more?"

"Not really."

Where was his passion? He showed little enthusiasm for riding my new Bandi, and his favorite horse time preceded and had followed his few earlier lessons, hanging out with Albert, his instructor Jessica's very first horse, too old and lame to serve. Once, when Al's feet weren't sore, she let Elliot ride him, a rare privilege. They bonded. On top of a full bag of carrots, Elliot raced back and forth to procure handfuls of fresh pasture grass, feeding them only to Al's soft and grateful muzzle. I was told keeping him riding would be my main challenge, that boys drop out once they realize the young American horse world is ruled by girls. I wondered if he would slowly drift away.

But one weekend Elliot's city friend Max accompanied us to the farm. Upon entering the barn Elliot took a deep breath and, with unadulterated sensual fulfillment, he proclaimed:

"I *love* the smell of a barn."

"You LIKE that smell? That poop smell?" Max said, eyes popping, incredulous.

YES, Elliot! I rejoiced inwardly. He *did* appreciate barns; they just had to be full of living, breathing, smelly creatures. You either get it or you don't, and Elliot got it through the nose. Well-kept horses produce a clean natural smell, appealing once you acclimate. An occupied barn holds scents, sounds, sights and routines that orchestrate music to the senses: the hollow clop of horses' hooves along the concrete or dirt aisles, or the occasional kick against the stall walls; the sweetness of bales and the tang of manure, itself vegetarian and inoffensive, produced of digested grass, hay and grain. A seasonal rhythm: in warm months, the day-in horses, having spent their nights outside, hang their heads over their stall guards, heavy with their version of wakeful sleep, nodding and watching. In cold months, the day-out horses, rested from their night in their stall, enjoy their sunny paddocks, the bright snow quenching their thirst, or huddle in their sheds against a cutting wind.

Horses are herd animals, and they communicate vocally and bodily. Wherever they are, they whinny and neigh greetings and warnings to each other and keep a watchful eye, tracking each others' comings and goings, shadowing their buddies. Their ears and lips "speak" two additional dialects. Flat back ears and meaningful nips show displeasure across the paddock fences, despite electric dissuaders. Inside, a horse startles, upset or angry, and disturbs the peace—her loud cries echoing against the worn wood. An impatient kick that bends the thick stall wall, restless neighing and pacing is soothed or rebuked by a human voice, a minor test of wills, and all settle again. I watched one trainer force an irate, anxious-for-his-dinner horse back out of his box stall, re-entering six times until his barging gave way to a tiptoed, mannered grace. Being dragged around by a horse is a losing game: we must teach them consideration of puny us.

Barn visuals and procedures addicted my human pleasure receptors—the long, narrow, dimming aisles that end in large squares of light where the double doors stand open to blazing summer glare; the sun and shade of the in and out that test our apertures; the dust that floats in the trapezoidal slants of illumination cut from skylights and barred stall windows; activity and rest that ebb and flow in gentle cycles. Stalls are mucked out and animals fed to a regular schedule, with clean bedding and hay snacks delivered by wheelbarrow or a pair of strong arms. Everyday, an industrial barn vacuum sucks the long aisles clear of wayward hay, shavings, hair and dirt, but it is a losing game. The filling of water buckets can't be hurried, but the feed tray can be rolled along more quickly to pacify the hungry. The staff moves at a calm, steady pace to conserve energy and keep to the horses' schedules. There is no getting ahead of this work, no benefit to rushing. It is relentless.

But step outside into the light: the enclosed stalls and barn aisles spring open to vast pasture, fenced and open, with, if you are fortunate, views of hills and rivers, a few pretty houses and a big open sky. Posts and boards recede and overlap, wavering in the heat's haze. Distant horses quietly graze, and nearer ones work under their riders, both deep in concentration. Exuberant riders, scared riders, exhausted riders, sweaty, dusty riders, thankful riders, frustrated riders. Same goes for the horses. It is magical.

Horse people share an immediate animal bond born of barn time. At Riga Meadow, where Bandi temporarily resided, the gamut ran from little kids in pony club, to youthful riders working as stable hands to earn their rides, on to many oldsters returning to their childhood passions after a mid-life of work and family care. I admire their dedication, especially the "mature" ones. When I first saw Mrs. Hackshorn, in breeches, boots, clutching a crop and a helmet, I never imagined that she rode. At a walk she pitched forward nearly ninety degrees, and sideways forty-five. Her head, arthritically locked, was cocked in line with her tilt such that her full body revolved to shift her view. That she moved at all challenged the laws of gravity. I figured she was a horsewoman once, but now playacted the part, wandering the barn to keep a feel of what once made her happy.

One stifling day I stopped at the entrance to the indoor ring, yelling "DOOR," as is the custom for admission, to see who was riding.

"Is that the old lady I often see around here?" I whispered to the stable girls ardently watching.

"Yes."

"I can't believe it. How old is she?"

"Ninety-four."

I watched Mrs. Hackshorn walk, then trot around the ring. Scolding the horse all the while, she suffered no nonsense. Barn manager and trainer Linda gave her pointers, always respectful, and still with an eye toward improving her riding. In no way did she humor her.

"I see I get no extra credit for taking up riding at forty-six," I said to Linda later.

"Mrs. Hackshorn is amazing and gives all of us aging riders hope."

We sighed, imagining ourselves ancient and crooked.

"I really hope that I'm still on at her age, or even close to it."

"Me too. She's an inspiration."

"Does she canter?"

"Yup."

"Wow."

A barn family is an oasis. Most of us do not know much about each other, maybe a little snippet here and there, and other family members are rarely present. Riding talk and action are all-consuming: horse needs crowd out chit-chat. Home life is separate—a proverbial million miles away. We sparingly share our outside sorrows and sagas with each other, and cannot dwell on them long. The barn is a place to forget, to work and canter our troubles away. But some tragedies crack the code. One boarder at our farm unexpectedly lost her teenage son with Down's Syndrome to pneumonia. We all deeply mourned for Pat who lost her sweet, sweet boy. I sent a heartfelt note, but refrained from open expressions of sympathy at the barn. Words are inept, and I hoped to keep that time and place where her children rarely ventured pure and free as possible. Illogical of course, because you cannot outrun that kind of grief, but maybe the barn "space" allows brief respite. Another friend who boarded at Riga Meadow also lost a child, a grown daughter to suicide. I sensed that for her, too, the barn is that rare place for a pause in the pain, the broken human wrapped in bubble-wrap, for an hour or two, against the hard world.

That Elliot's friend Max was nervous around the horses made sense for a city boy, but the feel for barn life is not something you can necessarily acquire through exposure, like a taste for beer or oysters, at least not in the deepest sense. Elliot turned barn rat right from the start (though less in our under-construction barn devoid of horses) and so too, for the most part, did Jane.

Jane was four when the farm became ours. Like Elliot and me she loved animals unconditionally, but our exposure had been limited to dogs, zoo visits and backyard interlopers. Eager to ride, she also fully realized the height from which she could fall. But she happily romped around the barn, feeding carrots to the horses, while I policed her around the hazards.

"Jane! Don't run. Remember, horses like *caaallllmmm*."

"Jane! Don't go in that stall without a grown-up."

"Jane! Remember to hold your hand flat so you don't get bitten."

"Jane! Don't crawl between that horse's legs."

"Jane! Don't clomp around the hayloft. Angel's in her stall and it spooks her."

"Jane! Be careful on that ladder."

But to a five year old, running is imperative. And, even her flattest hand can be mistaken for a carrot. And, the cool, cave-dark loft invites exploration of mice bones and secret spaces. I pretty much knew she would bond to horses—the percentage of horsey girls is pretty high among those regularly conditioned. Scott and I even debated where it might lead.

"Do you think the horse thing will be good for Jane?" I asked.

"I guess. That is, if we can steer clear of the fancy show circuit."

It is a big "if." We know people, rich and not so, who spend much of their disposable incomes on top horses and their free time at horse events. One family's sixth grader is released from her private school every Friday to fly down to Palm Beach to compete. It is a life, not a hobby, and wears thin in a hurry for the non-riding parents and siblings.

"Do you think we can control it to a sane level? Maintain it as a pastime rather than a passion?" I asked.

"I don't know. It's pretty laid back around here, at least. It certainly isn't the Hamptons, Bedford, or even Millbrook.... so maybe. I don't relish weekends traveling the East Coast with a horse in tow. Hockey is bad enough—the early mornings, the long trips...."

"… the freezing cold and the sweaty equipment in that awkward, stinking bag," I finished. "I know what you mean, though. I hope she can just enjoy it, like Elliot. But she might be really good at it, in fact with her strength and balance she'll probably be great at it, and girls are different about riding."

"Maybe having our own farm will reduce the perk factor and she'll take it for granted rather than as a novelty she'll yearn to maximize. You know, how rationing Skittles makes her crave more, but give her the whole bag and she rarely finishes them."

"I thought we always worried about our kids taking their privileges for granted?"

"Maybe in this one case it can work for us and undercut an overly-serious dedication."

"The upside is pretty compelling, though. Maybe her love and care of farm animals will balance a grow-up-too-fast, urban life." I always plugged the benefits of beasts to Scott whenever I could to atone for all the times our dog peed on the carpet, had diarrhea in Elliot's bed, or begged food. "And think of her confidence: after all, if you can coerce a thousand-pound animal to dance and jump, go and whoa, what *can't* you do?"

He gave me the "poor mutt" look.

I winked. "And it will keep her away from boys."

"Now you're talking."

"Are you maligning your own gender?"

"Definitely. And with good reason."

I thought about the girls I had met around barns. They consistently presented wholesome and refreshingly naïve, not jaded, materialistic and boy crazy. And parents of riding girls have confirmed my impressions. A few deeply regretted that their teenagers traded horses for valley-girl pleasures, heavy metal, and love, never turning back, but more found their girls put off serious dating until their late teens. One parent worried about her late-blooming daughter with nary a date until her twenties. Eventually, the single girl married a NYC cop. He was part of the equine division; she first saw him tall in the saddle patrolling Central Park. I liked the romance of this story, and the virgin maiden aspect especially appealed to the dad, if not the husband, in Scott. A horse-crazy daughter seemed a decent hedge against the awful extremes of, say, a drug-addled Goth, or a runaway, pregnant teen. Not that I lack confidence in my parenting skills or anything.

So, we never saw it coming.

In June we paid another visit to the Billingsly farm. We toured a veritable paradise of critters—two donkeys named Hoot and Holler (Ken is a trader), ducks, and peacocks (though four ran away to the wild side), not to mention the horses.

"Where's Elliot?"

We found him in the henhouse determined to catch one of the skittish birds. Feathers were flying. Nimble Tammy crouched and sprang to impress us on her first try and handed a beautiful multi-colored hen to my thrilled son. The time flew by and the overly ambitious family trail ride scaled back to both kids having a quick spin on the Icelandic named Cody. Elliot bounced to the double-time trot the breed is known for, with good sport Tammy running alongside.

Icelandics are small, steady and fun to ride, but their gaits are hardly elegant: horse and rider resemble fast-forwarded cartoon characters. Tammy agreed they give you a good laugh, and except for the jangling, touted their safety. On our drive home Elliot confessed his renewed appreciation for the smoother trot of the warm-bloods, and when I broached the idea of reliable Icelandics for our farm, Bobbi looked at me like I couldn't possibly be serious, shook her head and shot me down. "No, Quarter Horses are the way to go."

It was Jane's turn on Cody. I lifted her up to the saddle.

"I don't want to." She had a death grip on my neck.

"What do you mean, Janie? You love horses," I said rhetorically as I struggled to hold her noncompliant body aloft.

"I don't want to!" More adamant, she wriggled away.

"Janie, Cody is a nice horse and Tammy will be right there with you. Elliot had a fun time," I said, conscious of having told Tammy that my brave Jane adored horses.

"Don't be afraid, Janie," urged Keira and her brother Andrew.

"Yeah, Janie, you should try it," Elliot piled on, the six against one tuning her radar to manipulation.

Scott helped me wrangle her fighting form onto the saddle, both of us sure she would rise to the occasion. Instead she panicked, kicking to get off and cried, hard. Her agitation did not abate, not even after we gave up. Shaken to her core, we beat a hasty retreat to our car and home. A change of scene helped her switch gears, but I feared she was ruined for horses, in the manner of "the bad dog experience that makes you afraid for life." *Great; and now we owned a horse farm.* My crafting of a family hobby unglued in three minutes. First they were bored by the construction of our farm, then Elliot showed little interest in Bandi, and now Jane was scarred for life. Come to think of it, Scott's enthusiasm leached at any mention of Bobbi and me finding him a horse. He would cut us off with a quick "There's no rush." Plainly, I'd been forcing my horse fascination on my family.

I had anticipated that my guys might resist the animal scene, but I had counted on Jane. Why is it that females especially love horses and all that goes with it, the riding and the competition, the caring, grooming, feeding, the barn life? Men, Europeans in particular, eventually take their share of medals and ribbons at the upper echelons of English saddle horse trials, but you don't see many boys hanging around East Coast barns in the United States. Is it a power thing? Do girls in a paternalistic society empower themselves by controlling these large brutes? Do they practice adult loss and mourning when a horse goes lame, crazy or sick, as they invariably do? Despite these hardships, do girls value freedom from the *Sturm und Drang* of adolescence, home conflicts, schoolyards rivalries, the malls and back alleys of teenagerdom? I would love to spare my daughter all that plus sexually transmitted diseases, eating disorders, vanity, and guy-induced submissive feminine behavior if I could. I would choose to protect her longer from any cruel, destructive rites of passage. I would rather her heart be broken by horses first and humans later. Or is the connection simply that the "nature" of horse speaks best to the "nature" of girl?

But Jane was truly frightened of Cody. *Is she a girl who doesn't get it?* I bided my time and wondered. Several weeks later, and after we all got to know Bandi better, I retested both kids.

"Elliot, would you like to have a lesson on Bandi?"

"Sure, when?"

"How about tomorrow? After mine?"

"Okay."

"Jane, would you like to have a ride on Bandi?" I casually added.

"Yes."

The next day set a perfect stage: a bossy blue August sky lending a purplish green clarity to the hills that can make a person weep. The Taconic range of mountains hazed away from Riga Meadow's flat pastures, while the gray barns, nearer, sizzled in the heat. Grazing horses half-heartedly swished their tails against slow flies, both creatures spoiled and lethargic with late summer warmth and abundant food. I tacked up Bandi, expecting to show Elliot and Jane what I had learned, but after feeding Bandi some carrots, their waning attention scooted them off to investigate neighboring stalls and otherwise horse around.

I led Bandi from the dim closet of the stable to the sun-drenched path toward the outdoor ring. With Bobbi waiting, I got right to it, wanting to warm up and settle Bandi before the kids grew impatient. I had hoped they'd show some interest in seeing their mother ride, but appropriately self-centered, they used the time to fight with one another and make mischief on the fences, eventually requiring my sharp rebuke from my mount. Elliot slunk off to a hay bale to read his book, while Jane remained to keep up a steady patter.

"Mama, is it my turn yet?"

"Not yet, Janie. Soon."

Ten seconds later, "Is it my turn now?"

"*Not yet*, Jane. Try to be patient."

Twenty seconds later, "When is it going to be my turn?"

She climbed on the fence again, opening and closing the gate. With each bang Bandi's ears twitched and his head jerked around.

After my distracted thirty minutes, I spied my good-natured son still absorbed in his book, and flipped Jane to number one for take-off. Up she went, tentative, but game. We wrapped the leathers short enough for Jane's feet to reach the stirrups with her squealing whenever Bandi shifted his weight. Bobbi placed Jane's fingers properly around the reins.

"Sit up straight now, Janie, like a soldier."

"Like this?" Jane joked, going stiff as a board.

"Exactly. Now we're going to walk around."

Bobbi maintained a loose grip on the lead line as they giggled and chatted. Bandi acted the protector, and Jane was rigid, not with fear, but delight. After a few rounds, Bobbi gingerly hoisted herself onto the saddle behind Jane, and they rode around together.

"Do you want to trot, Jane?" Bobbi asked.

"Yes."

"Okay, here we go."

Bobbi eased into a slow trot, and Jane did her best to stay on her seat. She cracked herself up by dramatically emphasizing the reverberations in her voice as she bounced along to Bandi's swaying butt. They transitioned between walk and trot a few times before Bobbi halted.

"Whoa, Bandi," Bobbi commanded.

"Whoa, Bandi," Jane imitated.

"Do you like it, Jane?" I asked.

"Oh, yes. Let's keep going."

"Well, it's Elliot's turn now."

"I want another turn."

Bobbi completed another small circle.

"It's time to get down now, so Elliot can have a turn."

"NO!"

I had never seen her so adamant. By the time I pried her from the saddle she had dissolved herself in anger, bordering on a tantrum, a weapon she'd only ever engaged twice before. Embarrassed in front of Bobbi who doesn't have kids, I feared she would judge mine spoiled, ill-behaved brats. I wanted her to like them: soon she'd be teaching all of us.

"Oh-oh," Bobbi said. "That's what happened the first time I got off a horse and look what happened to me."

We laughed, and Jane pulled herself together. Elliot rode serenely, and Bandi behaved beautifully. Three of us were on board. We would have to see about Scott.

CHAPTER ELEVEN

The Bandi Diaries

·◁════════▷·

BARN LIFE WAS TRANSFORMING ME. I had fallen hard that first horsey summer into a polarized relationship: I loved my horse, hated my riding. With so much to learn, I was both daunted and intoxicated by a challenge antithetical to my daily life as mother and spouse. Horsekeeping and riding is intellectual, emotional and physical, requiring extreme concentration, calm wits and no small dose of bravery. Between Mommy brain and genetics, I lacked all three.

My immediate challenge was steering. I was warned that tugging on the reins, my first inclination, should be my last resort. Ideally, the lower legs and ultimately the "seat" (this complex misnomer includes the abdomen, lower back, pelvis, glutei and thighs; in short, everything from the lowest rib to the knee), are all; experienced horses sense direction requests by subtle weight shifts emanating from my eyes and head through to my butt in the saddle. This "connection" was that simple and yet frustratingly elusive. When I trotted toward a turn Bobbi would repeatedly mantra:

"Look where you want to go, about three paces ahead. Use your right lower leg to tell him to turn left, and position your left leg as a post around which you want his body to bend. Loosen your thighs."

My legs felt tragically connected to my upper body: right and left

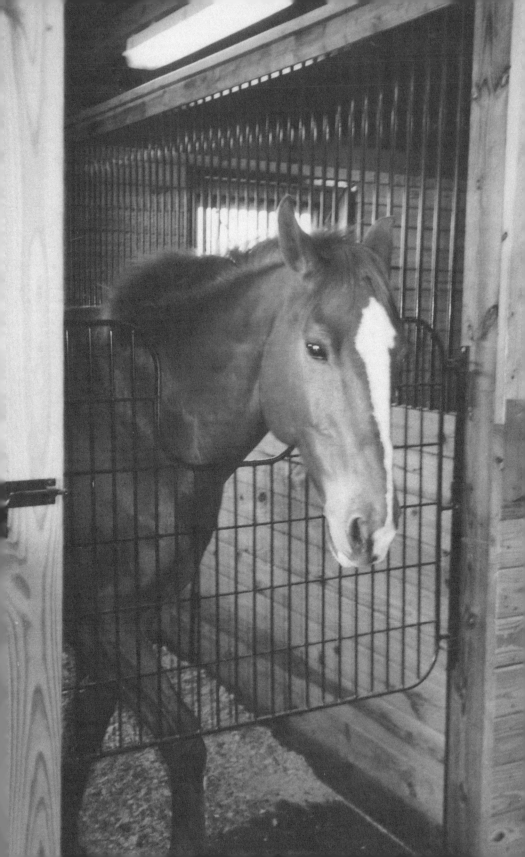

refused to operate independently and when I engaged them my arms pulled on the reins. Afraid of losing my balance I gripped my thighs to steady myself and Bandi stopped, as I had just issued the "halt" command. *Why is this so complicated? Can't I just tug on the left rein to go left?* I trotted on again, and Bandi cut the corner courtesy of my weak inside lower leg. My "posting" strung along like a wet noodle, and my strenuous leg commands didn't faze Bandi, so, compensating, I brought up both my hands and crossed them to the right of Bandi's maned neck, an intuitive but misguided attempt to drag him out to the rail.

"Keep your hands low, just above and at either side of his neck at the withers. *Where are the withers, again?* Pull back just slightly on the inside rein to turn his head in the direction you want to go, and keep your inside left leg on to keep him from cutting the corner." *This is Twister on a conveyor belt.*

I reengaged my legs to little effect as Bandi cut the next corners even shallower. Sweat was dripping into my eyes. Like most people, the inside muscles of my legs from groin to ankle are weak, having rarely been called into such strenuous service. These and the boney part of my pelvis killed for two days each time I rode until I "earned" my seat. And I'm not talking minimal discomfort, more the realm of moan out loud pain that starts off with a bang the next morning and builds to cataclysm the day after that. No matter that I had practiced Iyengar style yoga for five years, a branch that emphasizes correct postures, held long and with precision. Going into this horse thing, I expected the burn of saddle rubs, but smugly reckoned I would escape the deep muscle aches. I figured yoga found and toned every muscle in my body. And it did, except for my inner thighs. My teacher, Michael, confided that he personally never experienced soreness anything like he did after riding. And he can practice yoga for six hours a day. Certifiably, riding engages these muscles like no other "exercise."

In desperation I purchased "comfy rumps." This white polyester girdle-type underpant with a yellow foam cushion built into the crotch resembles something my grandma used to wear, but held promise against pelvic bruises and rub burns. I tried not to glimpse myself in the mirror or let Scott catch me in these beauties (decidedly *unsexy* underwear would be heavy ammunition against riding in his book), and I surreptitiously perspired in them through several lessons. But there was no remedy except more time in the saddle. For several weeks after Bandi's arrival my cowboy stance elicited snickers from my family, particularly my groaning wobble upon rising from a short sit-down or a full night's sleep. Scott laughed a little less when he realized what it meant for our sex life. But the pain slowly dissipated and didn't return even after I returned to New York City and could manage only one ride a week instead of four or five.

While my seat conditioned, my steering hardly improved, becoming a joke around the Riga Meadow barn. One day Bobbi and I worked in the smaller dressage ring, an area "fenced in" by calf-height portable plastic barriers arranged as a large rectangle. Still nervous at the speed of the canter, I was working hard just to stay on. There is generally an end of a ring that horses take exception to. In the same manner that they meander as slow pokes leaving the barn and thunder like Thoroughbreds heading back, it is usually the far side of the ring they cut, and cozy up to the near end. Home exerts a gravitational pull on these creatures, and even if they are well-trained to legs, hands, seats and eyeballs, it's in there.

"Okay. As you're coming into this turn, you already know he is stiffer and less willing this leftward direction. Look ahead to where you want to go. He'll feel your head turn and your body shift. Use a little right leg to tell him turn left, and keep your left leg on to push him out to the rail and bend him around. If you have to, give a little squeeze with your left rein to turn his head in the direction you want to turn, but not too much or he'll think you want to slow down to a trot."

Okay, I briefed myself, *I know what to do. It all makes perfect sense. Right leg turns, left leg pushes and bends his middle out. Don't pull up my hands. Look where I want to go. Breathe.*

We aimed to turn. I looked left toward eleven o'clock. Bandi looked right at the barn at two o'clock. I looked right to see what he was looking at. It was hard to squeeze and work my legs independently, especially just a fast squeeze with the lower right, but a firm pressure with the lower left, keeping my thighs loose. *How can I be so spastic?* Bandi cantered toward the corner with no bend in him. I tried to squeeze my legs a little harder but discovered that my sloppy general squeeze just meant "go" more. I tried to figure out what he was looking at stage right. He headed more right than left and picked up speed. *Uh-oh.*

"Look where you want to goooo...," Bobbi yelled, her voice receding into the distance.

But I was fixated on where Bandi wanted to go, back to the barn. A zombie, my panic led to inaction. Next thing I knew we had stormed the six-inch barricade out of the ring. Instinct pulled my arms up sharply on the reins and, miraculously, he turned around and stopped. *Whew: at least my arms work when they need to.* Panting, I remembered the scene in *Seabiscuit* when a horse bolted for his stall and rammed his jockey into the side of the barn, maiming him for life. I was a little squeamish about that.

"Well, that's a first," chuckled Linda, teaching in another ring. She shook her pig-tailed head.

"Those were some superb jumping skills," Bobbi joked, walking over to retrieve us. "Why don't we try that corner again?"

During my walk of shame back to my loser's circle of a dressage ring I soothed my dignity with inverted pride at having accomplished something that could still amuse such veterans. I was the day's class clown but there was a silver lining: Bandi took that "leap" as smooth as could be, indicating that jumping him might be easier than trotting and steering him.

After several weeks attending to my turning and cantering, Bobbi tested me out in the grass where rails did not keep us both honest. The open field loomed vast and hazard-filled, but I trusted Bobbi, and knew that when I stopped anticipating and simply did, like a robot, what she told me, it worked. We mapped out our imaginary ring in which I trotted and cantered, sometimes steering, sometimes not. Once or twice I really got in a pickle, with Bandi totally ignoring my commands, turning left toward the barn even though I was clearly commanding, vociferously with legs and eyeballs pumping, or so I thought, right.

"Bandi, you naughty boy! You're taking advantage of your mother," Bobbi scolded.

I thought so too, and grew frustrated. But I am wary of blaming my horse. A few weeks earlier, Bobbi told me about a student who always blamed her horse. "It's almost always the rider's fault," she emphasized.

"Let me straighten him out," Bobbi said.

Ha, ha, Bandi, you're in trouble now, I thought.

I slipped down and gave her a leg up. She trotted a perfect oval and eased into a lovely, controlled canter, steering perfectly with little apparent effort. All "seat."

"See. He can do it."

"Yes, I see," I mumbled. "Does he realize he can get away with more with me, or is it truly that my commands are so bad?"

"It's a combination. Your aids are a little confusing sometimes, and he is still getting to know you. But he's also smart and pretends to be confused when he really isn't."

I didn't like my options—bad rider or push-over.

"It's the same with the reins. Whenever you find your reins too long, it's because Bandi takes them little by little through your hands, so gentlemanly that you don't even notice until you go to canter and they're looping and he strings out long and unbalanced on his forehand."

"But I want to give him some room for forward motion and not be too strong on his mouth." I had heard about riders who yank and rest hard on the reins. Attached to a metal bar or "bit" in a gap between teeth, such rein action not only hardens horses' mouths making them resistant to any commands, but can also injure or turn them just plain nasty.

"You're not too strong with your hands. Bandi always looks happy, and his ears are never pinned back when you're riding. He likes you, but he's testing you," Bobbi said.

"Great. Just what I need, one more child testing me," I sighed heavily.

"Give more with your arm at the elbow, but don't let him steal length of rein through your fingers. Think 'elastic,' but keep a connection."

Every skill is qualified with a "but, do this, this and this, too." I rubberized my arms and resigned to keep trying—but maybe tomorrow, I'm shot today. I have some strengths, like decent balance, a strong, postured back (thank you, yoga), and soft, giving hands. But my legs are weak and asymmetrical: the right one creeps too far forward of the girth and the left too far back. It is fascinating to Bobbi that Elliot's legs twist exactly the same.

"Do you feel your left leg behind the girth and the other forward?" Bobbi asked, and I said yes, even though I couldn't tell at all, by touch anyway, where that girth was. The girth is a five-inch-wide strip of leather that snugly runs under the horse's undercarriage to secure the saddle from slipping side to side. It was difficult enough to see past my saddle, spread legs and stirrups; but feel it? My lower leg was encased in thick socks, "full seat" riding pants (which have suede on the butt and down the inside of the legs), ankle boots and then half-chaps (suede and leather armor that zips on over everything else), all in the interest of getting a better grip. I took a guess and slightly shifted each leg.

"Now you're even," Bobbi said.

Feeling so totally *uneven* I wondered if my back, injured and operated on in the past, is so corkscrewed that my legs are permanently askew.

My ankles also present a problem, particularly my left. The challenge here is to push my heels down angling my toes upward. This one is all about safety—if I fall off, my feet will slip more easily out of the stirrups, decreasing my chance of entangling in the leathers to get dragged or stepped on by a bolting, panicked horse—a gruesome image I wish I could edit from my mind's eye. Horses don't want to step on you, and are pretty nimble, but they can't fly; if you land beneath one you're in trouble. Being dragged seems even worse than a clean fall despite Three Stooges skits and spaghetti westerns. Proper ankles also push the rider's weight back in the saddle rather than pitching it forward off the toes. This gains importance in jumping. If the horse refuses the jump, there is a better chance of braking your own forward momentum and staying on, or falling off to the side or back. Falling forward, or "rotationally" onto or over the jump and onto your head or neck is never good, and a collective breath is held in the crowd at any show in this case, exhaled in relief and subdued applause when the rider rises, dusts him or herself off and, astonishingly to me, gets back on, usually more pissed-off than scared.

Despite these excellent incentives to keep my heels down, it is fairly impossible. For balance and security, gripping those stirrups with my toes is a primal instinct. My faith in my superhuman pedal digits directs them for all they are worth earthward and curling around in an attempt to maintain a hold of that tiny little stirrup rung. My heroic efforts to lower my recalcitrant heels results in two horizontal feet at best. Only when I am practicing jumping position and my butt rises off the saddle, gravitationally forcing all my clumsy weight into my heels, do I gain some downward angle. I have no trouble with this in yoga's downward dog—my ankles bend to a slim wedge, so it must be some weird psychological security blanket—my toes will glue me to the horse. I suspect I am not alone. Riders everywhere hear "keep your heels down" ranking right alongside the standards "keep your hands down and thumbs up," "shoulders back," "relax your elbows," "loose thighs" and my personal favorite, "look where you want to go." Again, I am better with my right ankle, but the left is, like the leg it is attached to, a booted rebel. I've had a right hip replacement, and I find myself contemplating whether a matching one on my left might even things out.

My next challenge soon presented itself: a trail ride, suggested by a fellow boarder at Riga Meadow. With Bobbi as my bodyguard, four of us set out to explore the two hundred and fifty acres of trails bordering the farm. I was a cocktail of nervous and excited, and my imaginary film entitled "Things that Could go Horribly Wrong, and No Doubt Will" looped in my head. Trail riding seems awfully exposed in comparison to a contained ring. Multiple horses may not get along or grow agitated at venturing far from home into the unknown. Even well-trod trails harbor terrors as nature changes daily. Uneven footing, streams, downed limbs, slippery hills, a gravelly patch, a muddy puddle of water and narrow passages are expected elements you would hardly notice on foot, but pose a possible hazard for even the steadiest horses. Things to stumble over are omnipresent. Hikers, dogs and vehicles can appear out of nowhere and may not care a crumb about spooking your horse. Indeed, some nitwits try to scare the horses for their own hee-haws.

But the lure of the open trail is part of the American West dream in many of us: cantering windblown through a field of tall grass; meandering a pine needle laden path; clopping over rivulets and river stones; making forward progress through natural beauty without the heat of asphalt or the whine of an engine; just the smell and sound of horse, the conversation of friends enjoying the same moment in nature. Isn't this what it's all about?

In theory, yes; in fact, I was a wreck the entire two hours, a long time to be tight as a bow string. Though Bandi rode pretty steadily, I alerted to each minute change in terrain, every rustle in the brush, and all ear twitches and head jerks of the leading equines. I rode more fearfully attuned than the horse beneath me, and I, supposedly, had the bigger brain. Oh, me of slender trust. Extremely solicitous on my behalf, my companions graciously passed up a long canter down an old railroad bed through the perfect alley of trees lined with soft, even footing.

"This is the safest place to canter—but we'll trot on, don't worry," one sighed at the missed opportunity.

But even trotting made me nervous. Bandi, energized and happy, rushed to keep up with the pack. His forward, bouncy trot that I couldn't reliably slow, unbalanced me, and I hung on the reins. Walking down

steep hills required a counterbalancing body angle that I hadn't ever practiced, and because of my steering, I nudged tree trunks with my knees and
head-butted a few low branches. On the last leg of the journey, with the
barn in my sights, I relaxed enough to enjoy the field of wildflowers and
open views of the hills receding north into the distance. *Thank god we're
almost home. I made it!* But my moment was eclipsed by a neighbor's dog
who chased us, barking and threatening a closer lunge until, at the last
possible moment his owner called him off. Bandi didn't seem to mind, but
I monitored every flicker of his ears as a barometer of his inner state.

Mission accomplished without mishap yielded an endorphin rush,
but I can't say I had enjoyed myself. It felt like those calculus tests in
college—you apply the formulas and get a decent grade, but without
the satisfaction of really understanding the material. My lack of nerve
defeated me. *Why am I such a coward? What happened to my teenage fearlessness on those New Jersey hack rides when all I wanted to do was gallop,
and then gallop some more?* I relished the rush of speed then, the float-
ing glide of a fast canter, the stretch of the hacks' muscular necks with
manes flying, the ground disappearing fast under dusty hooves, my
friends going just as fast, the control I believed I had, sure that I'd stay
on. *When, exactly, did I get old?*

Recreations never live up to memory as I discovered on my tenuous
trail ride as an older me. But there were other pleasures besides the riding: the before and after skills better suited to the forty-seven year old
that I had to master. I learned each task slowly. It began with simply
walking Bandi from his paddock into a grooming stall. The first time
Bobbi ceremoniously asked, "Would you like to lead your horse?" I
thought *Yes*, and then quickly, *No way*. The halter and lead rope were
a tangle of leather, buckles and twisted hemp with infinite options for
attachment. Bobbi guided my brain and hands.

"And, don't forget to close the stall door or paddock gate behind you,
or your horse may decide to sneak past you and escape."

So I led, and Bandi bumped his nose into my back and kicked my heels.

"Don't get underneath him, push him out if you have to, and stay alongside. Look ahead to where you want to go."

I've heard that before. Over a few weeks I got the hang of it, and felt overdue to attempt a solo "lead-in." So there I was, heart racing even though it sounds like the easiest thing in the world: 1) place halter over horse's head and secure, 2) hook lead line onto halter, 3) open gate, 4) walk horse into barn. Steps 1 and 2 went well, but I faltered at unchaining the gate one-handed while my other hung on to Bandi. Bobbi warned me not to wrap the lead line around my hand or arms in case a thousand-pound animal decides to bolt and you, entangled, are yanked or dragged by an arm that eventually detaches from its socket. While fumbling at the gate, Bandi stepped on my foot, only for a second and not full pressure, but it still hurt, let me tell you. Once I unlatched the gate, facing him I gave a short tug on the rope.

No go.

Another, harder tug.

Nope.

His big eyes looked right at me, very attentively, with ears up and head cocked, cute as could be, but would not budge. I leaned back heavily into a protracted heave, against which he settled back stronger. No way could my one hundred and twenty pounds win this tug of war.

I decided to try Bobbi's trick of flicking the loose end of the lead rope under Bandi's belly. Quickly, he pranced out of the safety of the fenced-in paddock. I jumped out of his way. We took a few steps, with me looking down, minding my toes. I realized I should have been "looking where we were going," *duh*, rather than at him or my own precious body parts. As I made this adjustment, he stopped abruptly and ducked his head down into some long green grass, hoovering away. Because their paddock grass is well picked over, a good feed requires a human escorting them to the virgin tufts that thrive in between the fences, barns and rings. It is a special treat, reserved for after-work or special bonding time—but we were just getting started. Bandi knew he was on borrowed time so he braced his forelegs and planted his nose down, mowing bites of grass back and forth as a typewriter slides along its carriage, his left eye daring me to interfere.

So I enjoyed watching Bandi munch until my reverie broke with the realization that I was establishing a bad habit. Bandi bullied me into this treat while Bobbi had cautioned *me* to tell *him* when to indulge. I pulled and tugged. He ignored me, casually munching, and I got my foot stepped on again trying to leverage my weight against his. I glanced around the farm to see who might be witnessing my ineptitude and could offer advice. Finally, I gave him a little boot under his chin, a firm yank with the lead line, and marched ahead with conviction. I heard Bobbi's voice in my head: "Keep looking where you want to go."

Bandi tried dipping again, but I maintained some authority until, agitated and in a hurry, he began to hustle me to the barn. I didn't want him ahead of me, so I fast-walked, which only encouraged him to trot and me to run. We bumped our way abruptly into the stall, and though I managed to turn him around properly, he wedged me against the wall, and his hoof found my foot again. He thrust his head into his corner pail and greedily gobbled his grain. *Aha! Dinner time.* Relieved there was a reason for his bad manners, I also realized I had been horse-handled. He pegged the novice at my first approach in the paddock. Already dejected, I then remembered that horses should not eat just before a ride, which is what I intended to do. Powerless to battle his face out of his bucket, I gave up. I gathered up my grooming materials, put away my tack and called it a day.

"Tack" is a familiar word but not a tangible I had ever thought much about. Defined in the OED as "a thing for fastening one thing to another, or fastening things together," it was originally a nautical term. In the horse world it morphed from "tackle" especially designating saddle, bridle and all the bits and pieces that fasten horse to rider. Logically, tack is kept in a "tack room," one of the most pleasurable places to linger in most barns. Stocked with soaped, oiled, and well-crafted luscious leather equipment, this horseless room is a prideful, cozy place in the thriving barn, often furnished with sofas and carpets and decorated with photos, ribbons and trophies that boast riders' exploits and horses' great moments. I was beginning to see how hard-earned wins are and thus justly celebrated. A tack room is also one of the few climate controlled areas in barns, mainly to protect the expensive leather, and offers precious refuge in New England where the air is usually too cold, too hot, or too wet.

In its broad assortment, tack, for me, was an unexpected pleasure. Ralph Lauren hit the bull's eye glamorizing his style with the horsey Polo image—beautifully polished equipment and purpose-driven, tailored, hardy, tight-fitting clothing combine to suggest aristocracy, tradition, leisure, wealth and dedication: the sport of kings. Having heretofore lacked the confidence to pull off the street version and wear the fashion label "Chaps" *sans* horse, Bandi entitled me to legitimately immerse both of us in all things equine—the real deal.

When horses trade hands, they come mostly naked except for the oldest, driest leather or cheapest nylon halter and most threadbare lead rope the seller could excavate from the dregs of her moldiest tack trunk; surprising, given that horses need a wide-ranging wardrobe pretty specific to them in size. Plus, their names tend to be emblazoned on everything, for vanity but also to keep these expensive items in the possession of their rightful owners and in their barn home (a well-run barn has a place for everything and everything in its place) so as to be at hand when needed: searching for your girth cuts into precious and expensive lesson time. Nevertheless, horse people are loath to part with any of their tack no matter how personalized to the horse they have sent on, hopefully, to greener pastures. Bobbi taught me the trick of putting my name on most things, rather than my horse's, in case of an early tragedy or a short-lived love affair.

Bandi arrived customarily empty-hoofed, so both he and I needed everything. In her infinite wisdom, Bobbi organized a trip to the saddlery store. It was time to return all things borrowed and set ourselves up right. I always wondered who bought kitschy key chains, jewelry, toothbrushes and underwear horse-motifed beyond reason, and now I knew. I went at that tack shop like a robin at a worm: socks to saddle, supplements to "stud muffins" (Bandi's favorite treat—maybe he relives his stallion days), fly spray to stirrups, chaps to curry comb. Orgy best describes my first saddlery experience, rivaling the frenzy of the "shop" that took place in the nine months before I gave birth to my first child. But a baby is an abstemious monk compared to a horse. Many necessities are required—saddle, bridle, leathers, stirrups, saddle pads, girth, halter, lead rope, grooming tote, brushes, combs, shampoos, conditioners, blankets of varying thicknesses and warmth, polo wraps, bell boots, half-chaps, breeches, boots; and then so much more that was simply fun—cartooned mugs of horses riding people for the tack room, stirrup decorated ankle socks, toys that "neigh" for Jane, wicking two-tone shirts for Elliot, bridle bit necklaces and horseshoe earrings, a wild mustang printed scarf, horse head bookends—all new, clean, shiny and full of possibility, adventure and yes, fashion. It is not unlike setting up house upon marriage or moving to a new place: that guiltless, mandatory refitting that deeply satisfies those with a domestic bent. The biographer Percy Lubbock noted what Henry James said about "housekeeperish" Edith Wharton: "[n]o one fully knows our Edith who hasn't seen her in the act of creating a habitation for herself." A dedicated horse person as well, I'd bet good money that Wharton appreciated tack, perhaps was "horsekeeperish" too, let's say. She maintained an exquisite carriage house at the Mount, the estate in the Berkshires she bought in 1901 and designed herself.

With a first horse, you start from scratch, and it's an experience that does not intersect or synergize with any other. Every bit of tack and rider apparel has a distinct practical purpose, often complex in arrangement. The puzzle of a bridle, for instance, falls into place once you understand the way the metal bit in the toothless area of the horse's mouth connects to the head stall and to the reins, onward through to the rider's soft hands, loose elbows, erect back, strong core, steady seat and long legs (one can dream). A foreign language, tack's meaning needs translation and then several personal and experiential applications for all of its secrets to unfold. Fluency comes with regular use. Beauty resides in tack's practicality, produced by thousands of years of specific adaptation of horse and rider in harmony: an ancient knowledge passed down hand to hoof in leather and metal.

Bobbi and I pondered, compared and stacked the check-out counter with fragrant, gleaming tack, unscarred leather in hues ranging from deep black to golden tan, miming the varied color of horses. We mused how best to highlight Bandi's chestnut coat and mane and laid his wardrobe as a new bride collects her *trousseau*. We indulged as only two animal lovers can anthropomorphically carry one another away without embarrassment about their mutual, excessive zeal for equines. The grooming tote and its contents held many wonders. I discovered that a curry comb is not toothed but rather a rubber mitt with little prickly knobs all over it, and how the varied size and stiffness of a brush cleans and polishes body, face, tail and mane. I chose colorful heart-shaped sponges that Janie would appreciate, magnolia-scented shampoo, the tortuous looking hoof pick, and a scraper to squeegee the water off of him like a wet window. I purchased Showsheen spray to coax that extra shine from Bandi's tail and mane, and selected everything in our farm's colors of brown, cream and, my favorite, green. I indulged in a stunning black saddle pad trimmed in gold braid that I imagined would set off Bandi's reddish highlights luminously. Glucosamine, worming agents, fly masks, saddle soap and leather conditioner, more sponges, riding pants and shirts, half-chaps and paddock boots, riding gloves and a crop rounded out the mountain that hid the increasingly friendly salesperson.

An inveterate shopper, my enthusiasm did not end at the tack store. I soon discovered whole new landscapes of mail order to conquer, and the bible of the horse shopping world, the Dover Saddlery catalog, is as thick as a Sears. When Bobbi first sent me one, I paged through, paus-ing on the fashion accessories that I could relate to, but skipped through the technical pages of bridle bits, straps, vitamins, performance enhanc-ers and the like; but now, armed with a little knowledge, I found myself reading the fine print on even these. The *piece de resistance* was Bandi's tack box, a furniture-quality trunk made of mahogany and designed to house everything that didn't hang or reside in the tote, with a lift-out wooden grooming tote to replace a plastic one.

Little did I know that Bobbi had ordered a handmade, stained and shellacked wooden tote as a gift to celebrate my first horse. Plastic is sensible for some things, but as with children's toys, its convenience lacks wood's heft and better-with-age patina. Some people now use vinyl saddles and nylon girths that can be hosed off, thus erasing hours of tack conditioning from an already colossal time-sink, but Bobbi and I agreed that the feel of wood and the smell of leather is worth the time, price and effort. We did not rebuild a wooden barn just to fill it with synthetic substitutes. Snobby perhaps, but traditional, high-maintenance tack enhances the whole sensual experience, one that an enterprising son of a house painter from the Bronx, Ralph Rueben Lifshitz, translated into a ready-to-wear fortune. Even cost- and time-conscious Scott agreed. Nostalgia for the more elegant past inhabits many of us.

My tack trunk, complete with oval brass plate boasting "Bok" in script, would take four to six weeks to arrive, as would the special order protective cover, in cotton/nylon green with cream trim and again "Bok" embroidered in cream thread. The mahogany trunk's treasure chest look sang to the young girl still stubbornly rattling around my drying bones, and its design specificity also satisfied my passion for order. Well-run barns require ship-shape tidiness with ergonomically designed racks for the curves of the saddles, name-labeled hooks for bridles, shelves for blankets, feed rooms for, well, feed, supplements and no mice, and trunks and boxes for everything else. So much stuff for one horse mul-tiplies with more, and Sharpie Rub-A-Dub markers are imperative for me to know my own. I labeled everything to avoid interrupting a busy Bobbi to ask yet again, "Is this my bridle?" I looked forward to setting up our wood-paneled tack room, the one area of the barn that needed little work and sported some nice old touches like the horseshoe hooks to hold bridles, crops and helmets. I happily day-dreamed a full tack room, wall-to-wall with equipment, a floor spread with creased, dusty boots and the trophy case filling up with the accomplishments of ourselves and our customers. Horse/house/barn-keeping all rolled up in one new microcosmic world.

Bobbi and I ran out of steam at the saddlery, and as it was the middle of an exceptionally hot and humid summer, we put off choosing the assortment of blankets and rain sheets for autumn. I signed the credit card bill averting my eyes from the total, and we heaved all the loot into the roomy trunk of my insulted Saab convertible that before had held nothing more strenuous than a tennis racket or two. We planned a riding date to try the saddles I borrowed, having chosen a few via the wooden "horse" they use to rough out sizing. I favored one, mainly on looks, but Bobbi sagely insisted I actually test drive them on my horse before committing. There are size and "twist" considerations (I am still unclear about the latter even after several explanations), but also the forward tilt and cushiness of both seat and knee pads.

Despite our whirlwind spree, we only scratched the surface. From wound care and digestive management to tail clippers, mane braiders and hoof oil, I foresaw years of new territory ahead. In the end, some items fit Bandi improperly, and I shuttled to the store to exchange several, including the bridle. Bandi's head is a weird combination of a "horse" and the smaller "cob" sizes, requiring a much more expensive "choice'"

Buying tack is one thing, learning to use and maintain it is quite another. To my surprise, the time-consuming grooming of a horse and keeping of the tack rivals the riding in "tactile" pleasures. On a riding day I wake up and wriggle myself into stretchy, shape-conforming, high-waisted breeches (bloated days aren't so fun), snug elasticized shirt (no hiding my muffin top here either), cushioned argyle socks and comfortably broken-in paddock boots, all purposefully tailored for movement and getting dirty. Though I never had one until now, a uniformed job always appealed to my sartorial deficiency. I comb my hair into two low pigtails and pin down strays, not overly fussing, for a helmet will soon plaster all, short and long, to my sweaty head.

Once the kids are breakfasted, dropped at camp and the day's schedule aligned, my drive to the farm is light and free, especially in the fresh of the morning with The Beatles blaring *Good Day, Sunshine*; my time alone—what the pundits term "Mommy time"—and what a fun way to exercise. As I crunch onto the gravel driveway, I encounter a few early riders out in the field, but just the sight of the sun-kissed farm is enough to have me offering gratitude to the power—God or science—that created fields, mountains and horses to inspire people to make barns, pastures and paddocks.

Retrieving my half-chaps from the back of my dusty car, I struggle, bent over and stiff, to zipper them on. I gather up a few sweet molasses and grain stud muffins from my stash in the muddy trunk, for now my mobile tack box until our farm is ready, and slap my barn hat on my head against the bright sun. I stride out to Bandi's paddock and call to him—"Baaaannnndiii; hey handsome. Hi, Bandi." He has begun to recognize me as carrot and stud muffin dispenser, and if I am lucky he'll whinny or blow through his nostrils in greeting as he saunters over. I give him ample treats, perfectly willing to buy his love. A stud muffin results in a strenuous licking exercise that long outlasts the actual morsel. It's funny to watch, peculiar to him, and I pat his forelock, rub his ears and give him a kiss on his soft muzzle. He smells like chewed grass and dewy earth.

We walk slowly to the barn, against the work to come, and he feigns an itchy leg or pesky belly fly to sneak his face down into the fluffy grass. But I am on to him now, keeping our heads up and our direction steady. "Oh, no you don't, Bandi. I'm not that green anymore." His improved manners match my increasing confidence and ability. Once gracefully into the stall, I remove the lead line and step outside, hooking the canvas stall guard across the opening. Bandi checks his grain bucket in case dinner came early, grunts in disappointment, takes a consolation drink or sometimes a pee. Business done, he sticks his head out into the aisle looking for me and more treats. He watches attentively as I lug saddle, saddle pad, girth, tack box, helmet, crop, bridle and a five-pound bag of carrots from the stall-converted mini-tack room to his stall. It takes two trips, and Bandi grumps if I make the first pass without initiating the carrot feed. Occasionally, he'll give me a nip—teeth to shirt or lightly on skin—to remind me of my treat covenant. He is gluttonous, but affectionate, too.

I arrange my materials. I hoist the saddle, pad and girth onto the rack that handily swings up on the wall outside the stall. I drop the tack box on the floor, its scrape on the concrete echoing down the tunneled aisle. I hang my crop on the hook of the stall guard in plain sight, but still I almost always forget it. Draping the bridle on the bridle hook, I unlatch its complicated figure eight resting position that Bobbi requires for tangle-free neatness. Initially, I despaired at the sight of the bridle as all those straps and buckles made it, and even the simpler halter, all but impossible to configure. But after several weeks I've mastered both the figure eight and the positioning of at least my own familiar bridle and halter correctly on and off my horse's head.

I offer half of a carrot to Bandi, enjoying the pull of his soft lips against my flat palm, and step into the stall. Leaning into his chest with my hands and shoulder to maneuver his large body back, I hook the cross tie straps to the brass loops either side of his halter where his mouth meets his cheeks. With another carrot and a neck scratch I talk gently to him: "What a good boy, Bandi. Are you ready for a ride? Did you have a good night?" One rider confessed embarrassment about conversing with her horse so she sings instead. I continue to prattle on and try not to feel silly. I take up another half carrot and with the rubbery curry comb I massage Bandi's back, sides, legs, chest, neck, belly and haunches in a circular motion against the grain of the hair to loosen the caked mud, dust and dander. In the summer all three are abundant, particularly if he has rolled around the bare patches of his paddock, and the loosened particles float airborne, visible in the sunbeam slanting through the one high, small window on the back wall. I know I breathe all this in, because it comes out later, copiously, when I blow my nose. *Eeew, gross*, I thought the first time I panicked at the blackened *(lung?)* tissue, *what the hell?* But there is no avoiding internal and external contamination in large animal, summer barn territory. In winter, though they are bathed infrequently if at all, the blanketed horses stay cleaner atop the frozen ground and snow. Muddy spring is the worst.

I work over one side, give Bandi a carrot and proceed to the other. Another carrot and I take up the stiff round palm-held brush to smooth over his hair, now with the grain, with short, deep flicks to out any remaining dirt. It requires many pressured strokes to get a dirty horse gleaming—they roll in a dirt patch to coat themselves as protection against heat and flies—and my arm gives out before he is anything near dust-busted.

"It should be a full-body work-out, with sweat," Bobbi would later tell my kids when they lazed through a grooming.

Feeling a cheat, I decide the bath after my ride will find the rest. I brush his right leg and he begs, either by scraping his left foot on the floor or by twisting his head down, well past his knee which he pulls up and under himself like a circus elephant. I confess to promoting this trick on occasion for friends and especially kids, but try not to reward gratuitous performances. I push his head away, "Don't beg Bandi: you're not a dog. I'll give you carrots for free."

Next I hoof pick, a task intimidating, back-breaking and probably the reason grooms were invented. The hoof pick is a small plastic handle with a triangular metal point at a right angle on one end and a stiff brush, like for a barbecue grill only pedicure petite, on the other. Starting with his right foreleg and facing toward his rear, I bend over forty-five degrees, carefully keeping my feet to the side of his leg, and run my right fingers down the elongated tendon below his knee to his hoof. A cooperative Bandi lifts his foot and relaxes into my firm left hold. Using the metal point my right hand picks out the impacted dirt and manure from around the inside of the shoe, careful to excavate under the ends of the U where stones like to burrow. I avoid poking the "frog" part of the hoof, a hard cuticle that runs from the back edges to a point in the center.

An uncooperative Bandi refuses to raise or keep his foot up or will even kick sideways at me to shake my grip. And, because I am positioned just beneath his haunch, awkwardly angled and intent on the task at hand, my chance of getting punched or stepped on, should he quickly stamp his foot down, is high. It pays to be alert and light-footed. I now realize the power of horse legs. If the jerking hoof clips my hand I'll suffer a gnarly bump that spreads into a blue/green bruise. Sometimes, with resolve and muscle I can restrain a restless foot with a firm grasp and a sharp "WHOA." Even with a peaceful Bandi it takes a while to chip out the dirt, often concrete-solid and stuck, and my weak back tires and starts to ache. After just one foot I'm sweating like a linebacker, with three more to go. I move to the hind, which on Bandi goes a little easier because he relaxes more. It is heavier though, and lower, and I find myself wedged claustrophobically against the back wall of the stall. I take a breather, give him a carrot and hobble to the other side, not bothering to fully straighten up.

That done, I bring in another carrot and the saddle pad. Placing the pad slightly forward of the withers, I drag it back to smooth the hair and align the pad into the curve of his back. I exit again and lug in the saddle and girth. Gently positioning the saddle on the pad, I aim to keep the kneerolls just behind Bandi's shoulder blades allowing freedom of movement. Threading the girth billets through the saddle pad keepers, I buckle the girth, four attachments in all, loosely across his front belly. I will tighten it more snugly just before mounting. Only one more carrot before bridling: bridle on means work, not grazing. I tuck my gloves into my pants. Retrieving the bridle I remember to close the stall guard behind me and put on my helmet. I place the reins of the bridle over his head and unhook the cross ties. Confidence, speed and dexterity are helpful here now that the horse is free to bolt, especially when tacking up in a grooming stall where the front side is open to the aisle.

I stand next to the left of Bandi's neck looking in the same direction. Holding the top of the bridle in my right hand on the right side of his face with my arm under his neck, I steady his head with that same hand on his face between his eyes and nose while unbuckling and lifting off the halter with my left hand. Threading the halter over my left shoulder to free my left hand, I slip the metal bit of the bridle into his mouth, inserting my fingers into the toothless part at the back of his lips to get him to open and take it above his tongue all the while keeping a firm hold with my right hand. Some horses do this more willingly than others, and Bandi, thank goodness, is amenable every time.

With the bit set back to the corners of his mouth I am afforded enough slack to slip the top of the bridle up and over his ears, pushing them forward and through, one at a time. I shift around to face him while buckling the throat latch where his neck meets his head, remembering to insert the strap end into the looped leather keeper. I even out the cheek pieces and tuck the nose band straps inside these, buckling them underneath his muzzle, again securing the end neatly in its keeper. All of this straightening and buckling can frustrate since the multiple bridle parts are connected yet mobile and can slide and shift into innumerable combinations of unevenness. Though sorely tempted I don't dare unbuckle anything unfamiliar; once, I second-guessed a Bobbi-calibrated strap and wound up with three disconnected pieces of leather in my hands and my tail between my legs. So, I pull on one side only to cock up the other and conclude a degree in physics might help. Bandi eyes me—*that's not right*—and I fiddle some more. I lift the reins back over Bandi's head, holding them under his chin. Hanging the halter on any rail I can reach, I remember my crop as I unhook the stall guard.

Finally ready, we clip-clop down the long aisle and out to the ring. I feel done-in already and the riding hasn't even started.

At the mounting block I cinch the girth strap one or two holes tighter around the thickest part of Bandi's body. Some horses breathe deep to expand their rib cages against the girth; later, the resulting wobbly saddle can topple a novice rider dangerously sideways. Other horses nip at you while tightening, but Bandi doesn't mind the squeeze of his girdle. I pull down the stirrups along their leathers releasing them from their high enfolded safety position that prevents them banging on the horse's sides or catching on anything should he get away. Leading Bandi alongside, I step up onto the mounting block. Sometimes it takes a few circling attempts to parallel park him accurately. I slide on my cotton-crocheted, tan leather-palmed gloves and loop the reins back over Bandi's head, taking up the slack. Grabbing some mane hair with the reins in my left hand, I step my left foot into the left stirrup and hoist my right leg over his back. If he walks off, I "WHOA" him and sit heavy, tightening my thighs. Inserting my right foot correctly into the right stirrup, I rest my crop along the side of my left thigh and head off for a warm-up walk. There is an awful lot to remember, and I worry that I am not hooked up properly.

After my hour lesson and a leisurely walk to cool him down, I dismount by releasing my feet from the stirrups, swinging my right leg over the butt end of him and sliding down and slightly away on the left side. Mounting and dismounting is always from the left, a tradition attributed to right-handed soldiers in accommodation of their left-hanging swords. I breathe relief and satisfaction. I lavish Bandi with good boy pats and, still holding the reins, thread the stirrups up the leathers to looped safety position. I loosen the girth as a thank you, and we head back into his stall. I unbuckle and remove the bridle and girth along with the saddle and pad, undressing him in reverse order, and restart the carrot stream. I replace the halter on his lovely face. Collecting the lead line, shampoo, scraper, sponge, fly mask and fly spray in a bucket, we walk to the outdoor wash stall, and I cross-tie him between the two posts.

Adjusting the water to slightly warmish, I hose him, careful to keep a hand on his rump to let him know when I pass behind. It is counter-intuitively wise to stay in tight to the back of a horse and absorb any short kick or swing widely out of range (their legs are longer than you'd think) to avoid one altogether. The tendency is to venture just far enough to receive the strongest blow. A behaved horse won't attack you unless surprised, but a perfectly distanced kick is not worth the risk.

I fill the bucket with shampoo and water and generously soap sponge every nook and cranny I can reach. After a good rinse, I drag the scraper like a windshield wiper and flick it to remove most of the water: this tool's efficiency is satisfying; the cascading water hits the ground with a splat and immediately his copper coat dries and lightens. I run my hands down each leg twice to hand-squeegee the excess water there. Then I give him the once-over with chemical-free marigold fly spray, replace his fly mask, attach his lead line and unhook the cross ties. Leading him some distance away from the washing station, I stop and say "Okay… *Now*" and allow him a hearty graze in the special grass, while I bask in the aftermath of a safe ride and good care taken. I scan the blue mountains in the distance, enjoying Bandi's serene, musical munching. Laying my head against his shiny smooth, sun-warmed sides and neck, I stroke and talk to him and train his errant mane off to the dressage-preferred right side. He casually sways his tail against the flies, I swat those he can't reach, and we sigh in unison.

It is an opportune time to observe Bandi for any injuries. One time a raw gash glared on his left haunch. A branch or a nail must have cut him, though we never determined the culprit. With some cleaning solution and salve, he healed up nicely. Another time Bandi's long penis caught my eye as it emerged from its neat pocket. I recoiled at its scaly, filthy condition.

"Joy," I called to a barn employee as she washed down another horse. "What is all this grey stuff on Bandi's schlong?"

"Oh," she replied, a little embarrassed, "that's just old skin and dirt."

"Can I pull it off, or should I wash it somehow?" Compelled to pick, I was also afraid to reach under there and mess with it lest he take offense and kick me in the head.

"Well, there is a soap you can use, and he may let you just peel some off."

By the time I weighed Joy's words "*may* let you," Bandi had retracted, all clean and tidy again. The idea didn't appeal to him either.

"But how do I get to it now?"

"You can just reach in there, but you better have Bobbi show you how," she tossed over her shoulder, suddenly remembering some pressing business in the other direction.

I always hate to end Bandi's after-bath grazes, but, perpetually late, I also always need to hightail back to my neglected family. Tugging Bandi's face out of the grass I lead him and his skuzzy sheath, with authority, back to his paddock, and pat him goodbye with one more carrot. I trek to the barn and wipe down the bridle, saddle and girth with a damp sponge and saddle soap, ferreting inside all the tight loops. I tuck and hang all tack and materials neatly into their places and scurry home— tired, dirty, unbelievably thirsty and thoroughly happy.

This was the procedure each and every time I rode, two hours total if I'm efficient, with slight variations depending on the season: in colder months, brushing and blanketing would substitute the bath, with extra indoor treats supplanting the fresh grass graze.

I ASKED BOBBI about Bandi's scaly member the next day.

"Oh yeah, it can get pretty disgusting in there. The scunge actually has a name: 'smegma.'"

What a great word, I thought, vaguely Yiddish, and later consulted the OED: "A sebaceous secretion, *esp.* that found under the foreskin." *Yuk. No wonder no one wants to deal with that.*

"It certainly looks like it sounds. Is it unhealthy? Should I clean it?"

"I'll get some special soap and a sponge and show you how."

I intuited it wasn't one of her favorite jobs either. And I figured horses have been living in the wild without busybodies washing any part of them, let alone their nether regions, so nature must guard against infection. Though we did eventually get the soap and sponge that was the last I heard of it.

Months later, in our own barn, I heard Bobbi prophesy many times that we would have to get her friend Terri to clean the horses' sheaths. *Why Terri?* I wondered. Enjoyment? Technique? Remuneration? No: I deduced Terri's job as chief sheath cleaner piggybacked another thankless role: motherhood. Mothers deal with diapers and vomit and all kinds of ick and therefore become immune, or at least seasoned to retch-inducing tasks. Likewise, I didn't mind too much peeling off what I could given the chance, that is when Bandi relaxed and dropped. It is gratifying in the way of picking at chapped lips, or a hang nail. My mental tally confirmed my theory—the childless among our crew were much more squeamish, and I am still awaiting my sheath-cleaning lesson.

I wondered what else I might expect in the gross department. Do they get trailer-sick, like kids and pets in cars?

"Do they ever throw up?" I asked Bobbi.

"No. They can't, the way they're designed. That's part of the reason they colic; the bad stuff has only one way out."

BY THE END OF THE SUMMER, I grew fairly confident about grooming and riding. The former became second nature and the latter less scary. Some skills noticeably improved—trotting, steering, and at the canter I occasionally managed the half-halt, that minimalist tightening of the outside rein and quick release to gather back a strung out gait without breaking into a trot. While turning, I could shift his head in the direction I determined, curving his body around my inside leg, and sometimes even push him into a corner he attempted to shave. I tried a little "jumping" too, just a few cross rails that Bandi mostly trotted over.

But once or twice he cantered, and I actually got some air. Honest and smart at the fences, Bandi paced himself and made it easy. I just fixed my position up out of the saddle, heels down, eyes up and hung on. And it's easy, if all goes well. If it doesn't, well, I hoped I would find that out later, after the sheath cleaning.

I achieved a milestone over that summer as well. I rode several times alone—that is without Bobbi minding me. I brought Bandi in from his paddock, tacked him up, rode both in the ring and in the field, trotting and even cantering. Then I washed him down and returned both him and me safely to our respective homes. My solo flights taught me that the anticipation of riding generated more anxiety than the actuality. I began to feel like a real horsewoman: not expert by any means, but with enough knowledge to get by. I was never more sweaty, grimy and parched in my life, but fitter too, my body realigning itself. It got increasingly easier to straighten up after zipping on those half-chaps and hoof-picking. I imagined that with caution this sport could be safe, enjoyable and good for me both physically and mentally. Then I overheard farrier Hilary and Bobbi discussing the recent death of a trainer they both knew just across the Hudson River in New York State.

"I can't believe she wasn't wearing a helmet," Bobbi said.

"I was out there just last week and yelled at her for not wearing it, and she said with certain horses she didn't need to," Hilary replied, shaken.

"Was the horse trouble?"

"No, but it seemed to have some kind of neurological problem they were trying to figure out. For some reason the horse went down, she hit her head, and that was it."

I took the opportunity to harangue Bobbi to always, *always, always* wear her helmet and to never take any chances at our farm. Part of me lived in perpetual fear of a serious accident. Not two weeks later she reported another incident.

Bobbi's friend Jane agreed to help with a horse the owner had purchased by video. A large dark bay with impressive moves, Sebastian's supposed one bad habit was bolting. Jane, a very experienced rider, took him on. Their first outing went well, but he dumped her on the second.

"Did he bolt?" I asked.

"No, she was prepared for that. He actually bucked her off," Bobbi said.

I knew bucking is a big no-no in a horse. I certainly would not want that trait in mine. But to expect one bad habit and get another upset my tightly-held theory of preparedness.

"She expected to be sore, but went to the hospital later that night because she was having trouble breathing and thought she might have punctured a lung. But apparently she just bruised her heart wall."

Just? I thought and started, once again, to rethink riding. I was still glad we had bought the farm, but maybe Scott was right about its use—preserving the land by growing hay would have been a whole lot simpler.

CHAPTER TWELVE

When in Doubt, Show

·⊂━━━━⊃·

RIGA MEADOW SCHEDULED A SHOW at the end of September to fundraise for their pony club. A Herculean effort undertaken in the dog days of summer, jumps and fencing were dismantled and re-painted, fields were cordoned off to nurse the over-heated, done-with-growing grass, white picket fence-potted plants clumped together awaiting their places, and tractors roared around grooming riding rings. Making the place pretty seemed of paramount concern as if the equally fussed-over horses, always buffed to their toniest for shows, would notice. But for riders and spectators a classy setting inspires even more horse devotion. Everyone asked if I would enter. "No way," I'd immediately answer, incredulous. I pegged showing for the experienced and talented. I remembered the humiliation I had witnessed at a clinic, let alone a show.

In June, Riga Meadow hosted a former Olympic rider and a well-known instructor, here designated as "Trainer," to teach a one-day riding clinic. Barn locals and others further afield paid for an hour lesson, in groups of two or three, with the expert. I came to watch Bobbi with her younger horse Toby and also to meet Karen, an applicant for our farm's position of live-in stable hand. Bobbi warned me this trainer was a yeller. I have generally considered workshops supportive rather than abusive, so I was curious. Karen and I settled in some lawn chairs under our sun hats to observe; it was a perfect riding day, lukewarm and overcast.

"You really can learn a lot from auditing these clinics," Karen said.

"I wonder if she still rides?" I queried. Trainer looked rather out of shape: she limped and carried extra pounds. She unfolded her director's chair in the corner of the outdoor ring and loudly proclaimed that her knees ached, so she would sit a lot.

"Okay, who's the first victim?" Trainer yelled, rubbing her hands together and chuckling, amusing herself.

Three women on horseback lined up.

"Tell me about your horses," she commanded.

Riders specified ages, habits, strengths, weaknesses and what they were currently working on. With a queen's wave she dismissed them to walk and trot the ring. She zeroed in on faults, interspersing tidbits of horse-think in the process.

"Your horse should have a good reason for walking a diagonal line without bending his head or his body, and it is up to you to give him one."

Everyone attempted a leg yield, edging their horses along a diagonal line without actually turning. Kathy's horse resisted and got feisty to boot.

"Don't pull on his mouth so hard—what's your name again? Yes, Kathy—I have trouble with names—your horse should respond immediately to your aid. Use your legs, and if you need the reins, tug once, firmly, but not hard, and release immediately. If he doesn't respond, ask again, but DO NOT engage in a tug of war with your horse, because he will just get hard to the bit."

"But he always..."

"No excuses. Just do what I tell you."

Trainer turned to the other riders who performed the leg yield marginally better. Kathy was jittery now, anticipating failure, and her horse sensed it. Trainer requested the canter and repeated transitions to the trot and walk. The riders cantered, well spaced-out, stopping and starting as directed. Then Kathy could not get her horse to stop and sped to the inside past a rider that Trainer was addressing, distracting them both.

"Kathy! Make that horse stop. Ask, and if he doesn't respond, ask again."

Kathy hung heavy on the reins, afraid to loosen them. It takes experience, faith and confidence to pump rather than slam on the brakes. She was also off balance and generally frazzled. I know from my own inexperience that it is almost impossible in this situation to have the wherewithal and poise to give the horse some room again, temporarily out of control, before retrying the request from a more settled position.

Kathy managed to stop, ungracefully, and fell in line with the group.

"Canter to the right," Trainer instructed.

Once again Kathy's large horse cantered too fast, filling the gap. She attempted a circle but wound up cutting back in the other direction, passing to the inside of one of the other riders. It wasn't dangerous, or that close, but it infuriated Trainer.

"Kathy! I am tired of teaching people who don't listen! You are a selfish rider, selfish! And you will have a selfish horse!"

"I'm sorry. But I feel unbalanced and am having a hard time controlling him, today. Usually—"

"Don't give me excuses—just do as I say. You're not trying Kathy, you have to try harder."

"I'm sorry; I *am* trying, but..."

"I don't want to hear it. You are mean to your horse, and you refuse to try. I can't teach you."

Trainer refocused without animosity on the other two riders for the ten minute remainder of the hour, with Kathy trying her best to control her horse and follow instructions. She endured another lecture when they lined up at the end and departed the ring in tears. I squirmed in sympathy for her: singled out, sniveling, mortified. All of us shrinking on the sidelines felt it easily could have been us in that ring with a bad case of nerves and an uncooperative horse. And, we all knew that hearing an instruction and actually performing it sometimes takes, as we say in yoga, many lifetimes. She looked to be trying and paid good money to be instructed. I wondered if the expert Trainer perceived something in the rider that our less-experienced eyes didn't catch. Still, it didn't seem enough to warrant such a personal attack.

"I have a theory," I muttered to Karen.

"What's that?" she whispered. By now everyone feared attracting attention.

"Maybe Trainer doesn't like her because she's so thin."

Kathy is tall but so skinny you try not to suspect anorexia. It seemed unlikely that her bony arms and legs could maneuver her reluctant animal, and in contrast her thick, muscular horse only rendered her more stick-figured.

"Maybe," Karen replied. "It certainly seemed uncalled for, criticizing the rider more than the riding."

"Trainer can't be too pleased with her unhappy knees when she was once a fit, top level athlete. At any event, I'm not letting myself in for that kind of treatment anytime soon."

That said, I did learn much about riding by watching the next few sessions. She is indeed an expert horsewoman, and many experts are impatient and demanding.

Fortunately, she recognized Bobbi's experience, and Bobbi described her Toby eloquently, while emphasizing his dopey youth. She took Trainer's instruction and never explained away any behavior, smart woman, though sorely tempted at times, I could tell. Her relief at avoiding abuse in front of me was palpable, and she was pleased with Toby's unreliable manners for that one hour. Bobbi later expressed dismay at Trainer's earlier behavior, but was not surprised. She had fully prepared to be, and indeed once had been, the victim herself.

"You have to let it roll off when it happens to you, but she was awfully hard on Kathy."

I had glimpsed a tradition of humiliation in the horse world.

Relief flowed again through the crowd when Trainer did not yell at

the farm's owner who rode a client's horse known for his antics. Someone surreptitiously alerted Trainer about Linda.

"What? Do you think I'm not going to yell at her just because she's in
charge?" Trainer retorted for all to hear.

SO THE UPCOMING RIGA MEADOW SHOW with all its possible
embarrassment seemed out of the question. But then, over cross ties,
Bobbi joined the chorus of people persuading me to enter.

"I was thinking of riding Bandi in the hunter event. He'd like to jump,
and Stacey made me promise we'd give him some opportunities to do what
he loves." Fresh from a ride, she brushed Angel to a dark brown sheen.

"By all means; I'd love to see Bandi strut his stuff." I gave him a peck
on his muzzle, and he sneezed. I blew his wet shower out of my own
nose and wiped my face with my shirt.

"Why don't you enter as well?"

My reaction was again "no way."

She peered at me with a sideways grin. "I'm going to bring Toby over
for some events too. I think we'd have fun, and you can certainly do the
long-stirrup (meaning grown-up as opposed to the child "short"-stirrup)
walk-trot division, and maybe even the walk-trot-canter."

Yeah, right, I thought. "But what about my steering? I'm not even
comfortable sharing the ring with one other horse, let alone more," I
puffed from hoof-picking Bandi's heavy left hind.

"So, don't do the canter, just the walk-trot."

Like that helps, I thought. "How many people are in the ring at once?"

"It's hard to say. Could be two, could be ten. More than that and
they'd probably divide it into two groups."

"I don't know." I bent to the right hind hoof.

"Remember: everyone will be going in the same direction, and if you
come up too close on someone, just make a little circle or cut across to a
less crowded spot. This is perfectly acceptable."

I hesitated as Bobbi fed Angel two carrots and walked her smoothly into her stall.

"I'll think about it." I hoisted Bandi's saddle to the curve of his back. He whinnied for Angel.

"You can always enter and then pull out at any time. Even just before your particular event. Horses scratch all the time. We could even put Jane in the kids' lead line walk-trot. She'd have a blast, and they all get a ribbon at this stage."

"Would you have a hold on her the whole time?" I looked her right in the eye.

Her baby blues returned confidence. "Absolutely. Bandi seems to sense when he has kids on him and behaves even better than usual."

With that, Bandi let fall an odiferous splat of manure and looked at me with sweet pleading. Though I suspected it was all about his mess (Bobbi later gave me a tote bag that said "behind every good horse is a woman cleaning up") and more carrots, I took his expression as a sign.

I smiled, "Okay, Bandi, we'll give it a go," and collected the shovel and broom to scoop the poop.

Competition was beginning to sound like fun. I still had several weeks to change my mind. And, technically, it wouldn't be our first. We attended a low-key show in a neighboring town when Elliot was seven and riding with Jessica. As a novice, Elliot entered one event—lead line walk and trot—in which the horse is tethered to the instructor, but the child's form is judged for posting and sitting. Nine kids competed, and Elliot's excellent posture, quiet hands and balance were accented by his hunter green show jacket that we found, second hand, at the tack shop. We beamed at his skill and effort.

The judges ordered the line-up, and places five through two went to other riders. His place came down to first or one of three unrecognized lasts. When the loudspeaker rang out "Elliot Bok riding Sultan," Elliot smiled, but Scott and I went wild, probably against all protocol. So, my one show experience was warm and fuzzy. Elliot lacked a horse this time around and would have to wait, but Jane and I would debut, me on Bandi in the adult walk/trot and Jane in the children's lead line, also on Bandi. Bobbi assured me we would all be fine, even five-year-old Jane, who didn't know the word "post" and had been on a horse about four times. Despite our return to New York and only weekly riding, I felt sort of ready, and in the coming lessons, Bobbi would review a few pointers about competing to increase my comfort level.

BY THE DAY BEFORE THE SHOW Riga Meadow Equestrian Center had been transformed. The outside grounds still buzzed with last minute preparations so Bandi and I joined three young riders atop ponies in the indoor ring. It seemed every show entrant had the same plan for getting ready, but sharing a ring, which demands steering accuracy and etiquette, rattled my nerves. Around and around we motored, changing direction as a group to avoid face-offs. I grew steady and confident. *Maybe I am ready,* I thought. As I trotted a left past the barn door at the far end of the ring, a loud tractor started, gunning its engine. I didn't register it amidst the other commotion, but Bandi jumped straight up, simultaneously spinning a one-eighty to the left, quick as lightening. Sailing off to the right I thudded hard on my side and replaced hip. I sensed flight for a flash second and hit the ground before I had time to freak out. Previously, I had talked to Bobbi about falling, about which I was petrified.

"Is there a way to fall so you don't get hurt?" I asked, trying to sound more calculating than cowardly. Having inherited a tendency towards doomsday scenarios from my eastern European immigrant ancestors, I cannot fathom innocuous falls. Those must be the exceptions that prove the rule. My mind immediately veers toward the worst case, and I picture Superman in a wheelchair.

"Well, the best strategy is to not tense up and try to roll away from the horse," Bobbi answered. "But it happens to everyone, and eventually it will happen to you."

I've had maybe fifteen rides in my life, but managed to stay on, and I had convinced myself that sheer will power would stick me to the saddle, no matter what. In actuality, there is *maybe* a nanosecond to consciously avoid coming off a quick-darting horse or to engineer a *graceful* landing, at least at my level of non-skill. Even Bobbi admitted there is precious little time to plan. Experienced riders with an excellent seat can anticipate a spin, spook or buck and prevent or "sit" it by keeping a tiny part of their brains and bodies ever at the ready. But "experienced" wasn't even in my vocabulary yet.

I had placed too much faith in Bandi and myself. One minute I confidently entered my turn at a happy trot—"Look at me, moving sooo well, feeling at one with my horse, ready for this show"—the next I was eating dirt, clambering to my feet, my brain yelling "Holy shit" over and over in an internal loop of panic; hearing Bobbi asking me from afar, rather calmly I noted—*doesn't she ever get riled? What kind of drugs is she on?*—if I was okay; watching my horse tootle over to the narrow open door, pause, and then bolt, a copper streak, out across the farm; seeing Bobbi, on foot, chasing after him. A series of cinematic scenes. My hip felt fine—big relief—and none of the kids lost control of their calmly coping ponies—bigger relief. Ashamed to be the grown-up that found trouble, I sprang up and raced to the door, feeling responsible for my runaway beast. I vaguely registered that no part of me hurt. Upon racing the length of three paddocks Bandi slowed by the silos where one of the stable girls caught him. I met Bobbi hiking him back to the scene of the crime.

"Are you sure you're okay?" Her uncharacteristically knitted eyebrows made me suspect I wasn't, so I re-extended all my limbs and shook myself out.

"Yeah. I can't believe it, but yes."

"Well, congratulations. Now you're really a rider." Her smooth brow was back.

"Thanks, I guess. What happened?"

"He spooked. He went left and you went right." She smiled, forking her arms.

"Should I have stayed on?"

"Possible, but not likely. He *is* a Quarter Horse, remember."

And why, then, do I own a Quarter Horse, I wondered?

"Is Bandi alright? Does he know what he's done?" I wouldn't fully realize what he had done, how he fated us, until weeks and months later.

"Oh yeah, I gave him a good talking to. Any horse can spook, but I'm kind of surprised he went out the door. He's a smart horse to find that narrow exit. I don't think he still feared the noise, but when he realized he'd dumped his mother—'Oh-oh, big trouble'—he decided to run for it."

Small comfort. I'd rather have my own incompetence fell me. At least that I am in control of, could work on. But to have to deal with my own problems and his seemed a tall order. How to anticipate the loud noise that I can't predict, not to mention imagined bogeymen in the scary bushes? Another horse's panic? A bullfrog skipping across the path? A bee sting? A horse-hating dog in hot pursuit? A crouching piece of rusted farm equipment? A sunbeam menacing a funky shadow? All likely scenarios out on a trail, but I considered the indoor safe—sort of hermetically sealed. And the whole point is to *eventually* enjoy the great outdoors, atop a tamed wild animal, feeling like I'm in Marlboro country (minus the yellow teeth and lung cancer). What I want is the thrill of victory without the agony of defeat. Is there such a horse?

I am learning no. Horses are like husbands, wives, kids, friends. They harbor complex personalities and neuroses, unpleasant behaviors and stubborn habits alongside their unique, endearing gifts. We choose partners whose negatives we can tolerate. Children are a crap shoot and we diligently nurture and fix them, rarely giving up even on intractable problems. But friends we accept or reject, depending. How much does one tolerate in an equine? Was it more my fault or his?

I survived my first ejection and that counted for a lot. I was told I should be relieved that I "got 'that' out of the way," and get grateful I wasn't hurt, except for the slight tweak in my back that developed more from post-traumatic stress that froze me rigid as a barbell. I knew I needed to skip gingerly past this inevitable milestone, but I tend to obsess.

I composed myself enough to climb back aboard Bandi as soon as we returned to the ring. To my credit, I trotted and even cantered, slowly inching Bandi back toward the offending far end. He didn't want to go and jigged away while I pushed-pulled him toward his fear and fought my own tension back from the cliff's edge of panic. My nose would grow if I denied my great relief at ending the lesson.

Putting on a brave front, I accepted condolences from riders and workers alike. This did not help. Everyone was unsettled and seasoned at the same time: they had all been through this major "it"—"the first time *it* happened to me, blah, blah, blah...," and though they pretended like hell to have gotten past it, their eyes betrayed them. Their own falls were all right there, vividly clawing beneath the bravado. Their overly compensatory confessions didn't hide their insecurity about tempting fate, on the contrary, they rang more of appeals to an equestrian saint (Anne, George, James the Greater, Martin of Tours?) for protection. I did not buy their queasy "You'll get used to its." Their body language drenched me like a menopausal flash: no matter how long or how well one rides, danger always persists, a third, shadowy companion to horse and rider. I felt indoctrinated into a club alright: one where the inner circle's shared secret comes weighed down by "de"-enlightenment rather than the anticipated liberating revelation. My honeymoon period had ended.

Linda gently put her arm on mine.

"You okay?"

"Yeah. I think I am, physically at least."

"Well, it happens to the best of us. Now we can put your name on 'The List' we keep of all the people who've had a spill while riding here."

A strange kind of glory, but I took my door prize. I pictured a wall of fame for fallen would-be heroes, a before and after smiling rider morphed into worry-laden risk assessor and back again. Scott later suggested "the list" satisfied insurance requirements, deflating me further. But there was some comfort in the numbers who get back on. I continued to hear many a tale on my way out of the barn.

"Oh, my horse used to dump me all the time," confided sixty-plus-year-old Mary.

"I've fallen off so many times I've broken every bone above my waist at least once," boasted Margaret Ann.

"Did you ever learn how to fall?" I interrogated each, desperate to plumb the physics of how to avoid breaking every bone above my waist at least once.

"One time I did try to roll over my shoulder blade. They tell you to avoid the neck and spine, and I guess I did, but that was my worst break: cracked my collar bone clean in half."

My quelled panic threatened to surface, and I bee-lined home, feeling every muscle in my body turn to glass.

I planned to keep mum about my fall. Scott was already edgy that we spent less time together walking and biking. I feared feeding him ammunition against my new pursuit, especially when I teetered on doubt myself. We had never had a sport or any significant leisure activity independent of each other, and even though the master plan included a horse for him, he'd already broadcast a clear disinclination toward time-consuming grooming, training, and a thorough education. Driving home, I didn't cry the tears of fear and relief I felt and calculated about two hours to a stiff martini. And, the show loomed first thing the next morning.

I returned home at 5:00, late as usual; by 5:05, as we readied for our date night, I spilled the beans.

As expected, he offered little comfort. The silent "I told you so but we both know I don't need to say it, if you were out walking with me it wouldn't have happened, maybe you're taking this whole thing a bit too fast and seriously" hung opaquely in the air as he shaved.

"Why can't you be supportive about my riding and the farm?" my words more an accusation than a question.

"What do you mean?" He held his razor aloft and looked at me, genuinely shocked. "I *have* been supportive—about the cost, about the time you spend away from the family, away from me..." scrape, scrape, scrape, rinse.

"Time?—*Time* away from the family? I'm *always* with the kids, all week long, all year long." I argued at him in the mirror, feeling I might strike him if face to face. "You are constantly gone and have been for the thirty years of your career. Work always came first. And now, when I've found something I love that doesn't include you—not for my lack of trying I might add—you accuse me of desertion? How could you?" I shook with indignation, left-over fear from my fall, intimidation from the Riga Meadow yelling Trainer clinic, nerves about the show in less than twelve hours, the possibility that I've been neglecting my family, and my rising doubt about whether this whole horse farm thing was a giant mistake I wasn't sure how to get myself out of.

"That's not fair and you know it. My career pays for all of this. I'd love to have the leisure time you have, but the real world doesn't work that way." Scott calmly wiped his throat with a towel.

I fumed and sputtered—"wait a minute: you know you love your work"—but he ignored me.

"Plus, I spend more time with you and the kids than most other fathers with big jobs that I know. You say so yourself, and you have to admit that we don't do half the things together we used to do. I've been pretty good about that."

"Yeah, right," I protested. "You give me the silent treatment all weekend, and if I'm late, forget it, I'm punished." I turned on the shower. "And you never spend any time at the barn. The other non-riding husbands and fathers are there more than you, watching their kids, helping their wives... and it's *your* barn."

"I do not punish you. That's your guilty imagination."

"Is not."

"Is too."

"Is—," we were getting nowhere.

"I can't help it if we live in New York all week and that the riding can't take place during the hours I have more time. Does that mean I shouldn't do it? Does your schedule always have to come first?"

Of course it does, I knew; there's that stubborn little detail called "income."

My anger looked back at me from the bathroom mirror. I was filthy, bedraggled, old, and stuck. But Freya Stark's words bolstered my fighting spirit: "Absence is one of the most useful ingredients of family life; and to do it rightly is an art like any other."

"No, but what do you expect me to do, quit my job?"

"No. Let's just forget this whole farm thing. Sell the fucking lot or plow it under as hay for all I care. It's not worth this torture." I tugged off my sweaty riding pants, got tangled up and almost fell.

"That's not what either of us wants and you know it. Let's just calm down—" he put his hands on my quaking shoulders, but I shook him off.

"The kids and I have entered whole-heartedly into this adventure and you haven't. Is that our fault?" I shoved my hairy, smelly clothes into the laundry basket.

"Let's not bring the kids into it. But does it have to be an all or nothing pursuit? Can't you take it easy?"

"You just don't get it, do you?" I escaped into the steam of the shower, slamming the glass door against any rejoinder. I didn't get it either, but I was cornered. I was scared to ride, but more scared to quit. If I did eventually decide to curtail riding, I wasn't going to admit that to him. I'd ride, crash even, for spite if I had to.

We had planned a dinner out, but unable to converse civilly I suggested we see a movie first. As much as I did not relish the idea of spending the night with my husband, I also didn't want to deal with the kids. I needed to escape from everything and hold off thinking about the show until I relaxed. A vacant romantic comedy did the trick, and Scott and I carefully stayed off-subject through dinner, but I didn't sleep much that night, wondering if the farm was both too dangerous and ruining my marriage, and whether to put Jane up on Bandi. Bobbi, a very experienced horsewoman, would have a good hold on Bandi, but who would be holding on to Jane? If speedy Bandi decided to spook, it's a long way down. Would quashing Jane's excitement be responsible parenting or over-protection? Her four-year-old friend Toby, the boy she planned to marry, was scheduled in the same event, and I did not relish her likely fury at not being allowed to "show with Toby." Do horses *really* take especial care of kids or is that our stupid wishful thinking?

Six a.m. finally rolled around. I slipped on my pressed, white collared shirt, tailored dark green blazer and struggled into my stiff, new show boots that I neglected, as Bobbi recommended, to break in around the house. I gathered my expensive, state of the art GPA helmet (the only one in the store that fit my small head—it cost an astonishing $400), and my black net show gloves.

"Don't dressage riders wear white gloves?" I asked Bobbi.

"Well, white is the tradition but they draw attention to your hands. If you wear white, your hands better be good."

I paused in the mirror to smooth my lapels. I looked good but felt an imposter. *I could still pull out*, I coached myself, and dug deep for courage. I came up empty.

THE BARN WAS DECEPTIVELY PEACEFUL AT 7:30 am. By the time I had Bandi tacked up at 8:00 the scene morphed into a three-ringed circus—people, horses, trailers everywhere; cars parking; dogs barking; announcements broadcasting with that feedback squeal; mounted riders and trainers conferring and practicing in every direction. Stomach acid climbed my throat. Later, the on-call farrier Hilary would tell me I had looked green. Now, atop Bandi, trotting around the open field, I grew petrified when I needed to be loose and calming to my horse. Confident riders cantered toward, past, around, behind, shouting "Outside" or "Jumping" or "Right" or "On your Left." Amidst such a free for all, my unease cascaded from my head through my queasy gut and thumping seat bones into my increasingly agitated horse.

Bobbi had warned me that some horses find it harder to show at their own barn. It's easier for them to face complete novelty than their home upended. We suspected this largely contributed to Bandi's uncharacteristic jitters the day before. Again, small comfort: I wasn't in a position to calm his nerves like the more experienced riders who physically and psychologically control their beasts, and I knew, because so many people have told me, that Bandi—a veritable four-legged tuning fork to my invisible, cacophonous frequencies—could sense every firing of nervous energy racing though my body. I remembered what Mary had suggested on my first, stiff-as-a-plank trail ride with Bandi:

"Press your tongue up against the roof of your mouth. It's an acupuncture pressure point that relaxes the nervous system."

It worked a little then, but now I figured I needed a jackhammer to pulse out my anxiety. Entering the ring I managed to steer clear of the dozen or so other riders, who, thankfully, were no longer allowed to practice their jumping. We were ordered out and the show got underway. My event was third: a little breathing space but not too long a wait. For thirty minutes I hung around, trotting tentatively through the maze of riders whenever Bandi, restless, tossed his head and pranced. He seemed mad.

"Would you like me to canter him around to settle him a little?" Bobbi exuded enough calm for all three of us.

"Would you mind? It's a little crowded out there." I hopped down. *Sweet relief.*

"Your steering is fine," she said, reading my mind. "But I can burn off some of his energy." Off she confidently trotted into the chaos.

This helped Bandi, but with my feet on *terra firma* I seriously considered scratching. I hated my cowardice so I tried to hold on. If I quit now, the next show would seem that much harder, and this was about as much "hard" as I could take.

Showtime. I remounted and walked through the gate into the ring under a crowd of about sixty spectators. Bobbi's last words to me were "Breathe." I smiled because my yoga instructor repeats the same advice when I'm laboring through revolved side-angle pose. I fell in line to walk around the ring. Except for the occasional bark, child protest or distant loud speaker announcement from the jump field, all was hushed, or perhaps I just went inward with concentration. Throughout my ride, I maintained my personal space by circling to the middle. I redirected focus to my form—back straight and centered, thumbs up and elbows loose, heels down with legs along the girth. The judge commanded the posting trot and then a transition to walk as we changed direction for more of the same. This ordered procession contrasted favorably to the chaotic warm-up outside the ring, and the horses all calmly rose to the occasion. Bandi moved at ease beneath me.

Then, astonishingly, it was all over.

That's it? Did it last even five minutes? My confidence just knocking at my opening door, we lined up as directed, awaiting the results.

I assessed our ride. We hadn't ridden our best. Typically lazy, or, in rider parlance "slow to my leg," I had to nag too rhythmically to keep his motor going. We cut a few corners, but getting respectably through was enough. Bandi stood proud, still and alert, poised like he'd been there, done that, many a time. These equines are so like us—anxiety first, concentration on the task at hand, and then calm. Glancing outward, I saw Bobbi with a thumbs-up, and I spotted Scott, Elliot and Jane meandering across the field from the parking area. They had just missed my ride. I caught Scott's eye with a little wave. He pointed me out to the kids and they tore over. *They got here just in time to see me lose,* I thought, but the sight of them so excited was heartening.

I watched Janie smiling and waving, both kids hanging over the fence as they announced the third and second place winners. Janie gave me a pumping double thumbs-up.

"And in first place, Roxanne Bok riding 'Steal the Show'."

Can't be, I thought. *Eight fairly experienced entrants, and I took the blue?*

I choked up from the emotion of the last eighteen hours, but refocused on getting out of the ring without incident.

"Yea, Mommy!" Jane hopped up and down. "You won. You won!"

"Congratulations, Roxanne," Bobbi said, not overly excited.

Scott smiled at me, and I teared up again.

In disbelief, I seriously considered it might have been rigged as reward for my falling off the day before.

"Did I really ride well?" Bandi stood calm and wise as Yoda now that we were done.

"Yes. There is no doubt about it: you were the most elegant out there." She was serious in her brief analysis of the other riders.

"I guess what they say is true: bad practices lead to the best showings," I concluded, as we collectively retreated to the barn. And that was the end of the celebratory gloating, because everyone dispersed to ready for the next rides. Exhilarated but already drained by 9:15 a.m., I noted there was plenty of show left.

Having just missed my event, the kids and Scott now had to wait several hours for Jane's turn. Watching riders and horses you don't know is the kind of drudgery that tests and proves familial love. Shows are deadly boring unless you ride yourself or have a vested interest in a horse or rider, and then their bit of glory is over in a flash. Not to mention all the down time, getting horses and riders in and out of the rings, re-grooming the footings, righting the knocked-over jumps and checking their heights, tallying up points, awarding ribbons, making announcements, giving the judges breaks. It's lethal unless you're gaga about equines.

Around 11:00 a.m. Bobbi rode her Toby in the hunter pace and won the blue. We justly celebrated for a few seconds. Jane's turn finally came, after much moaning and groaning and snack diversions, at 1:00. Scott and Elliot whined less but were equally restless. The sun beat down upon our hatless heads. We all traipsed into the relatively dark barn to get Bandi, who had been resting in his stall, tacked up again. Jane's spitfire excitement made all tasks more difficult. She and her friend Toby gig-gled and tore around. "Stop running, guys," I repeated. She tended to scream and run when hyped, two things that don't go down well with horses. My relief at my own success was short-lived: I began to fret about a revved-up Jane on Bandi.

Out again into the airy brightness, we lifted Jane into the saddle. Spotlighted by the sun, she shone. At this point Toby the boy, hit the wall in a tantrum. He had been waiting since the early morning for his moment too, but his lesson horse was still occupied elsewhere. We marched away listening to his pitifully loud, crying complaint. I felt guilty having our own horse when most kids rent, borrow or share.

Bobbi triple-looped the stirrups, and I laughed at Jane's short legs in full straddle but still barely reaching down Bandi's broad sides. Never-theless, she kept her proud, erect posture, held the reins with thumbs up and hands down, and flashed a genuine, movie star smile. With the mountains and green pastures in the background Jane starred in her own real-life *National Velvet*. She was all head up there with that big black helmet and found it hilarious that her feet kept escaping the stir-rups. Bobbi walked her around the grass, stopping to engage admirers, and led her into the ring. Four more riders followed. Except for the now pacified Toby, they were obviously experienced, and the two younger girls boasted jackets and hair ribbons that matched those in their horses' manes. They were unequivocally adorable; Jane on the other hand, in her white tee-shirt and sneakers, looked the cowgirl in comparison. *I could have done fancy*, I thought. It never occurred to me that this was also a runway, though I should have guessed from the glossy catalogs. Their little Ariat-footed boots urging their horses on, steadily the two fashion plates posted to the trot, even wild-man Toby, to my surprise. Jane trotted once in front of the judges, but then strenuously gesticu-lated to Bobbi that once was enough, and on the next pass they just walked. Outclassed and under-trained, Jane still had fun. Most impor-tantly, Bandi behaved.

There was one last worrisome detail Jane warned me about before the show.

"Mama, I'm going to win the pink ribbon."

"But Jane, blue is first place, and all the colors are good."

"Nope. Only pink."

She was determined. I didn't know what place pink was, but of course the odds were against her.

These littlest entrants lined up. Jane waved furiously at us, nearly knocking herself off her mount as they awarded all the ribbons. They announced her name first and an ecstatic Jane shouted "I won!" The judge held out the green ribbon to which Jane shook her head furiously. Bobbi quick-talked, and Jane was handed the pink. Bobbi was quite right—pink is fifth and green sixth. Sometimes things just work out. All the other riders also "won," with one of the snazzy girls taking the blue.

This time Bobbi giggled like a debutante escorting a triumphant Jane out of the ring, and we celebrated royally on Jane's behalf, last place or no.

"That is a beautiful pink ribbon, Janie," I cooed. "You were fantastic."

"I even bounced a little, but then it hurt my bottom." She vocally dramatized the jerky motion: "Ugh, ugh, ugh—did you see me, Elliot?"

"Yes, Jane. You did great." He winked at me. "It's hard to post."

"You did great, Jane, just perfect. We are so proud of you." Scott squeezed her tough little leg as he, Elliot, Bobbi and I escorted Bandi and his charge to the barn, a winner's circle of love.

Scott and the kids left, having had enough about three hours ago. I stuck around to see Bobbi ride Bandi in three more open course jumping events. My back was killing me from standing and anxiety, like a dried old newspaper crease it felt ready to crumble to dust, but I wanted to see the whole show through. During her warm-up, I looked over just in time to see Bobbi hopping back up on Bandi. *Did she have to adjust her saddle,* I wondered? Not likely. I had seen her adjust everything—girth, straps, saddle, pad—even talk on the phone, all without dismounting. My heart sank. Bobbi rode the course and took red (second).

"He didn't dump you, did he?"

"Yes he did, the bad boy. After the jump he decided to go left. I planned right. I went one way and he went the other." She still seemed surprised.

"Are you sure you're OK?"

"Yeah, I'm fine. I landed gracefully. I should have been paying more attention, but he's been so good at the jumps...."

"Did he not listen to your aid?"

"It's not that he didn't listen, because there was no aid given. He should have continued straight until I sent him right."

"So he didn't spook?"

"Nope. But he's strong and sometimes gets his own ideas."

Throwing a novice like myself is one thing, but dumping the expert Bobbi is quite another. Had we bought a lemon? Was he too good to be true? Is this his issue? Could I live with it? Was I recklessly endangering my daughter?

Bandi and Bobbi did well through the next two courses, though she had "a good talking to him" after another jump, strongly pulling him up and making him go right, which, like Melville's Bartleby, he clearly preferred not to do. They took two pinks. I reminded the disappointed and flustered Bobbi that we barely knew Bandi and that she had only ridden him about three times, preferring me to do the riding while I was still around weekdays for the summer. There'd be plenty of time for her to fine tune him once I returned to New York. "I'm probably *un*-tuning him," I consoled. We decided that he did well, given all the change he'd faced in the previous two months, and is a very eager, willing jumper— not easy to find. Bobbi gathered up her red and blue ribbons for our trophy case in our new barn, but wrinkled her nose at the pinks—"I don't keep *those*"—so I took them for Jane.

By 3:00 the show ended, but the day was far from over. Bobbi had to get Toby home and look after her other horses. I untacked Bandi, gave him a shower and let him have an hour or two in his paddock before dinner. I cleaned my saddle and bridle and reorganized. Seriously wiped out, I headed home at 4:00. Fried by eight and a half hours of standing and worry, I had no appetite and had a hard time relaxing on the evening drive back to the city: usually Scott complains because we're all fast asleep. Deep down I was pleased about my win and that I hadn't chickened out, but the surface static of worry tuned out a purer satisfaction. I had my blue ribbon and silver plate, and a sleeping Jane clutched her handful of pink ribbons all the way home, but still I felt conflicted: joyful at Jane's and my success yet queasy about my fall and Bobbi's, all courtesy of one ratty Bandicoot. Was it all too hard? Even when it goes well? Did it make sense to own and operate a stable and not ride?

The next day I awoke still rattled. I hoped my Monday morning yoga class would sort me out and help me conquer my fear about riding again, or having anyone I deeply care about ride at all. It was a back-bending yoga day, my most challenging. During the preparatory poses, I grew increasingly nauseous. Michael intuited my discomfort and said "That's it for you, hit the showers." In yoga that means Supta Baddhakonasana, a passive, restorative pose I gratefully reclined into for the rest of the class. Still, I felt lousy all day. Michael explained that any trauma, like a fall, is subversive for the body, and that arching backwards in particular releases built-up toxins from the liver and internal organs. I guess I had toxined to the hilt over the weekend, a horse bender.

THE NEXT WEEKEND Bobbi was judging a dressage event far from home. I faced riding alone, me and Bandi, or not at all. My window of opportunity was Sunday, high noon. The barn was quiet, and in solitude I tacked up Bandi. As we exited the barn door rain started but stopped before I could cop the wet as an excuse to cancel. Bandi was as mellow as he has always been, up until the weekend of the show. Grateful, I still realized that my rides on this animal, maybe even any animal, forever would be different. I know that I am not the exception to the rule, and neither is Bobbi. If we ride, we will fall off, will and skill notwithstanding.

Is my fear overplayed, I wondered? Am I a coward or is riding a crazy idea? Should I fight against my aging body and mind's tendency to avoid risks that seemed miniscule when I was younger? Maybe this is wisdom talking? Sitting, trotting, cantering and jumping on the slippery back of a one-thousand-pound prey animal, hard-wired to flee danger justifies caution, no question. And I bet I could spend a lifetime finding that truly bombproof horse. Those "safe ones" don't have any "go" left in them, a frustration of another kind. And, dollars-to-donuts, it will still find enough energy to spook.

My internal debates churning, I gathered power in numbers. Plenty of people ride, and plenty deal with spookier and naughtier horses than Bandi could ever be. And check out those cowboys on the broncos; in comparison this is child's play. Like so many aspects of living, it's a mind and confidence game as much as one of skill. Live in the moment, keep loose and confident, take falls in stride, leave anxiety at the door, don't anticipate the worst, expect the best, and accept whatever happens. Become a monk in a saddle. Can I get there? Right now, any jig on Bandi's part makes *me* want to bolt for the hills. That Bandi immediately senses my unease renders me more uneasy and *vice versa* into a vicious cycle, a closed loop of haywire circuitry. But if I cave now, next thing I know, I'll cower against more fears—give up skiing (knee and head breakage), tennis (wrist and elbow breakage), yoga (back breakage), driving (full-body breakage)—and I'm an old woman with a death grip on a purse taking baby steps to the drug store on my one outing of the day, my cane thrusting, my paranoid eyes darting around for muggers.

No: better to stretch myself, body, mind and will. Reach toward the hardest tasks so merely hard ones seem a cakewalk. Risk lives everywhere and must be embraced as an antidote to premature old age.

Right.

But then again, acres of doctors' offices and hospital wards brim with middle-aged weekend warriors refusing to accept the inevitable.

Right, again.

Where's the middle ground? Does equestrianism ride this envelope or limn lunacy?

Maybe I should equate the devastating quadriplegia-inducing fall with the statistically more likely car accident. I don't think about a crash *every* time I press the gas pedal. I know many couples who fly separately to ensure one survives to parent even though highways prove more dangerous than runways. But all of these scenarios are unlikely. I may break a collarbone, or twist my spine a bit, but probably won't kill myself. I will emerge braver, more confident, able to leap tall fences in a single bound, "Look, out in the ring, it's a bird, it's a plane, it's Roxanne Bok, no longer lily-livered, but eager, strong and not shaking like a leaf."

Or, I could just quit, responsibly accepting riding as self-indulgent when I have two youngsters to raise. But what about the kids? Once I fell off that likelihood for them loomed real and inevitable. Cars we must contend with, unless you're Amish—but a ton of irrepressible muscle and energy with a small, obstinate brain and no automatic transmission or front and side airbags, we can skip.

CHAPTER THIRTEEN

The Devil Is in the Details

BY NOVEMBER, winter nipped at heels and hooves and "finished" remained a dirty word. The barn and outbuildings were all re-built and painted, although there was no end to the hanging of hooks and racks and shelves and myriad doohickeys necessary to organize a functional animal- and equipment-filled space. The main barn was a gut job in the end, and when we stripped down an un-insulated building with a dirt floor it begged the question of what was saved. Not much: inside, all surfaces now shined with golden new wood patched between the few stately old pine planks that remembered history and experience. Scott still joked that we could display the few bits of original lumber on one wall in the tack room, and his crack wasn't far off.

Painstakingly, all thirty-seven stall floors were dug out to a depth of two feet in order to excavate the accumulated manure packed down from years of poor or no maintenance. We pitied the determined, brow-mopping guys who, with pickaxes, chipped away at this compressed "concrete" for weeks on end. But now cement floors with thick rubber runners span the formerly dirt alleys, and a stone base under a cushiony mat carpets each stall. New "touch slide" doors with black coated bars and working hardware replaced the rusted, bent metal on all doors and windows. Footing beams throughout were replaced where rotted from inadequate mucking and drainage. Toasty warm tack and viewing rooms now boasted clean, damp-proof tile floors. The *piece de resistance*,

a heated indoor ring, while not huge at 80 x 150 feet (the ideal is at least 100 x 200), whet our riding appetites with mostly patinaed old wood that warmly glows in the morning and evening light, lovely new-paned windows that preserve the old barn look, and no dented metal anywhere in sight.

We resisted the lure of the increasingly popular steel barn, an economical and perhaps greener route, though a material colder in temperature and atmosphere. The new roof is asphalt shingle—a *lot* of asphalt—in keeping with the softer, quieter to rain and hail, and no doubt leakier standard. However, we did yield to one newer technology. Eschewing the dusty, must-be-watered-regularly-or-you'll-choke-to-death dirt footing, ours is "dust free," a secret concoction of wax and sand and who knows what else that took three days with a special churning vehicle, not unlike a mini-Zamboni, to install.

"Is it a softer landing for us?" I inquired after hearing the price.

"Unfortunately it's probably no more cushiony than grass," Bobbi shook her head.

"Well, buy me that Velcro saddle, then," I joked as I wrote the check.

The out-building foundations had been shored up with one hundred and twenty-six bags of concrete, refurbished with new wood and the same green roofing and brown paint trimmed with cream to match the main barn. Gary, our contractor, was rightly proud of his work. He reveled in our weekly tour, and Scott and I delighted in exploring each transformation, ostentatious or modest, the three of us lingering to drink it in. He was a rugged fairy godfather to our big pumpkin, and I appreciated the magic craftsmanship that resulted in barn doors with hidden hardware and grooved wall panels that joined with invisible seams.

"You do beautiful work, Gary."

"You've allowed me to do my job," he graciously replied.

The smell of sawdust promised a new start for this old barn that now radiated a palpable lightness, freed from the dreary dank of the last decades. Scott and I realized how happy such transformations make us and how right it felt to rehabilitate a farm, speaking both to his farming roots and my solidarity with animals. Our barn walk-abouts dissolved any remaining rancor from our fight about my riding, which we left alone to find its own way. Time management is tricky for both of us, especially when we can't resist projects that push us well beyond a reasonable fullness, but we'd work it out. Eventually the farm would heal the land and us.

Outside, beyond the double-sized riding rings still under artistic management by Kenny, the round gazebo beckoned as a prime destination. Originally used to showcase young, untrained horses, its one hundred feet circumference impressively radiated without any center support, but it leaned like the tower of Pisa. Gary hoisted and reinforced the sagging frame and halved the sides to waist height. We splurged on blue stone flooring to evoke a shaded terrace. Indulging aesthetics now, my plans percolated a rapid boil: ring the inside with teak benches and lighting and fill the middle with tables and chairs. Not only will it shelter us from the summer sun and thunderstorms, but also afford perfect viewing of the outdoor arena, the barn, the fields and the hills beyond. During shows, vendors can hawk their wares, and I envisioned breezy summer dinner parties with soft notes wafting around men with ascots and women in spaghetti-strapped, ruffled dresses dancing barefoot in the grass. A dreamy Ralph Lauren scene had carried me away perhaps, but to think that we'd considered taking down this lilting relic that now reigned as the crowning centerpiece.

In our earliest imaginings for this project Scott and I had just hoped for cheap and cheerful. But with Mrs. Johnson's legacy, Gary's touches, Bobbi's horse knowledge and our funding, Weatogue Stables emerged deeply beautiful in the way that form follows function. We uncovered the farm's original blueprints that beckoned us that extra mile, and we followed its design. Deceptively simple and re-colored to blend into the New England landscape, the farm re-birthed unpretentious and welcoming, an enterprise that will wear more comfortable with use and age. The disdain I initially heaped on the former owner, I supplanted with respect for the flow of the grounds and the layout of the barns, and I can now understand its former healthy life. I saw that Mrs. Johnson got it right: horses were everything to her, and she sacrificed much for her dream, but sometimes even your all is not enough. Many worthy farms arc a belled trajectory, with heartbreak obliterating success. I hoped we would fare better longer, and that Mrs. Johnson would find some pleasure in El-Arabia's resurrection as a boarding stable rather than a subdivision.

Our fencing man finally showed up, months late, but flew along faster than we could believe with 11,000 thousand feet of new wood. I apologized to our neighbors for the days of post pounding, 1,710 to be exact, only to be encored by weeks of hammering on the four boards in between each and every one. Mike still disappeared occasionally, but snapped to when, frustrated, we dictated a deadline for a particular section. Perpetually jolly, he was hard to yell at.

"Have you heard from Mike, yet?" Scott asked every week.

"No," I'd sheepishly reply, feeling responsible.

"We still have to get the fencing all painted before winter, you know."

I didn't have the heart to tell him it was already too late; the wood too "green" to take the stain. We wouldn't see the finishing touch of ink-black outlining the paddocks until spring.

"And just why is that huge mountain of dirt still lurking in the middle of the fields?"

I shrugged. I had no good answer other than Kenny was on the project part-time, a cost-saving measure to us. The topsoil mountain built from what is now the outdoor riding ring was half gone, but the unsightly rest sprouted tall weeds like a steroidal Chia Pet.

"I think that guy likes his job a little too much," Scott said testily. "This can't be right."

I also questioned Kenny's progress, but I wanted to pacify my impatient husband who was tired of all the mud. He understands the bushy look in wild spaces, but likes good grooming in his landscapes. Likewise, I'll never see my husband in a beard; I think he distrusts wooly guys.

"I don't know . . . drainage is complicated? If we get it right, proper elevations will rid that huge pasture of standing water—you know, what Elliot calls the skating rink? Plus, Bobbi rightly concluded that the last bit of driveway and parking area closer to the barn shouldn't be finished off until all the heavy equipment is gone?" I smiled my reasons and met his eyes in anticipation of a funny rejoinder. He squinted back he wasn't buying, but graciously let it go.

Underlying site work is expensive and necessary, but hardly aesthetically gratifying. In our farmed valley, streams, culverts and drainage pipes all pour the rain from our expansive barn roof and out of the pastures into the many streams running from the hills neatly into the Housatonic River. Many of these waterways have been enhanced by farmers of old, and Kenny busily tapped and redirected them yet again for our own purposes. Excavation also continued to run septic and water lines from the barn (which never had a bathroom), an undertaking held hostage by the mostly obliging building inspector, and what also prevented us working on the little cottage meant to house an on-site stable hand.

Thankfully, to hydrate our aesthetic thirst, the Italian stone masons arrived to lay the flooring in the gazebo and to snug a walled patio into the nook outside the main barn's tack room. They worked by hand: chipping, lugging, pounding. New England stone is beautiful and echoes olden times, and the artistry hasn't changed. I added the last minute, view-encompassing patio with Scott in mind, just in case he decides not to ride. At least he can comfortably survey his land.

Well, maybe.

"You know if Kenny doesn't sort out all that dirt we'll never get the grass seed down. You know what it's like around here in the spring." He frowned.

"I DO know. I'll have Bobbi talk to him again."

I had hoped my commiseration would appease, but undoubtedly we were facing vast tracts of mud-in-waiting. Our restlessness met some consolation in the new (though raw) fencing that contoured the paddocks and delineated the pathways throughout. The entire property finally cohered as "farm." Where the line of fencing meets the river and our northern boundary, we'd left enough room to mow a bridle path. Between this late addition, the open fields to the east and south, and the adjoining twenty acres of woods, we'd have plenty of territory to explore nature from our mounts. I looked forward to this more than anything else and pictured Scott, Elliot, Jane and me on our own safe, contented horses enjoying a family ride. It was a dream that seemed distantly within reach, *once* the farm was complete and *if* we all learned to ride well enough.

Preserving open space excited Scott and me, but underutilized farmland quickly reverts to brush and woodland. Hayfields must be cut and tended, and openness guarded. While a return to tree cover is generally desirable, Connecticut sports more forest now than one hundred years ago when entire mountains of trees were cut, round-stacked and slow-burned into charcoal to fuel the iron industry. Salisbury's strong iron ore was its heritage, significantly contributing to the Revolutionary and Civil Wars mostly in the form of canons, balls, guns and anchors. Much of this region's beauty relies on patches of open agricultural views that followed in industry's wake, but such vistas are shrinking as farms disappear.

That said, Scott is a tree hugger, and our farm lacked shade. Only a few ancient, questionable oaks graced the property, and these sat on the road or distant along the far fence line. On one of our more exciting days at the renewing Weatogue Stables we attended the installation of fifteen thirty-foot sugar maples to line the main driveway into the farm. They arrived in threes each laid out long on, and carefully tied to the bed of a trailer, five Gullivers among the Lilliputians. Their six-foot root balls were neatly burlap-wrapped and tied for protection—massive gifts of nature. Our landscaper Mari staggered their planting in two pseudo-organically unlined rows.

"I really wanted you to see them with some leaves before the winter set in," Mari told me as I practically wept at the graceful sweep of their branches, inviting arms that waved us in with every breeze and rustled benedictions in our wakes.

"This really makes the farm," I said, collecting myself. "They're tremendous!"

"I know. I went with the bigger ones because of the scale of this place. The land, the barn—I was afraid the twenty-footers would look like lollipops."

My mind wandered to the added cost of these giants, but deemed them worthy.

"Just think how much grander they'll be in ten more years," Scott mused, characteristically comfortable with delayed gratification and long-term investment.

But I knew he was pleased. Wealth has its privileges, as the old advertisement said, this time in the form of mature trees. We had long since stopped trying to contain all the "requirements" into some kind of meaningful budget. The overruns serially exceeded our re-padded projections, but so had the transformation. Our deepening satisfaction was such that, dangerously, we felt compelled to tack on whatever marginally made sense. Like kids in a candy store, the addicting sugar fueling a reckless overdrive, we simply couldn't get enough. At least I couldn't, and more restrained Scott was not enough of a killjoy to rein me in. And I knew the added touches satisfied such that even if Scott never climbed aboard a horse, he would enjoy this farm.

On one hand, I newly appreciated his generosity of spirit even though the Weatogue Stables business model of personal indulgence and land conservancy didn't fit his hard-headed capitalistic parameters. On the other, we both worried about what it messaged the kids. Regularly, we tried to keep ourselves and our kids thankful for Scott's business acumen that affords us an exciting NYC life and a refuge in bucolic Salisbury. Scott and I remember that money doesn't grow on trees having come from little, but our kids have only ever known prosperity. They can't help but take a lot for granted. We understand, but it pains us, more so since we can't resist the fruits of his labor—nice homes, pricey vacations, horses and a farm we don't have to kill ourselves working. Is personal philanthropy and talking them to death about the harder roads of others on our own block and around the globe enough or are our kids lost to Mammon devoid of their own bootstraps?

TOWARD THE MIDDLE OF NOVEMBER Bobbi deemed the farm complete enough to move in horses. The sun shone boldly for a late autumn day, a sign of approval. The morning clanged and banged with hammer-in-hand Bobbi hanging water buckets, installing gates and blanket racks, and organizing bedding, food and wheelbarrows. Elliot's hockey game sent us south to Danbury mid-day, so we returned just in time to see the horses arrive in shifts of two in Bobbi's trailer. We brought all of Bobbi and Chip's horses over, optioning immediate critical mass and avoiding the split of a well-knit group of five—the princess Angel, her younger brother Toby, and the three oldsters Theo, Glimmer and Katie. Room we had in abundance: should we be lucky enough to eventually fill all thirty-seven stalls, we could repatriate them.

So far, we boasted one boarder who lived in Avon, Connecticut, over an hour's drive due east. Nancy discovered us from a handmade flyer Bobbi persuaded a friend to post in her tack shop. Our new facility, the ample pastures, Bobbi's training and especially the all day turn-out overrode Nancy's longer commute. Previously her horse spent limited time outdoors because of the pricier suburban real estate. Chase is a six-year-old gelded Quarter Horse on full training board. "Board" means we perform all the daily horse care—feeding, hay and grain supply, cleaning, bedding supply, turn-out, and arrange shoeing and vet care. The training part consists of Bobbi either teaching Nancy or riding Chase four to five times a week. As our prized first customer; Nancy opted for a near paddock with a run-in shed to provide sun, wind and rain shelter, and a roomy center aisle barn stall between two horses for company. When chestnut Chase moved in our first day, he pranced and whinnied his satisfaction with Nancy's choices.

Scott opted for a hike and office work rather than hanging around the barn awaiting four-footed tenants. He promised to turn up later, so Elliot, Jane and I hung out with the new barn cat Ninja and the two bunnies Elliot had begged for and Bobbi had needed no encouragement to find. She located the bunnies through a newspaper ad and put together the wood hutch herself. Scott wisely pits himself against more pets as a bulwark to my tendency to stockpile, but since these mini-furballs would live in the barn I just gave the nod without the usual family council.

"Guess what?" I announced at the dinner table one Wednesday night.

"What?" Jane and Elliot shouted in unison.

"Bobbi got the bunnies."

Scott eyes darted: *did we discuss this?*

There was cheering all around, and I described the two female sisters (we hoped—despite dedicated peering, unlike horses' balls, bunnies' are hard to spot)—one black and white and the other mostly white with tan markings, both with blue eyes. Luckily, Elliot claimed the black and white one "his," leaving Jane surprisingly content with the white and tan. Elliot named his "Hera," after the Queen of Olympus and the goddess of marriage. Jane decided on "Butterfly Girl."

"Oh, Jane, that's a terrible name," Elliot said.

"No it isn't. I like it," she frowned, bracing for an argument.

"How about Venus, Jane?" I intercepted, wanting some coordinating names myself for the pair. "She is the most beautiful goddess of love."

"Venus, penis," she rhymed, wrinkling her nose but quickly adding, "how about bagina?"

Elliot and Jane giggled at her wordplay, and after a few more unsavory anatomical references, Jane went back to Butterfly Girl.

The next morning on the way to school I took another tack.

"Jane, did you know that the Roman name for the most beautiful goddess of the hunt is 'Diana?' Wouldn't that be a nice name for your bunny?" I played Jane's penchant for soft, feminine names like Vanessa, Sara and Olivia.

"I *like* that name. Diana, Diana, Diana!"

I silently congratulated myself; I knew Elliot did not relish the thought of yodeling "Come here, Butterfly Girl" to a bunny.

Diana and Hera were a huge hit. Bobbi, knowing I often felt left out of these first exciting days of official operation, periodically called me in New York to report on general progress.

"I'm performing my favorite task of the day right now," she sing-songed.

"Oh, and what is that?" I asked, "Making umpteen phone calls to corner Mike into finally finishing our fencing?" Poor Bobbi had attended to the countless details and phone calls throughout the renovation when all she really wanted was to train horses.

"No, I'm holding the bunnies. They are so cute. And soft. One is buried down in my jacket, and the other is hopping around."

I felt naughty about buying two baby bunnies when my "Bunnies for Dummies" emphasized adopting overly abundant, older rabbits. But my kids really wanted babies and were disappointed when they learned that our dog Velvet "had the shot" so she couldn't have puppies and that we were not going to have baby horses any time soon (they had forgotten my earlier promise of their own foals to raise). I figured bunnies were easy. I read that rabbits need plenty of holding to domesticate them properly, and we were certainly all up for that. The barn would soon bustle with plenty of visitors to oblige in our weekly absences.

Bright and early the following Saturday morning we walked over to the farm and found the designated bunny stall thoughtfully located next to the tack room. Baby bunnies rank high on the cuteness pyramid, and my kids carefully held and stroked them and clapped with delight as they popped and scampered. Free-roaming their stall all day, we confined them to the hutch with blankets at night against the cold and predators. They nibbled broccoli florets and lettuce from my kids' hands: animal heaven. Hera is the love bug and Diana more curious and athletic. Continually escaping from Jane's arms, I sternly enforced that she sit to avoid dropping the delicate creatures. Poor Jane: it is hard to get anything right when you're five. She'd either lose Diana or squeeze her. Out of concern, Elliot and I reprimanded more than we encouraged, exasperating Jane to tears at least three times each visit.

"But I want to hold Diana and she keeps running away," she cried.

"I know honey. Sit down, and I'll catch her for you."

"Why do I have to sit down? Elliot carries Hera around."

"Well, you're still little and learning how to treat animals."

I cornered Diana and scooped her up with a swift, firm hold.

"Here you go, Jane."

Tentative, Jane grasped too gently, and Diana's front half immediately wriggled toward freedom. Jane grabbed tightly at bunny hind quarters.

"Don't squeeze, Jane," I sharply rebuked as Diana squirmed away.

Empty-handed yet again, Jane's tears brimmed.

"Jane, I think your bunny just wants to motor around a little. Just watch how cute she is."

"But I want to hold her."

And on it went: Jane waiting impatiently for her turn to hold, then a little squeeze or grab, a scratch, a cautionary rebuke and tears. Elliot was old enough to instinctively learn barn behavior or at least to remember any corrections, but not Jane. Right after meeting the bunnies, we went in search of the black furball of Weatogue's mouser-in-training, secured in the feed room with food and blankets until he established our barn as his territory. Bobbi's friend, newly designated "Big Jane" to distinguish her from our Jane, found the kitten abandoned in a crate alongside the road. A vet saved his life, neutered and inoculated him, and Big Jane nurtured him until we were ready. She named him Ninja for the new motorcycle she received that same day.

Ninja befriended us immediately, meowing vociferously and sliding against us for pats and cuddles. Jane petted his sleek back, fascinated by his undulating tail. As she stroked it, I warned her never to pull. Sure enough, not fifteen minutes later, Jane ran to me in tears.

"Don't run, Jane!"

She admitted to pulling the cat's tail and got a sharp claw across the face.

Later, over a glass of wine at The White Hart, I said to Scott: "There are so many tears from Jane at the barn. I *think* she's enjoying it, but I feel I'm always yelling to keep every mammal safe. I hate being the harpy."

"But you *are* a harpy." His quick smile showed he caught me fishing for a sympathetic ego boost. I played along with my wounded mutt look. "Only kidding," he continued. "Look, it's our job to protect our young. Big animals are dangerous, and little ones look like her stuffed toys that she can do whatever she wants with. It's got to be frustrating and emotional for her not to be able to maul them with affection. Five year olds are not great at restraint."

"I guess it's a steeper learning curve for her than it is even for us," I sighed. "She'll learn to speak 'animal' just like we did—well not you, yet. You *are* remedial in the subject." I got him back.

He could have harangued me about my excessive zeal for animals, chastised me for Jane's cheek slash, and reminded me he didn't bargain for bunnies and cats, let alone horses and dogs, but he didn't. He looked handsome; his short, graying hair accented by his black and grey cashmere sweater atop snug jeans, all of him backlit by firelight emanating from an ancient hearth nestled in the smoke-mellowed pine walls of the tap room. I smiled, appreciating the comfort of our many years together.

"She'll learn," we both unisoned.

And somehow, despite the doubt, the fighting, the yelling and the crying, it all still spelled fun.

SO, AS THE HORSES ARRIVED TWO BY TWO in the late afternoon sun of our first official day of operation, I feared they'd pale in comparison to the bunnies and the cat. Bobbi's Angel and Toby settled in, alternately grazing and sprinting across the paddocks, and the out-to-pastures Glimmer, Katie, and the one-eyed old racehorse Theo wandered around like "what else is new?" A peaceful transition, but Bobbi's friend Terri and her daughter Meghan stood guard in case someone decided to go crazy. You never know with horses, and my family would have been useless in an emergency. Bobbi soon returned with the last two, my horse Bandi, and Cleopatra, a pony for the kids we leased from a girl who physically outgrew her but emotionally couldn't sell. Bandi and Cleo unloaded smoothly and immediately dropped their muzzles into the turf, munching away without so much as a casual glance around.

Elliot hung back, giving the horses some space. I held Bandi's lead rope letting him graze while Jane danced close circles around Bobbi and Cleo. I kept a sharp eye on all eight horse hooves. Jane begged for a ride, so Bobbi boosted her up bareback on Cleo and walked around the grass. Laughing hard, Jane sparkled. We persuaded her to dismount and led the two horses into their stalls to settle.

"That went well," I said, enjoying the feel of horses occupying our farm, at last.

"How could a horse not be happy here?" Bobbi teased.

"I think old Theo is wearing himself out with excitement." Through the open stall window we watched his running silhouette.

"Maybe it's been twenty years since he's done that," Bobbi sighed.

"Take it easy there, old man," I shouted.

As we congratulated ourselves on a smooth transition, Jane repeatedly hugged Bobbi's legs. Eventually she added "I love yous" to the mix. Bobbi and I kept up our patter as she hugged back. Finally Jane squeezed tighter with louder endearments and stuck her arm straight out toward Cleo. We finally got the message: she badly wanted another ride. Jane's manipulative ploy embarrassed me, but at least she didn't scream and demand; it was more a sweet desperation. We protested that Cleo was tired, that Bobbi had to get the other horses in, and that soon she'd enjoy plenty of rides with a real saddle and stirrups that didn't require looping to hold her feet. But Jane kept up her antics, smiling away until we caved. I could tell that Bobbi was channeling her own child self, the one that wailed at the end of her first ride.

We led Cleo to the indoor ring: her hooves' echoing clip-clop a barn's equivalent to the smell of cookies at a housewarming party. Jane would be the first to ride on the new footing, the youngest being appropriate inauguration. As they circled I saw that Cleo was, as Bobbi suspected, one special pony. In unfamiliar territory she steadily carried my precious cargo, mellow as could be. Elliot couldn't resist a short turn too, and delighted in the novel experience of bareback. Sated, we collectively rejoiced that the horses condoned our six and a half months of preparation and that even though Jane would spill some tears, the highs would more than compensate. Already my son was talking about how the bunny day was the best of his life so far and telling all our visitors how he couldn't wait to work at the barn in the summer.

"You know, Mom, I think I like taking care of the horses more than riding them."

I felt pretty good about that.

I remembered a conversation Scott had with Elliot during a walk over to the barn one day. It stemmed from Scott's explanation both of conservation easements, our plan for much of our land, now totaling 120 acres, and last wills and testaments, a natural segue.

"I want to be an investment banker and a farmer just like you, Dad." We turned onto the hayfield, our legs scissoring the tall grass.

"And why is that, El?"

"I want to give all my money to land conservation." Scott and I exchanged glances.

"That would be a good thing, but there are other ways to work with the land without needing so much money. You could be a forester, for example."

Elliot chased some crickets, came up empty and rejoined us.

"Why don't we live in Salisbury all the time? The country is so much better than the city. It's quiet and clean and more beautiful."

"Well, I have a job to do and that pays for all this: 'Money comes in pretty handy down here, Bub,'" Scott smiled at me as he quoted our favorite Jimmy Stewart line to the wingless angel Clarence in *It's a Wonderful Life*.

"You can give Jane the New York apartment, but I want the country house. That will be perfect because Jane loves the city best—"

I shot Scott a worried glance. "Got that, Mr. Potter?" I quipped, and cringed at the sound of "country house" issuing so glibly from Elliot's lips.

"—but I want to learn everything there is about horses, farming and conservation."

Later, Scott and I congratulated ourselves on getting some parenting right, despite Elliot's plan for divvying up the spoils upon our demise. These snippets alone were worth the expense and trauma of renovating the farm, even if Elliot evolves into a NYC subway conductor rather than the naturalist I anticipated. He already harbored an innate, genuine compassion for living creatures, a developing work ethic, and a strong taste for the beauty of the land—nature in general, and Salisbury in particular. I loved him for it, and believed Jane would get there too, by degrees, and with a few more bumps, bruises, scratches and tears along the way.

BOBBI WANTED TO KEEP THE FUN COMING, so Thanksgiving weekend we arrived to meet our new miniature stallion officially named "Miller's Red Blue-eyed Hawk." He is a ribbon-laden cart-driving phenomenon that sounded too cute to pass up. After a tear-free cuddle with Hera, Diana and Ninja, we walked out to the pasture that held Bandi and Hawk. Originally Bobbi matched Bandi and Cleo together, but they fell too much in love, and their pining when apart indicated an attraction too strong.

"Shouldn't they be together all the more?" I asked, mooning over their thwarted love.

"Well, it's like having more than one dog—you don't want a pack mentality against you, and the lovesick can't focus properly on their work."

Ah, there is a limit to her indulgence regarding the horses, I thought.

Bobbi explained the head game that determines who could safely cohabitate out in the paddocks. Horses prefer buddies, but can turn enemies quickly. They are social herd animals, and we walk a fine line between complete domestication and their wild "horseness." I liked the idea of my gelding Bandi infatuated, but my safety on board over-ruled his love life.

Carrots in hand, we found Bandi and Hawk following one another around the grassy enclosure. Hawk is adorably small: two hundred pounds of squat black and white fuzz, smaller than a Great Dane, with an oversized head, a ground-sweeping shaggy tail and a lofty mane. His luminous blue eyes beguiled us and his portliness rendered Bandi a fashion model in comparison, tall and lean. Hawk looked more like a pot-bellied pig than a horse. This Mutt and Jeff couple trotted right over, gently taking the treats we offered.

"Look Mom, he's sooo small," Jane squealed in delight.

"Just your size, Jane." Scott squatted to keep her fingers safe.

My supply to gluttonous Bandi ran out first. Elliot and Jane continued feeding Hawk. Bandi bent his head over his new buddy to check out what stash remained when up reared little Hawk, all power and might. He bit hard into the side of Bandi's neck and hung there for what seemed an eternity. We instinctively backed away, pulling the kids from the fence. Bandi reared and squealed until Hawk released. Their alternating guttural neighs and high-pitched whinnies shattered the peaceful scene we enjoyed not one second before.

"Mama! What are they doing?" Jane cried.

"WHOA, WHOA," I yelled, trying to distract them from snorting and frothing at each other.

Bandi and Hawk separated only to reposition themselves butt to butt and kick out hard, both landing solid blows into each other's shins. The ground shook under their slashing, stomping hooves. Nostrils flaring, their eyes, too, were wild, the whites glaring.

"WHOA, WHOA," I repeated and rushed the fence to interrupt them.

"Careful, Mom," Elliot warned.

The horses stopped, looked perturbed for a minute or so, and then walked around like nothing happened.

Petrified, Jane leaked tears yet again.

"What was that about?" Scott asked me, squatting to rub Jane's back.

"Wow. I don't know. I guess it was a food thing." My heart pounded. "Jane, honey, it's all right. Horses are like that sometimes. They are big and strong and they wrestle just like you do with Elliot, and sometimes it gets a little rough. But they're okay, and no one was hurt."

I wasn't so sure about that and expected Bandi's neck to be bleeding and one of them at least, leg lame. Cowed city rubes, we retreated to the barn to hug and squeeze the mellower bunnies.

After her training lesson with Chase, Bobbi expressed surprise at our carrot-inspired war.

"They've really been perfect together so far. They play with one another but never anything vicious." She pulled the heavy saddle from Chase's sweaty back. "I'll go check the damage."

Bobbi began apologizing for their bad behavior, so I explained the situation. I should have anticipated that food could provoke a hierarchical battle from the top horse, obviously Hawk in this case.

"I think Bandi was just curious about what Hawk was getting, but Hawk took offense."

"Well, Hawk is a stallion who forgets his size."

"Like the small bully in the playground who starts things and then gets the shit kicked out of himself on a regular basis?"

"Yes, exactly."

"Well, it was stupid of me to do the carrot thing."

"Don't worry. They're still settling in, and as we discussed, if we need to, we'll geld Hawk."

Later that weekend Hawk reassured me, at least as far as people were concerned. My kids crowded his stall, groomed, hugged and patted him with nary a hint of bad temper. Indeed, he was extremely affectionate, taking carrots gently without nips, and otherwise exulting in the attention. I'll give Jane credit—she's brave without rashness and recovers from her fears quickly and completely. Hawk and Jane bonded right away: he's sturdy against her unintended roughness and yet petite enough for her to relate to in the human-to-horse scale ratio. They matched. Jane trusted that despite his strength and stallion pride, he's a right pacifist around people. His job is driving, and Bobbi ordered his petite harness and wood and leather two-seat cart. We looked forward to seeing Hawk in action. Supposedly this little black-and-white ball of furry brawn can pull two adults, even uphill. After seeing him muscle Bandi around, we believed it.

CHAPTER FOURTEEN

Be Careful What You Wish For

THE WEEKEND AFTER THE HORSES MOVED IN I planned a lesson with Bobbi. Finally my dream was before me—to ride my own horse at my own barn. I arrived at two thirty to ride at three, pleased by the one minute drive to Weatogue Stables versus the fifteen minutes to Riga Meadow. How thrilling to pull into the farm with horses grazing in the pastures.

I noticed the place was uncharacteristically deserted except for the horses. It was Sunday after all, though weekends don't count for much when it comes to animal care, barn chores and lessons. I knew Bobbi was gone with Toby at a show. Maybe our new first hire had the day off. Petite with long, streaked blonde hair and a little girl smile though close to thirty, Meghan showed genuine excitement about our farm the day she helped move the first horses in. Her current part-time job assisting in euthanasia of the sick and dying at the local vet was burning her out. She grew up around horses: her mother rode and her dad was a retired jockey. She exemplified "real trooper," sleeping on a cot in the small, minimally heated, mouse-infested viewing room of the barn with only her rescued Boxer "Boomer" for protection until the cottage was complete. Not long after, Meghan left her vet job and became Weatogue's assistant trainer, concentrating on the many children who, one by one, turned up for lessons. She had a knack for horses and kids despite a few tattoos and an alarming (to me at least) pierced tongue. Bobbi appreciated her willingness to wield a hammer and lug heavy feed bags, as well as her self-directed work ethic and upbeat personality. Her ability to exercise the horses would come in handy as we filled up.

For my first ride at Weatogue I looked forward to someone helping me ready Bandi until Bobbi returned just in time for our scheduled lesson. But no Meghan and no Bobbi. I was disoriented not having all my systems in order for the new space. *Don't worry,* I coached myself, *by now I've walked Bandi in from the paddocks many times at Riga Meadow, and tacked up on my own.* Even so, I was leery and preferred some company, but decided to brave it. I arranged my tack by the grooming stall and walked outside for Bandi. Luckily he came right over to the fence and accepted the halter while Hawk stayed out of the way, saving me a skirmish or an escape.

As I led Bandi up the path, he repeatedly halted to look around, alarmed: ears back and twitching, eyes a little wild, body tense and edgy. I got more anxious, too, and wondered what I'd do if he tried to bolt. "It's okay, Bandi—you're a good boy. This is your home now." At the barn door he stopped dead, and it took some cajoling to get him in. I maneuvered him down the main aisle, and he bullied me as I clumsily circled him into the grooming stall. He whinnied and high-stepped, and so did I, admonishing him and minding my toes. After several attempts, and a little tap with the lead rope on his belly, he moved forward the two steps I needed to secure one cross tie. For the life of me the second one wouldn't hook. It's a tricky mechanism with the hinged bottom lip extending out rather than in, so that with a strong pull panicked horses can free the latch and take off. This bucks logic until you hear how much damage a freaked out horse can do to himself, others and the stall if he's stuck when all his instincts are shouting "Flee." A runaway horse will generally settle in the grass somewhere to eat or head for the familiarity of his paddock or stall.

My unexpected spasticity with the cross tie flustered me, all of my unexpressed anxiety loudly and clearly absorbed by my sensitive horse. Bandi grew more tense, and together we looped a vicious circle when I counted on a virtuous one. He, at least, had always been as cool as aloe, except that one pre-show experience, so this was new. With no rescue in sight I tore two nails forcing the second cross tie. "Shit," I muttered and sucked at my bloody finger. Though damaged, I forged ahead, grooming him in the same pattern we'd established all summer at Riga Meadow. I removed his very dirty blanket—he must have been rolling—unsuccessfully keeping my torn nail bed away from the manure encrusted tail strap. I fed him a steady stream of carrots through the curry combing, the brushing, and the hoof-picking. Our oversized grooming stalls allowed him ample space to push me around and twist himself sideways. He nipped at me as I passed from one side to the other, not altogether good-naturedly, even though the carrots flowed steadily. He pawed repeatedly at the concrete between the rubber mats of the stall and the aisle, echoing a grating scratching. A horse whinnied from the field, and Bandi stretched out his neck and head to issue a long, loud, plaintive moan.

What the hell does that mean? Will he bolt to his buddies the first chance he gets? With me on him? I gave him pecks on the nose and collegial pats, but there was no disguising our unease when Bobbi pulled up and unloaded Toby from her chrome trimmed, white metal trailer.

"Hi. Sorry I'm late. I called you at home, but you'd already left. How are you getting on there?" She bounced into the barn.

"Okay," I replied shakily.

Her eyes narrowed as she tuned in to the static between me and Bandi.

"I'm going to put the Tobster in his paddock and be right back in."

I bent to hoof-picking, which went better than I expected.

I wondered if it was appropriate for Bobbi to be AWOL so many weekends to show, attend clinics and judge. The busiest part of the northeastern horse circuit runs June through November, half the year, and Scott had already expressed his reservations about Bobbi's weekend absences, when our family and working boarders would ride. I defended her, arguing that her riding advancement would benefit her students and our barn's reputation, but at that moment, blundering in the grooming stall, I realized how much dedicated babysitting my family would need for the foreseeable future. Barn manager and trainers must be physically present to manage and train. And, she seemed to be habitually late. That I silently had to admit to my own perpetual "barn time" tardiness only peeved me further.

Bobbi returned, and we finished the grooming and tacking up together. She soothed and talked to Bandi. As she told me later, she could see the both of us were pretty much wrecks.

"Are you okay to ride?"

"I think so, but he seems riled up."

"Why don't I get up on him for a bit first?"

Now you're talking, I thought to myself.

As we walked to the indoor ring, I heard my daughter, her sitter Marie, and Jane's play date Lindy arrive. *Great*, I thought, *what a time for squealing, running girls.* The kids perched themselves on stools set catty-corner to the ledge of the ring wall, and we all watched Bobbi flawlessly walk, rise to a posting trot and then a smooth canter. Bandi was perfect, though keenly alert to every sunbeam, car rumble and wall kick sounded by Jane and Lindy's sneakers at the ends of their restless legs. But he seemed to trust that Bobbi would protect him from any monsters.

"Is it okay for the girls to be there?" I asked Bobbi, desperate to erase any possibility for spooking.

"Yes. He might as well get used to it." In theory, the more horses are exposed to, the more they accept without surprise.

To my relief, the bored girls noisily scrambled off to visit the bunnies and Hawk. I reluctantly climbed up.

"Breathe," Bobbi said, exhaling loudly as a guide.

I rode. My lesson progressed smoothly, and though I felt secure in the saddle and even managed to get the canter more easily than usual, my heart raced, and my trapezoidal muscles clenched painfully in anticipation of calamity. The breathing was moot. Our indoor ring had a double door at the far end just like the one at Riga Meadow. *Would Bandi drop his shoulder and jump that one-eighty that landed me in the dirt?* And, so jinxing myself, or, more accurately, inadvertently cueing my horse to what I feared, as we cantered past one of many windows he leapt toward the middle of the ring and ran a few fast startled strides toward the stalls. Pulling up sharply I barely stayed on. Quaking, I forced him back to that spot and continued around. Bobbi and I both gamely tried to ignore this mishap away, drawing little attention to it as you should a child's tantrum.

I cantered a few more circles, slowing him as he strengthened toward the barn end of the ring and prompting energy as we headed away. We motored nicely until again, at the same window, he sprang up, reversed direction and bolted forward, strongly toward the ring entrance. I felt my body air-born and off-center above him. Instinct urged me to leap off before falling, but I pulled hard on the reins and miraculously relocated the saddle. I barely resisted this panicky flee response, a weasely tactic to control my physicality, when I couldn't control Bandi's.

"Bandi, you silly boy! It's only a window," Bobbi exclaimed, walking towards me. "Are you okay?"

"Um, yes?" I croaked. "I was tempted to bail. Isn't that safer than getting tossed?"

"No. It's always better to stay on if you can."

Great. There goes my exit strategy.

"Maybe we'll try the stronger bit," Bobbi continued, "the Mikmar that Stacey mentioned Bandi likes. It might help him focus and give you more brakes. Can you canter once more to end on a better note?"

"No," I shouted internally. *How much do you want from me?* But I knew that Bobbi was fighting for my confidence. I also knew I'd be dwelling on this incident to no end even if I now managed the best canter of my short, sorry equine career. Against all inclination, I cantered again, half a length with heart pounding, and walked to cool him down. He picked up his ears at the kids roughhousing noisily on the hill outside the windows. Bobbi and I held our breath against a spook. Despite the cold day, Bandi and I were both sweating: our combined nerves generated a lot of heat. I should have walked him more, but I couldn't postpone my two feet on mother earth a second longer.

As I untacked, Bobbi and I ignored the eight-hundred-pound gorilla in the room that was my bad first ride in our new place. Instead, we discussed that the horses were still settling in. Bobbi apologized for not schooling Bandi the last two weeks given her lesson schedule and all the work necessary to get the farm in order. *And your show schedule*, I thought to myself. There were still so many loose ends, odd jobs. Dusk approached, and the warning chill of a long, cold New England winter penetrated the barn. I drove home, scared and upset with Bobbi and myself. Did we jump the gun on this horse? I admitted to myself that I hadn't truly looked forward to riding since my fall at Riga Meadow. And this exciting day that we anticipated for months was a bust. I didn't yet have a full file of good rides in which to bury the bad ones.

Scott arrived home contentedly weary from a harmless hike up Bear Mountain. *I could have been with him instead of risking my neck*, I thought as we relaxed in the hot tub before dinner and the ride to New York. Knowing he could make this very point was salt to my wound; still, it didn't take me long to unburden myself.

"How was your ride?" he asked.

"Not so good."

I paused.

No response.

"Aren't you at all interested?"

"That's not fair. Sure I am."

"I'm having a bit of a crisis about riding at all."

"Why? What happened?"

I poured out the events of the day.

"I wonder if Bandi's the right horse for me. I'm not even sure he likes me much. I mean, I know he's not the most affectionate horse, and this I accept. But I sometimes think that he's too much horse for wimpy me, and even though I may look like an experienced rider because I'm athletic and a fast learner, my 'head'," I knocked my noggin with my fist as we settled into the 101-degree bubbles, "has only so many hours in the saddle."

"Bandi has a habit of spooking, doesn't he?"

"Yes. Even once with Bobbi, though it seems to happen mostly with me. I think he's a little high strung and so am I—we might feed each other's anxiety. I spend the whole ride waiting for the dump and run and probably bring it on myself. I really wish I could be braver." In my frustration I felt like crying. "I know Bobbi wants me to learn to jump and go on hunter paces with her, and I love the idea, but I feel farther and farther from it the more I ride him."

"Maybe you need a quieter horse." He narrowed his eyes at me. "But we've discussed how this can't be a full-time thing for you. We have a life in New York, and you have two kids and a husband. As it is, we don't do half the things together that we used to."

I sparked, but couldn't flame that chestnut again. Beyond mad, I was just downright tired, deeply weary of the whole enterprise, with no fight left in me for Bandi or Scott. I knew Scott meant well, that he missed me, and he chastised kindly, but still I felt scolded for neglecting him. He was also right. To conquer my fear and master Bandi would take a lot of time and energy, both of which I lacked as a commuting parent of two kids running two households, not to mention the job of decent spouse. And I already felt sneaky, squeezing riding in around the edges when I'm least likely to be missed. Scott must have felt like the wife who lost her husband to golf, another passion that regularly takes three hours each outing. It didn't help that Scott selflessly had resisted pressure to swing the clubs in order to maximize his family time. Plus, I'd been spurring myself to ride, reluctant rather than champing at the bit.

"There have to be horses that don't spook. Why don't you give him some time to adjust, and if he doesn't, we get you a different horse. Don't feel guilty; it's not such a big deal. There has to be a horse that's right for you."

"I couldn't bear the thought of selling Bandi to another unfamiliar place," I said. For better or worse I loved that damned horse, and didn't want to be one of those people who change horses on a whim. I also suspected his jitteriness was more my fault than his.

"But I've already decided that I don't want Elliot or Jane on him even though we planned for Elliot to ride him sometimes," I continued.

"I agree. The kids should absolutely not ride him until we know he's safe. But maybe you could ride but only walk around, until you feel comfortable." Scott was trying his hardest to be supportive, but I could tell his heart wasn't in it. I was in this one alone.

"But I don't want to give up on myself or on my horse: it feels like failure. I should be able to ride him and not be so scared. It's not like he's trying to dump me. At least I don't think he's trying that.... But all I really want is a reliable horse that I can ride around the farm without fear—walk, trot, canter. I don't even really care about jumping fences, and I can't see doing shows or hunter paces at all." We both sighed, no answers in sight.

I pondered it the whole ride to New York, even through my attempts at conversation about what was going on at Scott's office. My dream was unraveling, and I keenly felt my lack of faith in my first horse. I saw the path where heartbreak lay. I imagined a new owner loading Bandi up, his eyes accusing me from the trailer window as I waved good-bye. I resolved to take a break from riding and speak frankly with Bobbi. If she and I bet on the wrong horse, it seemed important we be upfront with each other.

·⊂━━━⊃·

I CALLED HER THE NEXT DAY TO CONFIRM DETAILS for our official opening, a December caroling party inspired by our family visit to the Billingslys' farm last Christmas Eve. We chatted about the goings-on at the farm until I sputtered:

"Bobbi, I'm not so sure about Bandi."

"Oh?"

"I don't know that we're a good match. We make each other nervous. I'm not convinced he likes me—he takes nips at me and pins his ears back."

"Well, he always makes faces when he gets groomed."

"I know, but I'm afraid he might be too much horse for me." In defense attorney mode I explained my decreasing confidence and my expectation and fear of his spooks. "I don't want you to feel bad about our buying him, or about my first horse experience. I know every horse has his issues; I'm just not sure that I can deal with this one. I suspect he's going to take a lot more time and energy than I have right now. I want to enjoy riding and not work so hard."

I hung on the line, wondering if she'd peg me a dilettante.

"I know exactly what you mean," she said matter-of-factly. "It's no fun when you are waiting for something awful to happen and not fun to feel like you're going to get hurt. My friend Cynthia has a really naughty horse that she won't give up on, but I'm not comfortable riding him any more. He bucks and tries to toss you. Another student of mine also has a misbehaving horse. She says, 'He only dumps you if he knows he can get away with it.' That's not the kind of horse to have. Bandi is just being silly and has to be taught that when his mother is on him he must behave and focus no matter what." She paused. "I don't think Bandi is too much horse for you, but maybe not enough. The worst thing you can do is have a green horse—that's the most dangerous. Maybe you need an even more seasoned horse." She paused again, thoughtful. "But let's not give up yet. I want Bandi to settle in, and I want to school him more, possibly with a stronger bit for more control. You're a good rider. We'll figure this out."

I exhaled the breath I'd been holding.

"Well, my goals are shifting too. I need to go slower. Maybe someday I'll jump and hunter pace, but not right now. I need to feel comfortable even if I don't have time to ride for weeks at a time because of family stuff. Really, there's no rush. I can do this 'til I drop, like old Mrs. Hackshorn at Riga Meadow." I pictured myself old, and sighed. "Right now I think I'm going take a break for a few weeks to ratchet down and let Bandi settle in."

"Are you sure you want to stop altogether?"

My heart sank. *Won't someone just acknowledge it's okay to take a break?*

"I know; Scott thought that might not be a good idea, either."

"You could ride Cleo for a nice safe ride or just walk around on Bandi, find your comfort zone and go from there."

"I'm not too heavy for Cleo?"

"What do you weigh?"

"120."

"Not at all: we purposefully didn't get a small pony. She can easily take 130 or so."

I was still under the limit even with the three to five pounds I habitually shave from my reported weight. "Okay. Let's go with that this weekend."

"Right. If you want to ride, ride. If not, don't. We'll play it by ear."

CHAPTER FIFTEEN

Settling In

·◁▭▭▭▷·

"**N**OW I KNOW WHERE MY WIFE IS."
With Chip's announcement, we knew that the move into
Weatogue Stables had cemented. After frenzied months of chasing con-
tractors and hunting down supplies, Bobbi now practically lived at the
new farm, often twelve hours a day, six to seven days a week. Horses ask
for a lot, and with Bobbi around, they get it.

Everything was novel. The barn evoked a life-sized version of Calder's
Circus—a magical set filled with all new toys wrought from practical materials that, nevertheless, performed wonders. "What's this for?"
"What the heck is that?" were my constant questions. The answers
amazed and pointed to new acts I had to learn. I was a wide-eyed child
again.

Cart-driving Hawk, our miniature stallion, delighted us in that three-
ring way. The little guy began prancing around as soon as we wheeled
out his burden.

"He certainly seems ready to go, doesn't he?"

"It's his job, and he's excited to do it. It's been a while since he's
worked." Bobbi puzzled over all the straps that both harnessed Hawk
and attached him properly to the small bench seat perched between two
large spoke wheels, but she eventually fit all the pieces. A slatted floor
cum foot-rest slanted in attachment to two long wooden poles similar to
a rickshaw. Hawk fit nicely in between and was secured with leather at

various locations, with the reins stretching from his bridle at the sides of his mouth, across the length of his back and into our hands in the cart. Lacking side panels, human escape would be quick should the need arise.

Boisterous Hawk wasn't all that easy to handle, and I despaired I'd ever figure out the tack on my own. I thought this, at least, would be manageable right off the bat. But I appreciated his spunk: Hawkster was eager to show us his stuff, proud even. Surprisingly strong, when he shifted into forward it required nearly all my strength to hold him, but after a few more adjustments we sat ready for take-off. Elliot and Scott were at a hockey game, so Jane and I pioneered the maiden voyage. The cart comfortably seats two full-sized adults so Bobbi and I squeezed Jane between us covering our legs with a horse blanket to bind us together. Bobbi gently flicked the long driving whip above Hawk's muscular back. With a jerk he walked up the driveway, and we turned onto the road.

"This is fun," Jane squealed. "Can we go faster?"

"Trot on, Hawk," Bobbi commanded, and flicked the whip again. Hawk gathered himself into a nice steady trot. We couldn't help but giggle. Hawk didn't realize his size: he took his work seriously, unaware that he mimicked a coin-operated child's ride only with a linear forward motion. His teacup, barefooted hooves quaintly echoed a delicate clip-clop, clip-clop, along beautiful Weatogue Road. We waved at our neighbors, their curious faces pressed up against their windows, and traced the curves of the Housatonic River, sluggish brown with impending winter. A Currier and Ives scene freed from its frame, we rolled along marveling at the enhanced perspective courtesy of the slower pace, more open and relaxed than by car. A clarity of vision: the cut of individual leaves rather than a blur of green, the swifter current and eddies of the river, the very air unfiltered by windshield glass, the breeze frostier on our cheeks. Hawk genially accepted the few cars that passed us, each driver slowing with a double-take and lots of pointing, followed by enthusiastic waves and smiles.

As we approached some boulders on our right, Hawk quick-timed an about face and bolted for home. Bobbi jumped out the side and grabbed the reins near his mouth to set him back on course. It seems Hawk takes exception to large grey rocks, a prolific species in New England's glacier-dragged landscape. George habitually claimed our lawn grows them, and I suppose it does: long-buried, it's hard to begrudge ancient stones their patient exhumation to the surface air and light. We urged Hawk past his granite peril and continued on to disabuse him of the notion that he was in charge: the two-leggeds would dictate the terms of the ride. An hour later, cold but exhilarated, we tapped into the barn and heaped praise on our studly little stallion as we un-tethered him from his work.

I guessed driving would be a favorite pursuit around the farm and sure enough, by the next spring my kids and I would be directing Hawk around our hay fields, with Elliot entrusted with the reins. We found Hawk's canter comical, not in the least frightening, and we all laughed as we went. He still spooked at rocks, but we learned to jump out and give him courage.

Over those fall weekends at the farm we immersed ourselves in the language of animals and the rhythms of the barn. Scott entered into the spirit and found he appealed to the barn cats. Black-and-white "Smudge," Meghan's latest rescue, wove herself in and around Scott's denimed calves, purring for attention. Petting and talking to her, Scott rallied above his usual miming the motions of animal connection. I surreptitiously watched the two of them and hoped Scott had awakened to the many pleasures proffered by four-footed creatures.

Our top barn cat, Ninja, grew stand-offish with everyone, but liked to bring Bobbi heads or haunches of the mice he'd scored and happily berthed in the fake fur house I bought him for Christmas. In keeping with our black-and-white theme, Meghan toted home another stray (one of the hazards of her job at the local animal shelter), and dapper Tuxedo, who resembled an aging Elvis, became our very own king of Weatogue Stables. We couldn't accurately calculate his antiquity, but his spine sagged and his hind legs splayed, and he cowboy-swaggered like John Wayne into the sunset. "Bag o' bones" was no metaphor once you'd met Tux. Extremely affectionate, "old man" appreciated his cushy accommodations—Meghan claimed rescues are indeed grateful—and scored big with the kids. His seniority earned him sleeping rights in Meghan's cottage, anywhere he desired, usually in bed or next to her Boxer. Tuxedo's hearing was shot, his fur slick, his back too boney and his skin flaky, and Meghan had lain awake in fear of his occasional wheezing in the dead of night, but so far he's righted himself by morning. He had finally hit upon some good digs and wasn't departing without a fight. We knew his ninth life with us was precious and that when he'd die I'd miss checking for his low, slow frame as I backed my car out of the parking lot.

Balancing the age spectrum at the farm, the youngster bunnies grew so each week we noticed the difference. Out of rabbit spunk they would nip at us, and we anticipated the ritual spaying in hopes of better manners by dimming their nesting instinct. Their health also benefits and we'd avoid a bunny farm, though we still believed both Hera and Diana were female. The kids handled the bunnies and cats more adeptly each week and fawned over pony Cleo who turned out to be one terrific teacher. Jane soon rode her unaided around the ring, weaving haphazardly (she steered like her mother) and steadfastly refusing to trot, or "bounce." Elliot picked up the canter very easily on this tolerant mare, and both kids learned tack and groomed with increasing ability. Hoof-picking was a favorite task, one privilege of youth being a robust spine. Patient Cleo kept each hoof aloft while Elliot and Jane clumsily chipped out every piece of packed dirt, manure, stones and mud. It was wonderful to see them work and ride.

The clothes and equipment were piling up. Jane's little brown barn boots brought smiles, as did her miniature breeches, black velvet hat and hot pink gloves. I rashly purchased Elliot a set of full chaps in black suede, very cool, but installing him into them exhausted us such that we never attempted it again. I couldn't argue since he sticks to the saddle pretty well without the extra help. They look good hanging in the tack room under his helmet, however, and I imagine an older Jane might be more willing to suffer for fashion. I've further indulged myself too, with all styles of breeches, insulated winter boots, lined black gloves and tan and beige crocheted airy ones, and a black velvet helmet as an alternative to my matte-finish one reinforced with titanium. I spotted a clunky silver charm bracelet hanging a horseshoe, a four leaf clover, a hoof pick, a bucket, a bridle, a helmet, a stirrup, and a first prize ribbon, and I found a matching, more delicate one for Jane for Christmas.

The week before Thanksgiving found us content with the way things were going. Our first boarder enjoyed the barn and Bobbi's instruction, and word spread about Weatogue Stables. As the place grew into itself, I began to get my nerve back about Bandi. After riding the kids' pony Cleo once, I realized that size and familiarity were important. An embarrassing but instructive debut, I found her smaller size made me more rather than less precarious, and my top-heaviness ushered me gratefully back to my wide-bodied Bandicoot. His fuller mass below balanced my height, and I immediately felt at home again. I realized how far Bandi and I had come together, how accustomed I'd grown to his bouncy trot and smooth, forward canter. Maybe he was the right horse after all, and I vowed again to seal our deal.

Evening became my favorite time at the barn, when the horses are brought in from a full day out in the fields to be fed, re-blanketed, checked over for injury or ailment, and bedded down for the night. Bobbi mentioned the magical hours between four o'clock to seven, and on occasion over the fall weeks I'd sneak down and spend an hour or two helping to muck out and feed, dispense carrots, and listen to Bobbi and Meghan talk about the day and each horse's regular habits or, just as often, his or her newly presented physical or emotional quirk. With dusk falling, the hungry horses' impatient whinnying and chortling for food first erupts in frenzied munching and neighborly sniping as feed buckets are brought out and distributed quickly down the line, eventually resolving in a contented peace.

Satiated horses nod their heads and doze, root around their woody shavings, make half-hearted faces at their neighbors, breathe and sigh more heavily and deeply. Any remaining restlessness shifts to a hushed repose when human and animal work is done for another day. Horse Shavasana—relaxed and alert at once, self-contained with an egoless, calm mind. At these bewitching hours, a working barn maximizes its microcosmic spellbound aspect: a world so specific to itself, shiplike in its protected enclosure of care, camaraderie and knowledge linking human to human and to beast. I relaxed into its hold like I have never done anywhere else.

In twilight I stepped into Bandi's stall and fed him carrots one by one. The dew already chilled the aisles, but Bandi's cozy bedroom retained his radiating warmth. Together we leaned against the wooden side wall. He leaned tired, probably from fight-playing with Hawk, and soon he settled his heavy head on my shoulder. I stroked his face and massaged his neck at the withers. He fell asleep. I breathed deep to match his pace and slow my heartbeat. We sank into lethargy. I marveled at his trust: almost asleep on my feet, I was non-threatening—accepted. His head relaxed heavier. Both of us relieved from steady watchfulness, we rested calmly about fifteen minutes. Our exquisite interlude was over in a flash. Next door, Chase loudly kicked his wall, bringing ever watchful Bandi to that Quarter Horse-quick attention. I jumped cleanly out of his way, just.

I knew then the exquisite privilege of horses, what I now perceive when another horse person's eyes catch my sympathetic reflection: the shared experience of having entered the sanctum sanctorum of horse space, a slim cross-shadowing of us with "other." They let us co-opt their freedom in captivity. They need and we supply; we need and they supply. Traced to 3,500 B.C., the connection transcends species boundaries, similar to what I imagine bound Jane Goodall to her chimps.

But the evening heralds darkness, too. That December as fall crisped into white winter, we peacefully mucked, party planned and chatted to and about horses. The usual day's end routine. Our neighbor John Bottass wandered in. I was always happy to see him. An early supporter of our venture, he had also helped Bobbi with some crucial, couldn't-wait haying. I knew I could count on his help in a pinch. We all shook hands in greeting. I immediately noticed John's pale aspect.

"This is my sister, Ann," John said. "I told her all about the barn and wanted to show her around."

"By all means; show away." I swept my arm wide, liking the authentic feeling of farmerly camaraderie.

"You guys really did a wonderful thing for our town by fixing up this old place. It looks just great," he said as his eyes watered.

"John, how's your grandson?"

John's son Danny also lives on our road, working with John on the farm. Danny's fourteen-year-old son Daniel had been fighting brain cancer for several years. On Memorial Day, Danny and his family missed our annual party because Daniel spiked a high fever. They headed to Hartford Hospital instead. Danny was once again in the thick of a miserable treatment.

"Daniel passed the day before yesterday. He just couldn't make it," John said, maintaining control with difficulty, his pain filling the large barn.

"Oh, John, I'm *so* sorry," Bobbi and I echoed simultaneously. Tears sprang to our eyes, and I thought hard about what to say. But what words are there? The death of a child is the worst possible thing. The magical hour fell as fairy dust revealing that dusky melancholy that can petrify even the bravest, philosophically or religiously secure souls.

"Oh John, it's so very, very unfair," I said. "How is Danny?"

"Oh, he's not so good. Even though you think you're prepared, when it happens you really aren't."

"How about you, John?"

"Well, it's hard; see, Daniel was the one who wanted to be a farmer and take over the place after me. He had a knack for it and a love of the land. He even wanted to get us back into dairy farming again." John's words quavered, and I've never seen him be anything but strong and tough, often bordering on belligerent. Now his long, sagging body and ruddy complexion belied a permanent inner sadness. He looked ten years older.

My tears leaked as I repeated the paltry platitudes of brotherly sorrow, thoughts for, and offers of help to his family. I later wrote to Danny and his wife that our beautiful Canaan valley would always remind us of Daniel and sent a donation to the hospital in his honor, but my ineffectiveness scared me. *Please God don't take a child from me*, I selfishly begged. But there is no soothing balm, nothing to be said or done, no protection; we cower naked, soft flesh open to smiting. John, Danny and his family will suffer forever, this I know all too well from my mother's early death. We say the bankrupt words, send the checks, go to the memorials, give a prayer of thanks for our own kids' current, dubious safety, invoke a silent, psychic talisman by vowing to appreciate "the important things in life," but the death of a child, even more than that of a young mother, makes you doubt horses, love, the beauty of nature, any safety you think you've cobbled together, God, everything—a sickening sip of nihilism.

John and Ann took a look around the barn, and I talked it up as I intuited they sought escape from the grief of a mourning household, if only for a few minutes. A hard job to make small talk, but I prattled on.

"Be sure and save the date for our barn party," I said in parting.

"We'll be there," he said as they stepped out into the thick dark.

I gave the horses a final carrot treat, drove to my toasty and brightly lit, cheerful home, hugged my kids, and tried to be truly grateful for our health and well-being as a family. And I was. Still, it felt wrong to fully appreciate what was still good in our valley in the shadow of death. Is this what they mean when they say you have to experience the bad to fully live?

CHAPTER SIXTEEN

A Scatological Digression

·⊂══════⊃·

MY NOSE TOLD ME WE WERE FULLY UNDERWAY as an operating horse farm. The barn no longer smelled only like newly
sawn wood. It wafted "animal"—scented in that heavy, damp hair way,
a fuzzy mammalian body odor. This aroma permeates the raw wood, all
our clothes, boots and hair, and is highly specific: horse people immediately register it as a "nose" from a fragrance factory would musk or
vanilla. It's what induced Elliot to once sing out "I love the smell of a
barn." And, so do I. It prompts me to consider my daily life should I
have been born a horse, part of the herd snuggled together conserving
energy and heat on a cold and snowy plain; or spread out baking in the
summer sun, slow-moving with heads nodding heavy; or pack-running
through the rain, neighing, bucking and nipping my neighbors' manes
just for fun. It's a large-animal-in-mass-quantity smell, strong enough
to blot out even the most odiferous of us. It stakes its claim in the barn
to announce "Make no mistake: we are the big, strong glory of horse."
Back in the city, when I taxi past the carriage hacks along Central Park
South, it's my nose that brings me home to Weatogue Stables.

Part of this olfactory package is of course the waste. What comes
out the hind end. Manure. Poop. Shit. Nuggets. Call it what you will,
the flecked brown wetness of it splats with impunity on the shavings of
the stalls, the grass of the paddocks, the footing of the rings, the rubber mats of the grooming stalls, the concrete of the aisles or the sopping

floors of the wash stalls. Anywhere, anytime—riding or reposing, running or stepping. Even the cleanest barn broadcasts this aspect of animal odor, its fresh, tangy high note that relaxes into a mellow earthiness. Manure goes both ways: disgusting in a dirty barn, and almost pleasant in an orderly one. It is set off by its surroundings, like a plain dress enhanced or ruined by accessories.

Horses are herbivores, so their excrement is digested hay, grain and grasses with the occasional carrot, apple, peppermint, banana or clementine (skin and all) thrown in. "Manure" comes from the Middle English "manuren" meaning "to till or cultivate the land" and reflects the virtuous fertilization circle of waste replenishing pastureland. When equines are healthy and eating well they produce a shocking lot of it, and this, Bobbi tells me, is a good thing. Whenever a new horse arrives at the barn, Bobbi reports happily:

"He's pooping well," and we appraise the pile, nod and smile.

The statistics are staggering: an average 1,000 pound horse generates 50 pounds of manure each day, thereby producing its own weight in poop every three weeks. That's 18,000 pounds per year, or 450,000 pounds over the twenty-five year life span of the average horse. Seventy-five percent of it is water that evaporates, but still, that's impressive output. In the late nineteenth century, New York City boasted 100,000 horses producing about five million pounds, or 2,500 tons of waste each day. "Watch your step" must have been on the lips of every perambulator and boot cleaning a main chore of many a domestic servant. Imagine the lacy hems of those long Victorian skirts!

Bandi likes to dump a load at least once or twice every ride, always taking the time to stop and really enjoy it—so *male*. Some horses even grunt with satisfaction. When the Bandicoot relieves himself in the indoor ring, on our nice, expensive, carefully waxed, mixed and laid dust-free footing, I face a choice—get off and pick it up, enlist an innocent bystander "would you pleeeease … ?," or carefully avoid steering through it so as not to grind it into the "expensive, carefully waxed, mixed and laid dust-free footing." Organic matter left in the footing degrades its dust-free properties, requiring an expensive oil reconditioning. The way I steer, Bobbi always races for the pitchfork before I weave around again.

I have learned that horses are better able, or at least more willing, to hold their urine. Manure comes out arbitrarily, but they hoard their water for the stalls. If they've been outside, Bobbi's custom is to lead horses to their stalls for a few minutes before tacking them up in the grooming stall. This works pretty well for organizational purposes. The horse can settle a few minutes, take a drink and eliminate if necessary, and I can sort and arrange my tack in the grooming stall, thereby avoiding abandoning said horse to retrieve my saddle, bridle, hat, grooming tote, etc. A wise blueprint, but it's my habit to forget something, usually a different item each time. Mostly I miss my hat, but also gloves, chaps, clips to keep my hair out of my face, the crop, the soft brush—it can be anything. Twice I fancied myself complete only to see my sneakers still on my feet. Elliot once rode out to the back field, and trotted even, minus a girth. This item, you'll remember, is the under-strap that secures the saddle to the horse. "The kid's got good balance, I'll say that much," Bobbi said, shaking her bemused head. *Good thing he thought to tighten the non-existent girth before cantering*, I thought, picturing a free-floating saddle and Elliot parting ways from Cleo's bare back.

And then, even when I can pride myself on getting all the *accoutrements* together and on, I find I have to relieve myself, and so I leave said horse unsupervised in cross ties in the grooming stall and hope Bobbi doesn't wander by questioning "who left this horse unattended in the grooming stall?" Cross ties sound disarmingly secure but are misnamed. First of all, they don't cross, but simply attach to either side of the horse's halter at his mouth. Secondly, they don't tie but latch and are so rigged that with a good hard pull the careful design will release the panicking horse either to bolt to the feed room for a grain orgy, or, more likely out the door and down the highway to the fresh produce aisle at the Stop-n-Shop. If you're lucky, he'll wander off and graze in a pasture until, sheepishly, you retrieve him.

"What happened?" someone will ask.

"I don't know. I was in the bathroom," I'd have to reply.

But the main reason you allow your horse the stall is so he or she can have a good long pee sooner rather than later. I'm told horses wait to go *in* their stall, even if they have been outside all day long. *This is crazy*, I logically think: *I don't want them wetting my nice new stalls on the clean shavings, and anyway, why would they empty where they sleep and eat?* We go to great lengths to "housetrain" most domestic animals so they *don't* go inside. I'd like to think the horses would rather not pollute their grazing pasture, but the fact is they'll poop on it 'til kingdom come. No, Bobbi informs me they prefer not to get their legs wet—kind of like my dog preferring the absorbent Oriental rug to the kitchen linoleum. Likewise, the shavings of the stall receive the urine so nicely as opposed to the frozen or hard ground with its high rebound factor. If you've ever peed in the woods, especially as a female, you understand, but a horse can't squat low to minimize the splatter. Even soft summer grass is not as good as fluffy, thirsty wood shavings; it's impossible to keep paddock grounds soft and grassy with several thousands of pounds of horse eating most of the grass and hoof-beating down the remainder. And if your eyes have ever popped at the sight of a horse taking a leak, you can imagine how off-putting this would be should it occur in a grooming stall with only a rubber mat and concrete underfoot. Thankfully, this happens only rarely. When it does, the girls moan, complain loudly to the offending horse and hotfoot it for a wheelbarrow-full of shavings to soak it up.

I've never seen a horse urinate in either the outdoor or indoor riding rings, surprising, given their footings' inviting absorbency. Maybe it's the tight girth that keeps horses sanitary in this regard. Maybe they're working too hard. And only once I've seen one pee while being ridden, out in the field. The rider is instructed to stand in the stirrups to relieve the weight from the horse's kidneys for better flow. Though I've come close to having Bandi defecate on my head while I was bent down obliviously picking away at a hind hoof, he has yet to pee in a grooming stall.

Maybe this only occurs when your horse is pissed off at you (excuse the pun) for not feeding him carrots fast enough or because you've spared a few affectionate strokes to the neighboring homely-faced gelding that your horse, for no good reason, hates with a passion.

Poop in the grooming stall is common however, and though it pours steamy hot and potent as it lands with consecutive thuds on the rubber mat, it's only a swift shovel and broom away from the hopefully handy muck bucket. One quick, smooth, swinging scoop—that is, if you are talented. Bobbi and the girls are one-tool wonders, but I take several passes with both broom and shovel, smearing it into the mat treads a good bit first.

If you hang around horses any length of time, you must make your peace with dust, hair, urine and manure because all four are omnipresent. A barn is only totally clean for about five minutes if all the horses are out; upon completion of the tidying chores that take hours, it's already time for the newly dirtied horses to track everything back in, and, you guessed it, have a good long pee in their stalls. If you are a fastidious person, a barn will confound you. Your clothes and hair will all trap the foursome of dust, hair, saliva and the essences of waste just by a walk through. We are all Pigpens at a barn, and dedicated clothes, and a closet if you can spare it, are a must.

The same goes for hands. Most horse handling and grooming is difficult to manage with gloves on, with all those straps and small buckles and hooks. It takes naked dexterity, so gloves are best reserved for the actual riding. That means dust, hair and saliva on your hands at the very least, and probably no small amount of manure. Take hoof picking for example, required before each ride. Bend over at an awkward right angle. Persuade your horse to lift up his foot backwards by running your fingers down the back tendon of his leg, pulling and cajoling until he decides to accommodate you. Hold the hoof tight and high and ignore your screaming lower back, keeping alert for the moment when your horse decides enough is enough and tries to kick at your face only inches away as you diligently dig at the bottom of the hoof to remove the packed in dirt and, you guessed it, compacted manure.

On a good day, the hoof is mercifully clean already, or the manure and dirt release swiftly in one large, satisfying chunk. On a challenging day, the impacted matter sticks like concrete, with little stones embedding up under the edges of the shoe in which case you chip away at slivers the size of toothpicks. *Or*, it is full of soft, fresh, smelly, still food-pocked manure that streaks your boot seams as it falls out. Repeat entire process three more times. Upright yourself, groan loudly for sympathy, massage your sacroiliac, and simply accept that visible and invisible manure now happily resides all over your palms, deep in the crevices of your cuticles and wedged far under your fingernails where no nail brush can reach. Remember not to scratch your nose, lips or eyes, and take solace in the fact that all barn help seems remarkably robust.

Horses regularly roll in their paddocks and stalls, especially after you have slaved an hour bathing them, and it is common for mud and manure to dry crust onto their bodies. It's an insulation tactic, both to cool and to warm. Annoyingly to them no doubt, we laboriously brush this dust off, flying it into the air to coat our clothes, hair and lungs, and it is difficult to accomplish a thorough dusting with gloves on. Not to mention the various horse blankets, or "sheets" to contend with, another bare-handed job. These "clothes" keep your horse warm and prevent him sprouting too woolly a coat for indoor riding; winter sweat can chill and sicken. Blankets come in myriad weights, and the wardrobe can expand to include every level of protection from the summer lightweight cooling anti-sweat fly sheet to the total "dustbuster," a fitted, high-collared suit that makes a horse look like he's enclosed in a condom or disguised as the Archbishop of Canterbury.

My reliable Dover catalog sports nearly thirty pages of clothing as a testament not only to the power of marketing, but also that perfect blanket-free weather conditions rarely, if ever, occur. There is a combination of outerwear—light-weight, medium-weight, heavy-weight or "Rambo,"

fly-sheet, "cooler" or rain sheet—that can keep any horse, from the hir-
sute to the smooth-as-a-baby's-bottom completely body-shaved, temper-
ate day and night in the frigid New England winter. The trick is to figure out what is required each hour of our variable climate. The girls are
perpetually sticking their hands inside the blankets to feel the body heat
of the armless four-leggeds, who can't tell you "Hey, I'm dying over here,"
or shed their own sweaters should they sense a hot flash coming on. In
fall and spring considerable time is spent determining the proper blanket formulas for morning, afternoon and night. Consultations are held,
second opinions sought. It does my heart good to know my Bandi has
a blanket master figuring out his precise layering needs when the thermometer reads eleven below, even before the wind chill, and I am warm
and cozy in central heating with a fireplace to add to the atmosphere.

Even though Bobbi assures me horses don't feel the cold much, and
that they suffer more from the heat and pests of summer, I only half
believe her. Most humans cotton to warmth and abhor cold. We'd be
much more concerned about global cooling than we are about global
warming, the latter evoking an extended Caribbean holiday. To contem-
plate a New England winter getting colder and longer would give us all
religion about our wasteful habits and probably induce a voluntary ten
percent tithing to develop technologies against it.

So the blanketing makes all horse caregivers feel needed, at least
psychologically, and the basic models overlay the horse from the withers, down the sides and over his back end to the bottom or so of the
haunches. The blankets Velcro and buckle across the front of the chest,
and two straps run crossways under the belly. At the rear end it gets
complicated. One strap reaches either side of the blanket under the tail,
or two straps reach from the sides of the blanket around the inside of
each leg to hooks under the tail. No matter how cleverly you twist and
loop and otherwise fancy-knot the straps out of the way of the poop
and pee chutes, it is wasted effort. These fastenings are often urine and
manure-encrusted and must be unhitched by human, gloveless hands.

The problem compounds with mares in heat. Their legs and any blanket straps bring dried menstrual blood into the mix. Again, even in the cleanest of barns, the horse blankets quickly get disgusting, and you'll go broke trying to keep enough clean blankets and Tide on hand to satisfy a stickler. Furthermore, these cover-ups are hairy, big and bulky to wash and take forever and a long sunny day to dry. So, the best remedy is to de-hair and wash the blanket on occasion, make peace with the dirt, resist the urge to pluck that annoying horse hair from your tongue, and invest in a cruelly stiff nail brush for the shower. A surgeon's got nothin' on me in the scrub-down department.

"Why are your hands so red and raw?" Scott asks.

It defies my reason that no one succumbs to the dreaded, kill me now, twenty-four hour intestinal bug in this germ factory, including my kids who aren't as careful as you and I might be about the hands to mouth infection highway.

On the whole, however, properly cared for horses appear hygienic to humans, especially their noses and mouths. I have never seen them stick their faces in manure, sniff each other's butts or lick their genitals dog or cat-style. Their faces are satin sleek, with deep, expressive eyes sprouting long eyelashes and camel-like muzzles that are soft, dry, and, when they lower their heads to greet you, just at the perfect height for nuzzling. While a horse might shy from busy hands flitting about their heads, they often favor a face forward approach to identify people by their individual breath and smell. They rarely drool, unless exposed to moldy clover weed in which case they pour saliva in alarming flows. But this is exceptional; generally their faces invite intimate contact. I have always been affectionate with my animals, kissing and hugging them all the time. I'm not alone. The girls at the barn face-nuzzle their horses regularly and even let them bite off chunks of frosted donut, a half of a ham sandwich, a blueberry muffin top, or share a sip of Vitamin Water straight from the large-mouthed plastic container and go right on finishing it themselves. On their birthdays, Bobbi's horses receive name-inscribed carrot cakes, each moist slice shared and icing smeared between her and the honored equine.

During one grooming session I was lavishing Bandi a typical how ya doin' muzzle smacker and cooing at him about what a handsome boy he is.

"Bandi loves to roll out in the field when we let him out nude," Bobbi reported.

"That's for sure," Meghan agreed, "Especially after we clean him up real good."

"You should see him roll around in the manure out in his paddock. He gets covered in it, even all over his face. He must balance on his head to get it between his eyes like that, right Meg?"

I pulled my face quickly away from his and searched for evidence.

"You should see him in the morning sometimes. He's got poop all over his face and ears and head. I don't know how he manages it." Meghan shook her head.

"I guess I'll have to stop smooching him so much." I wiped my mouth on the arm of my jacket, on which I noticed the crease marks of brown dirt, dust, manure…whatever.

"Well, he usually keeps his nose out of it, so you're probably safe," Bobbi laughed.

I thought about Scott's reprimands regarding dog kissing.

"Do you have to do that?" he'd demand. "It's really revolting."

"But look how cute she is," I'd say and hold Velvet up to his face. "How can Daddy not love you, Velvie?…She smells so good. Come on, give her a little peck."

"I'm not that dog's father, and you're not its mother, by the way." He'd recoil in displeasure. "You're a real nutter, you know."

"But she's so cute. And dogs are very clean—we can't get their germs. Here, just give her a pat."

He rolls his eyes and does just that, a perfunctory knock on the head.

Now my affection has multiplied to horses, cats and bunnies. It's hard for me to understand his aversion; I feel so naturally connected to our pets. But it must be strange for him to have these, to him alien, creatures roaming his house. He has acclimated, but still must physically restrain himself when the kids take my lead. But, there is hope for him: on a trip to Anguilla, as instructed, he kissed a dolphin. We have it documented on the video we bought after our "dolphin experience."

When it comes to toilet habits—like human, like horse. Some men pee all over the rim, splash a close wall and leave the seat up. Others you'd never know paid a visit. Same goes for women. Though better in people's homes as a rule compared to men, women are just as bad in public. We hover, and splash, and leave the mess for the next victim, who hovers even higher and showers even more until you must hike the cuffs of your pant legs and teeter on one tiptoe to avoid contamination.

Likewise, some horses are neat and their stalls a pleasure to pick out. Angel, Theo and Cleo for example, poop in a tidy pile toward the backs of their stalls so that one organized pass of the toothed shovel scoops mostly poop with minimal precious wood shavings ending up in the muck bucket. Some horses are pigs. Bobbi's young horse Toby dumps in the middle of his stall and pirouettes the whole pieces into small bits that spread throughout his bedding—think chopped salad—and fall through even the smaller tines of the pitchfork. Not only is cleaning his stall harder, but his shavings must be replaced more often, *and* Bobbi gets to pick it out of his hooves during grooming, a triple whammy.

"Is Toby worse than Chase?" I asked Meghan one day.

"I would rather scrub Chase's wall twice a week than clean Toby's stall once."

This surprised me. As we spoke I glimpsed Chase's stall in all its glory. Poop stains of old smeared the back wall from the window down to the floor bringing to mind a brown, black and tan Jackson Pollock. We admired Chase's handiwork, and, as if he guessed our attentions, earlier he had deposited two manure nuggets, one large and one mini on the metal windowsill in between the bars, all artistically framed by the distant blue sky and lovely nearer scene of the fencing, grass and riding rings of our spring blossoming farm. A turd still life. I pictured him wedge-boosting his haunches to manage it, and we all shook our heads, marveling at his dexterity. I thought I heard him whinny his pride from a distant paddock—"Yep, that's my Chaseroo special—pretty impressive, huh?"

"At least it's in one spot," Meghan said, getting to work.

"Cleo and Angel are the best," Bobbi said. "They leave neat piles in one corner and never walk through it."

Women really are superior beings, I thought.

"The girls are better on the whole," Meghan said, echoing my thoughts. Our barn, run by females, is not above the occasional male-bashing.

"Bandi's not the neatest," I quietly acknowledged, feeling responsible in the way a mother might of a four-year-old child that still wore a diaper and breast fed.

"Oh Bandi's pretty bad. He poops wherever and whenever he feels like it," Meghan laughed.

"He especially likes the expensive footing in the indoor ring," I admitted. We've all cleaned up Bandi's double releases during a single lesson.

I ponder the germ warfare waging at our farm. My kids' favorite nook in the barn is the snack cabinet that I stock with the highly processed, guilty pleasures prohibited at home—goldfish, cellophane-boxed stick pretzels, hot chocolate mix and vanilla-flavored milk, fruit leathers, gummy bears and cookies n' cream granola bars—in an unimaginative but effective manipulation of cottoning them to barns and horses. Junk food and barn work go well together, and we all succumb. Disgracefully, I rarely remind the kids to wash their hands before digging in.

"Hawk is the funniest though," Meghan said. "He used to poop in the back of his stall, but when Chase moved in next door, he started pooping in the front right corner, as close as possible to Chase's food bucket."

"Oh that's rude," I laughed. "The ultimate insult."

NOT ONLY MUST ALL THIS MANURE BE PICKED UP, it must be properly disposed of, too. Usually this amounts to a big pile along the back tree line out of sight, unless you cough up the big bucks to have it hauled away. Our farm is large enough to get a good compost heap going, but according to Chip, it is not enough to leave it to ferment itself. Good composting technique involves stirring, airing, rotating and even temperature taking with a long triple yardstick of a thermometer. So far, no one has risen to the challenge.

Lucky for us our neighbor takes all the manure our horses can produce. Once a day, Bobbi rides the freshly loaded tractor across the street and up the narrow, graveled road, romantically labeled the "goat path," though its reality hardly conjures that cheese heaven of the Dordogne, into Ed's field. I rode with Bobbi once, excited about our new, authentically green and yellow John Deere tractor, fascinated that Bobbi could drive it. I crouched uncomfortably between the stick shift and the one seat, with a death grip on a small handle bar and my one buttock hanging ten, thinking *tractor accident* and wondering why I imagined riding sidecar would be fun. Bouncing eight feet off the ground with no seatbelt, I avoided Bobbi's cranking arms and legs that maneuvered this unsophisticated piece of equipment over ruts and through soft dirt into field position.

Rumor had it that Ed planted this field to lure deer. In hunting season, he and his buddies congregate on Ed's front porch, comfy in their chairs with rifles at the ready to get themselves some venison, all without the hassle of traipsing through the woods or hanging out in trees. Maybe they can even keep a hold 'a their beers. It's easy to criticize his method, take the Jed Clampett cheap shot. But I have eaten feedlot cows my whole life and therefore have colluded in barbaric animal husbandry. And the deer have vastly overpopulated the area, only to starve in harsh winters and increasingly suffer roadside calamity. If Ed can finagle couch potato hunting, who am I to argue if the results are the same as from those who rove camouflaged? It is still meat on a plate; fairer game perhaps, without beef's long, crowded trailer hauls to slaughter chutes of death. Ed probably appreciates the meal more than we supermarket hunters and wastes less after looking his kill in the eye and butchering it himself.

As concerned carnivores, Bobbi and I split half a cow from John Bottass's herd. I liked the idea of organic, free-range, antibiotic-free, well-treated even if short-lived protein. No doubt I have ridden past this fated cow by bike and car for all two-plus years of its life. I am confident it was "harvested" humanely. John respects his livestock, and Meghan accidentally witnessed its well-placed shot to the head and a bleeding neck slice right out back in a familiar field—no long truck transport, no tunnels of doom, no odor of blood or terrified moos of panicked, excreting, death-sensing cows. Processed and packaged by a meat locker in a neighboring town, I now have three freezers' full, an astonishing 350 pounds of all cuts of meat, some rather bony and brontosaurus-sized that I haven't a clue how to cook.

Bobbi and I entered Ed's deer patch, and she jostled that tractor into position. When I realized Ed's practice of the on site kill was no worse than John's for my half a beefer and considerably better mass production, I grew comfortable that Weatogue Stables continue to supply Ed with free deer-bait fertilizer. As we chugged along the slick, deeply creased field and Bobbi switched on the rotator blades of the tractor bed to literally spray the ground with finely chopped manure, I realized, with that sudden clarity of "ah-*ha*," the origin for the saying "When the shit hits the fan."

CHAPTER SEVENTEEN

An Unsteady Trot

·◖═══════◗·

A T LAST. The December day for our own barn-warming carol sing
dawned wintry and bright. The season prompted dewy memories
of the Billingsly's barn party, and though I doubted ours would measure up, I awoke eager to celebrate our venture with our long-suffer-
ing neighbors—all that whacking and whirring—and friends. Noreen,
who lives down Weatogue Road concocting indoor and outdoor garden
fantasies, contributed the just right touches: two enormous wreaths
with red bows and white lights gave welcoming color and warmth to
the front barn doors, and the icicle lights outlining the gazebo circled a
whimsical halo in the lonely, dark fields.

Inside the barn, she wove garland through the loft railings and along
the front twenty stall doors, beyond reach of dexterous lips and tongues.
Every horse boasted at least one ornament hung on his or her gate as
proof of their owner's devotion. As the main attraction, a twenty-five-
foot evergreen touched the rafters invisibly wired with red mackintosh
apples. For weeks afterwards the horses and my kids feasted on the
fruit. It tasted sweeter having been plucked from a fruit-bearing pine.

The sky covered itself with soymilk clouds, bluish gray and thin, as
the guests arrived. Our indoor cheer buttressed the descending New
England gloom as did human treats. Mike, The White Hart Inn chef,
prepared tea sandwiches of watercress and *chevre*, egg salad and pum-
pernickel, cream cheese and date, and smoked salmon, along with bite-

sized poached shrimp with cucumber, and marinated flank steak on *bruschetta* with salsa to savory us. Spirits and plenty of hot chocolate and mulled cider warmed us, and mini key lime tartlets, chocolate-dipped strawberries, and oatmeal and chocolate chip cookies sweetened us. The horses lounged photo-ready, occasionally kicking the walls and squealing to remind us chattering humans that they were the whole point.

In finale, several regulars from our local theatre company led us in caroling around the indoor riding ring. The shy crowd eventually joined into *The Twelve Days of Christmas*, singing in group rounds. Jane and Keira jingled sleigh bells and shouted *Frosty the Snowman* and *We Wish you a Merry Christmas*, while my son and his friends stormed the grounds, conquering the remaining piles of dirt. The supportive crowd expressed heartfelt congratulations and blessings, pleased to celebrate a rejuvenated farm and usher in our new venture. It didn't quite live up to the Billingslys' party, but that's my penance for imitation.

WE RANG IN THE NEW YEAR WITH A HORSE. For several weeks, Bobbi had had her eye on Willy the appaloosa for Scott.

"Bobbi wants you to sit on him to see if he fits." I casually floated the idea to my husband.

"Don't get a horse just for me." Suddenly looking crowded, Scott pushed out his elbows. "I'm really busy at work right now. And, anyway, do we really need another horse right away?"

"Well, he'd make a good lesson horse and a spare for trail rides."

"I thought we didn't want to get into the lesson business, only take on riders with their own horses?"

Killjoy, I thought, picturing all our empty stalls.

"Well, then a trail horse for when we have visitors. He's really nice, and picture how striking he'll look out in the field with all those brown ones." I decided to tackle him with aesthetics. "He would be our accent horse: an exclamation point amongst all those periods."

So Scott sighed in resignation, and Bobbi and I split Willy's cost and expenses. He settled right in, happy for all the attention. I quickly learned that "the pretty white horse," as Jane referred to him, required separate sets of brushes to deal with all that old lady grey-white hair, especially in shedding season, and we quickly excised black polar fleece from our wardrobes. Light horses, like peroxide-haired women, require copious maintenance. But he proved exceptionally dependable, especially with children, and his homely face and general good manners endeared him to all. Elliot requested regularly to ride him with his comfy canter and willingness to jump.

Willy did freak out once: he jerked his head in wonder at miniature Hawk—*what the heck is that?*—snorted and bolted to the far end of his paddock. Hawk has that effect on some full-size horses: he's not a deer, not quite a dog, not readily classifiable. He seems unnatural to the uninitiated, and I suppose he is, bred by human intervention. But Willy soon habituated to him, both alone and pulling his cart, though the Hawkster hitched to his work often stirred up the horses as he trotted along beating his staccato rhythm down the dirt road. As Bobbi explained, "The big horses want to know why we allow that horrible thing to chase that poor little horse."

Bobbi always takes the horses' points-of-view, and her willingness to interpret their thoughts—actually speak for them—though silly, endeared both her and the animals to Elliot, Jane and me. We not only learned horse behavior, but also, without embarrassment, easily fell into the fun pattern of anthropomorphic translation; that is, unless Scott was around, good-naturedly rolling his eyes.

Winter into spring brought a new girl, Brandy, to join the Weatogue team, working part-time until we got busier. An energetic twenty-three, she owned a raucous laugh and bonded with Bobbi's horse Toby, riding him regularly. We concluded that Brandy favored him for his voluptuous, naturally wavy brown tail that echoed her own mane, in the way people choose pet dogs that resemble them. She won over Elliot and Jane with her Cousin It imitations: she would cascade her own long brown hair over her face, replace her wire rim glasses and squeak just like the hairball creature in *The Addams Family*. She worked hard and valued the riding: part of the Weatogue pay package is training under Bobbi, no small perk. She and Meghan learn from an expert on well-trained, -behaved and -tended, healthy horses without the expense of ownership.

Meghan brought over her horse "Q" (for Quixote), a large retired race horse with an overbite so egregious he couldn't nibble carrots flat-handed: we would push them into his mouth end-to-end like you'd feed vegetables into a juicer. But hundreds of dollars later, the dentist maneuvered poor Q's bite into line by about seventy percent. My Bandi hid quite a few oral problems, too. Equine dentistry is the stepchild of horse care, with only about five percent ever treated. According to dentist Cheryl, most can benefit, and even minimal treatment can transform behavior on the bit and significantly improve eating comfort and general demeanor. During World War I the cavalry dentist-to-horse ratio was one to ten, testimony to the importance of the well-tended horse mouth. Sharp points tend to grow on their teeth, often to the non-masticating sides which slice away at gums and cheeks. These can be either "floated" away by hand files or power-drilled down, neither a sight for the lily-livered. My knees weakened amid the protein powder that smoked the air the first time I watched, and cavity-free Scott beat a hasty retreat from the whining drills.

But considering that rider control of these animals is largely through a metal bit in their mouths, good oral hygiene makes sense. While Q's transformation broadcast like a before and after make-over, Bandi's improved teeth showed up in his performance. He chewed less furiously in the bridle and also yielded to the rein more, relaxing his neck into the soft curve, that holy grail of dressage riding known as "going on the bit." Not that I can do it, maybe only occasionally by accident, but I have watched Bobbi on Angel maintain the perfect rein tension so horse and rider are weighted evenly and neither is pulling or giving too much. Bobbi managed it more handily with Bandi after his dental treatment. I guess we all feel like new when relieved of one, let alone multiple toothaches.

The dentistry seemed to settle Bandi some, but still he was not himself. Perhaps he isn't a winter kind of guy. Heavy weather means more indoor work, and he is not enamored of the indoor ring. Or maybe the change of barns, the second in four months, set him questioning the reliability of family and home. Still leery of riding him, our nerves reinforced each other's. On trail rides I was too edgy even to trot.

"Don't worry," Bobbi soothed tactfully. "It's such a treat for me to relax on a leisurely walk."

We plodded slowly along.

I decided against riding the kids' pony again. It was undignified, and I determined to see things through with Bandi. A small voice in the back of my head whispered the possibility of getting yet another horse, ostensibly for Scott to ride and an easier mount for me: an heir and a spare in addition to Willy. Collecting horses is a horsekeeper's devil-on-the-left-shoulder temptation. I tried to dampen the inclination, picturing a frowning Scott on my right shoulder, but new horses came through the barn now and then, and Bobbi is *au courant* to those for sale. We tried Big Merlot for a couple of days, but while he would fit Scott—we still hadn't lost hope of getting him in a saddle—he was largish and too green on the flat work for most riders. He seemed mellow, but did shy once in the woods at something we didn't perceive. I wanted that autopilot bomb-proof horse that required no work or tension from me, one that I could *trust*. But can a human ever fully trust a herd animal of prey? Can a horse give true and total allegiance to his owner? To love and protect her? To sacrifice his own hide and put her vulnerable, skinny neck first? To value and cherish her 'til death (by natural cause, not horse accident) they do part? Scott would say, "It's a *horse*, not a husband, you poor mutt." It is also what led nineteenth-century propagandists for the horseless carriage to proclaim the horse "an untamable brute which man had cowed and beaten into partial subjection, but which bursts his bonds occasionally, carrying ruin and death through our streets."

Yet there are many such storied relationships between human and beast, and people swear to their authenticity. Have I seen too many romantic movies and owned too many overly domesticated dogs? Has anthropomorphism warped my brain? Will I die alone with too many cats?

Reality check: horses are large, potentially dangerous animals. Tamed certainly, but not domesticated: still unpredictable, strong and not overly intelligent, at least in what humans consider intelligence.

Hugh Parker, a long-time breeder/trainer who worked for many years at El-Arabia, warned me: "Never trust a horse."

Okay, what then? Continue to live in fear, the only part of riding that I had mastered? Figure out how to keep my buns in the saddle during spooks, spins and bolts because they will happen, even to the "bomb-proof" loafer? Recognize that the automatic horse of my dreams is a fiction, except on a carousel? Learn how to fall? Drink more milk? Double up my disability insurance? Add more body armor—that hot, unflattering protective vest? Squat-thrust and crunch myself into thighs and abs of steel? And keep my kids at it?

Wait a minute: what happened to the fun?

At least the kids were progressing smoothly with no serious riding angst. Like animals, Elliot and Jane blissfully live in the moment and don't project. And so far, Cleo had been a perfect lady, just the right side of lazy. "It's easier to Go than Whoa" Bobbi always says. And Jane was going slow, policing herself by refusing to trot. "There's no rush," I repeated to Bobbi and Meghan. It was easy to forget Jane's tender youth in the midst of this grown-up adventure. She mostly managed to keep up, but her stubby, albeit strong legs offered limited leverage at even a pony's comparatively broad sides. We found her a proper saddle, one that didn't require several looped riggings of the stirrup leathers, but her feet still barely reached pony belly. Every once in a while she would remind us she was only five.

"I know all the parts," she boasted at dinner. "The brain is the boss of the body and helps you think."

"That's right, Jane."

"And the kidneys are down by the hips on the side—they help you bend." *Hmmm*, we thought, *that's half right.*

"And the big and mini contestants, they help make your food into poop."

Ah yes, only an amateur in this game show called life. But despite tears, rebukes and minor injuries, Jane still stoked fun at the farm. Meghan rescued another kitten, a steel grey with white paws. Janie love-mugged "Boots" on a regular basis in an effort to prove that, like herpes, a cat scratch scar on a cheek is forever, despite Mederma and youth's miraculous healing powers. The bunnies remained a delight, and the kids fashioned old boxes into "Bunny Inns," "condos" and "resorts" to keep these highly intelligent (or so I'm told) creatures entertained. Ever more elaborate, Elliot and Jane designed runs, windows, tunnels, lofts, doors, interior and exterior perches, pop-up holes and hideouts, and decorated all with drawings of bunnies and flowers, twine hung as beaded curtains, wallpaper patterns and directional signposts: they *are* sophisticated, tasteful bunnies, after all. Indeed, when Hera and Diana so trashed the first bunny inn that we removed it, the sisters went berserk. When the kids installed a replacement, we were instantly gratified witnessing the frenzied explorations. I could speak for the bunnies, but I won't.

Then there was the mystery and intrigue of the hay loft, accessible only by way of a hazardous twelve-foot vertical wooden ladder that beckoned like Combat to a cockroach (or like flies to ... well, you know, the brown stuff we've got plenty of). The cats scale it, both up and down, and so do my kids, except when Angel is in the barn: Bobbi's skittish horse snorts, circles, kicks and emits an unearthly scream at the sound of Elliot and Jane thundering overhead. A thick rubber mat pads the concrete floor beneath the ladder providing me *some* peace of mind: my kids may mimic little monkeys already, but many of their friends need agility training. Like cats in trees, they would get stranded at the top. As I coaxed quaking visitors backwards and down into the eager hands of confident Elliot and Jane or watched my barn rats help their skeptical friends overcome their fears of bunnies, cats and horses and demonstrate how to handle them, I was reminded of how far we had come and why we bothered. The Weatogue enterprise was a language all its own, and Jane and Elliot were learning it, right down to its most obscure rules of grammar.

Hawk rose to barn mascot and supplied steady entertainment. Kindly patient with the kids, he also learned to live and let live with Bandi. Though separated in adjoining paddocks, squat Hawk still squeezed between the fence and the shared automatic waterer to visit Bandi. They'd squeal and romp and occasionally succumb to violence. Hawk's strategy was to fit himself right underneath Bandi's belly between his four legs—a veritable mini-Bandi. Once inserted, he'd kick out in all directions, clipping Bandi's shins with his cutting hooves. After a few perplexed seconds Bandi uncovered the little monster who for payback, got kicked and knocked over in his rolling retreat to safety through the fence. He *is* a little stallion, with a Napoleon complex to boot, and fast, too; much to Meghan's dismay, Hawk beat her racehorse Q at a run. Though Bobbi assured me that Bandi's and Hawk's "play" was harmless, we'd decided to geld Hawk to lower that testosterone for his own protection.

Elliot was riding well. He developed a relaxed grace in the saddle, and though he did not aspire to show, he was keen to canter and jump. When Cleo stumbled forward in a canter and Elliot barely held on, he continued unfazed. How I envy that body confidence that kids possess, that invincibility I still faintly remember having had myself. How galloping at great speed was the whole point on my few trail rides as a teenager in New Jersey, faster and faster the only thought in my fool head. Now a slow canter induces the heebie jeebies and I rein in, envisioning the woman at our local equestrian shop, an accomplished rider who fell, hit her head, and lay in an induced coma for weeks. Yes, she was wearing a helmet.

"How is she doing?" I enquired about three months later, figuring I would hear all was well.

"Well, she is starting to recognize people, so that's a good sign."

Yikes! my internal alarm systems shouted.

Amazingly, she returned to riding after a year. *How do I interpret and apply that data,* I wondered?

Deep within my child-body memory I dredged up the security I once owned climbing those old iron monkey bars atop the concrete playground—how ludicrous the idea that I'd lose my grip or misstep my footing. How annoying my parents' warnings to take care. But now I watch Jane brazenly scale, flip and hang upside down, and the words "be careful" escape my pursed, old lady lips with each daring feat. I try to hold my tongue—the books specify that repeated warnings render children anxious and fearful—but shouldn't they be cautious? How easy to lose concentration or simply slip. Those precious heads, those delicate spines.

So I aggressively maneuvered myself psychologically to a tolerable place with the riding and the playground and the loft ladder and the high swing in our yard's willow. And then, just as I relaxed a little, a friend's daughter broke her arm in three places falling from a playground contraption. What is a mother to do but be anxious and spout warnings? That line between necessary and unnecessary danger is a moving target. I've known parents who forbade their kids public sandboxes (germs) and playgrounds (falling). That certainly seemed the wrong side of cautious until one kid nearly lost an eye to an infection from sand that feral cats used nightly as a litter tray, not to mention the fractures that added up. Recently, I dined with a man who spent the last fifteen years in a wheelchair due to a skiing accident. I lifted his wineglass to his shaking lips and un-strapped the spoon from his less paralyzed hand. Spasms racked his body several times an hour. Should we not ski? I thought of those crowded slopes of reckless, hormone-dazed teen snowboarders grinding the flakes to dust, thundering locomotives on my quivering tail: is riding really any more potentially injurious? Should limber kids push the envelope and oldsters quit when bones dry out and spinal tissue ossifies? Insurance actuaries and hedge fund managers are weaklings when it comes to risk assessment: it is parents who do the heavy lifting—24/7.

Though it was gratifying to watch Elliot progress in the saddle, his swan dive into barn life was a less anxiety-producing benefit of the farm. He anticipated working there all summer, in lieu of all camp activities if I would allow it. We negotiated an employment contract of mornings, evenings and non-camp days for $2.00 an hour. Once he started pulling his weight, we'd raise him to $5.00. Pay for honest work thrilled him as I don't believe in remuneration for household chores (the kids receive a small allowance as "sharers in the family resources," in line with some parenting hokum I once read). He even devised a form to organize Bobbi's daily riding schedule. I was pleased he embraced the physicality of mucking out stalls, lugging hay bales, scrubbing water buckets and cleaning tack, as well as extraneous tasks like making hot chocolate for everyone. The whole expensive, emotionally and psychologically stretching horse business "ride" paid off in spades when, out of the blue he announced, "Mom, this farm is the best thing that ever happened to our family."

In addition to the ever-present risk analyses of danger and non-profitability, time was another problem. There was never enough. Now I understood that those people in the dirty riding pants I see racing through the grocery aisles are not pretentious, but simply late getting home from the barn. I undertook each ride with the time-devouring proper grooming, tacking and cleaning up and expected the same thoroughness from my kids, even though Bobbi always insisted: "The important thing is to ride. I know you want to do it all, but we can clean up, just get in the *ride*." Because the forty-eight hours of a weekend flew by, and my husband awaited my often-late return, and the kids had other activities requiring parental accompaniment—"Mom! Where have you been?"—on occasion, I'd leave the dusty tack near the sink for the girls to clean and slink off. But I did master these tasks, and when time afforded, I enjoyed saddle-soaping the bridle, girth and saddle, scrubbing the horse saliva and chewed-treat encrusted bit, storing the clean bridle in a tidy figure-eight, hoisting my saddle to the rack, turning the saddle pad up to dry off and air out, all excuses to bask in the afterglow of the ride. This and the grooming—bathing, brushing, combing—rounded out the experience: giving back for the privilege, just being with my horse, meeting his needs, taking good care.

The barn activity induced a peace that I wanted to extend to my riding. I received B. K. S. Iyengar's *Light on Life*, an autobiographical account the aged yogi who refined yoga for the working masses (those who can't spend ten hours a day perfecting triangle pose), and brought his practice to the western world. I read it over several days, mounted safely on a steady, four-legged chair in the Butternut Mountain lodge while my kids careened down weekend-crowded, snowy slopes. *Train the mind to live in the moment through the discipline of the body*, Mr. Iyengar teaches, *don't anticipate the future or dwell in the past and time will slow and happiness will follow you all your days*. Nice advice and a good gig if you can get it, but the practice is excruciatingly difficult, even for those few minutes of Shavasana, or corpse pose, that top off each yoga session. The mind churns busy, busy, perpetual motion. The egotistical brain refuses to shush and allow the body to sensate without its interference. I sipped my hot chocolate, closed my eyes, and vowed to be *in the moment, live in the now* when I ride because I realized that the *thought* of riding, the anticipation of all that could go wrong (that too-busy brain), wracks the nerves more than the actual riding, or watching my kids ride. It is in the black of night, away from the riding ring that the "what ifs," those grisliest possible if not probable scenarios, sabotage the body's best intentions of release and rest, and brush away any stale childhood crumbs of can-do attitude and ability.

Light on Life worked. My next ride included a walk, trot and canter in the ring on my own. When Bobbi joined me for a trail ride afterwards I felt lighter, buoyant. Out in the field and woods I endured two "spooks": one when my Bandi picked a half-hearted fight with Toby, just because (who knows? perhaps Toby farted in Bandi's general direction like the French Taunters in *Monty Python and the Holy Grail*), and another when Toby shied at a puddle and both horses jumped. But I handled them with calm if not quite grace and shut the door on panic. Briefly reverting to type I wondered *why me: why does something always happen on my watch?* but refocused on the pleasures of the day, satisfied to have kept my bum in contact with leather.

CHAPTER EIGHTEEN

Spring

·◁═══════▷·

EVERYBODY WAS SHEDDING. The stiff and soft brushes over-flowed with hair after a single swipe down a neck or across a haunch. We discovered which horses tolerated the sucking whine of the industrial sized vacuum, the only tool up to the job of grooming these giant hair balls.

"It's still so cold, why are they already shedding so much?" I asked Bobbi as I sucked Bandi a hickey with the nozzle. It "popped" as I pulled it off, and he jumped.

"It's the light. As soon as the days get longer, the horses' hair gets shorter."

"No kidding," I replied, resting my aching arms.

In vain I sloughed off Willie's hair, which turned my dirt-hiding navy turtleneck into a white mink. The clogged brush was useless after only two strokes.

"You'll have to vacuum me off before I head home."

All those flying protein strands offended my own rather meticu-lous grooming, but the plague blew through within a couple of weeks. By May the horses molted sleek and thinner, some of them seal-skin smooth and shiny. Bandi was looking good—fit and toned, but still out of sorts. Bobbi called his previous trainer.

"He's probably bored," Stacey reminded. "Have you taken him hunter pacing or to some jumper shows? He really needs that."

So Bobbi, Meghan and I rolled him over to an event in Millbrook for his own entertainment, and he and Meghan performed well across the jumps. This, and the approaching summer set him right again, more like his old self. It became clear that he is an outdoor, over the fences kind of guy, not fancy or refined. He grew more affectionate, so we concluded he had decided to trust us and truly settle in.

The thawing ground sported islands of newly planted grass, and a relieved Scott fast-forwarded to wider swathes of green overtaking the recalcitrant mud and ice. We awaited the elusive three consecutive dry days to enable our AWOL fencer to paint our still raw posts and rails. Elliot jumped and cantered Cleo but my son remained content to snub the show circuit, much to Bobbi's dismay.

"He looks so good up there," she sighed, shaking her head. "He'd be great in competition, and Cleo is such a good, safe ride."

Maybe we were wasting a perfectly good pony, but secretly I rejoiced. Riding was his leisure pursuit, his non-competitive respite from NYC academic and sport life: he was in it for the sheer enjoyment of camaraderie between boy and beast. Jane broke through to trotting, enjoyed it, and even got the hang of posting. While she trotted still tethered to a longe line, she freely wandered the indoor ring at a walk and took pride in her earned independence.

Spring fever gripped us all, and in unison with the beasts we shed our layers of silk long johns, polar fleece and down. Finally the outdoor arena was complete, and the weather beckoned us hibernating, squinting New Englanders out into the light. One seemingly perfect day, I snapped the ritual photo of Jane's *plein-aire* debut on Cleo and, content that all was well in hand, ducked back inside to tack up Bandi for my own lesson afterwards. Soon enough, Bobbi and Jane walked into the barn, Jane atop Cleo, in tears.

"We have something very exciting to tell you, Mommy," Bobbi said in a chipper voice.

"Oh, and that is?"

"Janie is now a real rider." Bobbi snuck me an "it's OK" wink.

"I want to tell Mommy," Jane said through slowing tears.

"What happened, Boo-boo?"

"Cleo jumped and I fell off, all the way to the ground." She pointed down, indignant.

"Wow. That must have been something. Are you okay?" To deescalate her tension, I managed measured tones.

"It hurt my back," she emphasized, out to get some sympathy from spine-addled me. But I miserly mask any hysteria so my kids don't turn into hypochondriacal worriers like me (all parents devise cockamamie strategies to prevent their own phobias infecting the next generation). And I know plenty of cry-baby, body-nervous kids so I am hyper-vigilant against it. According to the gotcha rules of reverse-reverse psychology I will surely now produce one. So, I downplayed Jane's fall like an Oscar winner, but my internal sirens were rapid firing—bad parent, bad parent, bad, bad parent—spotlighting my billboard-sized headline "AM I PUTTING MY KIDS UNNECESSARILY AT RISK?"

My thoughts rushed on. *Boy, Bobbi certainly takes everything casually. Is this a virtue or a fault? Come to think of it I've never seen her upset or angry—is she on drugs? She talks awfully fast sometimes. Does she really know what she's doing? We're all landing in the dirt. Does she value her life as much as we do ours? Have I not seen her clearly because she fuels my dream? An equine addict, have I miscast the horse dealer my friend? Sometimes she is slow to get things done around the farm. She has even ignored Scott's direction and hired another part-time worker....*

Bobbi sensed my wild-eyed inner turmoil and haltered my bolting brain.

"I'm not completely sure what scared Cleo, but she went, 'oh-oh— monsters!' and hustled forward a few paces, and Janie lost her balance. It would have been hard for her to stay on." We both looked at Jane who was beginning to enjoy the drama. Bobbi continued: "She fell pretty flat, and she wanted to come tell you right away. I asked her if she wanted to walk in, or ride Cleo. She chose to ride."

"Oh, Janie, you are very brave. Remember when it happened to Mommy on Bandi?"

She nodded slowly, perking up.

"Now we're both members of the riding club. It happens to all of us, even Bobbi, but we get better at riding, and falling, all the time." I prayed it was true and swallowed my rising distrust of horses, Bobbi, myself.

Soon she was happy again, and by the next week back on Cleo without any thought of her fall. I noted well the beauty of children: natural little yogis, they don't dwell on the past. I wish I could bottle their carefree psyches; no wonder we rail at old age. Jane rarely mentioned her mishap, except to brag a bigger injury against her brother's hockey bruises, but it reminded Bobbi and me that Jane was only five. I reiterated our safety first policy and our vow to proceed slowly against Jane's capability of learning quickly. My motto for us all was: "There's no rush."

Unscathed by what could have, and indeed had happened in a flash, Jane re-trusted her safety to Cleo and Bobbi. Cleo's startle surprised us, but it can happen to the rock steadiest of horses, and goes with the territory. Plus it was spring, and several of the horses had gotten exuberant. We later figured out that Cleo reliably hops a few steps when prompted to trot with a whip on a longe line, but not off-longe. It's a subtle quirk, but enough to have unseated a tiny novice. I rethought Bobbi's nonchalant reaction to Jane's first tumble and realized there was no sense in all of us panicking nervous hen-style. Maybe the words "you have to break a few eggs in order to make an omelet" are a poor choice, but either I'd have to reconcile myself to the unsettling music or get off this carousel. Unlike us, Bobbi's seen it all, possessing perspective fore and aft of our maiden voyage. Her calm expertise counter-balanced our newbie theatrics. I aimed to take her experienced lead, but nevertheless anticipated some renewed soul-searching that night in bed.

Sure enough, as I lay rehashing the day's events, I recalled Bobbi's uncharacteristic agitation one winter day when Jane ran and slid across some iced-over puddles. I tossed a few perfunctory "careful"s when she got especially daring, but Bobbi twitched like a bird, unable to concentrate on our conversation.

"I can't bear to watch her. She might fall."

"Bobbi. She's only three feet tall and on the ground."

"I know, I know, but it's so slippery."

"It's very funny, Bobbi, that you're less worried about Jane four feet off the ground on the back of a thousand pound animal that doesn't speak English, but you freak out about a little ice. I mean, how far can she fall? She's an ice-skater for Pete's sake."

We both cracked up.

I realized that perceived risk is just that, and perception is skewed across our own personal graphs. Bobbi knows horses and what they are apt to do, and what kids can handle on horseback. She trusts from seasoned, first-hand experience that people who learn to ride fall and are mostly fine. She understands horses with a sensory awareness that gives her confidence and a sense of control that I lack regarding horses in general and in particular, if not icy patches and playgrounds. I shouldn't allow my unease about kid horseplay to circumscribe Elliot's and Jane's opportunities and experiences in the caring hands of an expert. I would trust them to Bobbi in this arena, taking the obvious, reasonable precautions, and let my kids map out their own comfort zones.

WE STARED DOWN New England's always disappointingly delayed spring, riding outside when we could. Once the snow melted, we drove the cart with Hawk through our fields instead of along the road. What a feeling, parting the awakening hayfields with nary a car in sight. Soon, Elliot and Jane were driving themselves with Meghan and me following on foot alongside, then farther and farther behind. We belly laughed when little Hawk cantered for all he was worth, his mini hooves pound-

ing a puny thunder on the still hard ground, the cart meandering leisurely despite his dedicated effort. My healthy, happy kids bonding with
an animal against a backdrop of plump seed heads waving in the fertile fields, and trees, young and old, about to burst into leaf evoked deep
gratefulness and contentment. If I had died then, I would have said I
had truly lived.

By early June we mowed a path around the perimeter of the fields so
Hawk and the horses could trail with ease. I enticed Scott into a drive
with Hawk; the kids and Bobbi following along behind.

"Look Bobbi, Mommy and Daddy are so romantic. They really love
each other—maybe they'll kiss." So we did.

Jane gets it, I thought! The moment was not lost on this five-year-
old. The scene echoed her fairy tales come to life, with Scott and me
the prince and princess. I enjoyed the role; as a teenager she'll probably
paint me the mean old crone.

Scott didn't relax in the cart, perhaps aware of his extra weight for
Hawk who seems too small to be so strong. Irrationally, I also held
myself up to lighten the load. I pondered whether Scott would ever ride.
I had stocked up on gear just in case: an oversize Charles Owen velvet
helmet, size twelve black Ariat riding boots (not quite as cute as Jane's),
and an extra-large pair of gloves lay quietly in my tack trunk against
that special day, be it this summer or when our kids depart for college. I
decided not to nag. Riding desire can't be foisted upon you.

Two other events sprang us into summer. First, we gelded Hawk.
Taking some of the testosterone, or "starch" as I referred to it, out of him
should render him more agreeable and safer among the other horses.
We didn't want him perpetually alone in the paddock. Few horses like
the solitary life of a stallion, or, at least we don't like it for them unless
they're meant to breed. Instinctively herd and pack animals, horses are
happier in groups, especially familiar ones. When one of their paddock
mates is taken into the barn before them, they fuss, neighing and calling to each other "Where you going? Come back, come back...." Often,

when one horse is to be ridden, we take his or her buddy in too, just to avoid upset. Bobbi, Meghan and Brandy systematically bring the horses from the fields in ordered groupings so that no one is left out there alone.

Doctor Kay arrived on castration day, spiffy in his bowtie as usual, a WASP mohel preparing an equine bris. He has been vetting in the area fifty years, his practice changing with the times from dairy cows to horses. He adeptly tranquilized Hawk. Bobbi sat on the little stallion's neck, who mostly slept through the procedure that Bobbi admitted was not particularly pleasant to witness.

"At one point Doctor Kay said 'Just where did those testicles get to?'" Bobbi told me later. "He just flung them across the stall, and we scooped them up at the end."

"Oh," I said, rolling my eyes. "I'm sorry I missed it."

But my sarcasm was disingenuous. I envied Bobbi experiencing every aspect of a working farm, even the gory bits.

The second event glinted as a sure sign of spring's renewal. After months of chorusing "poor George," our unlucky caretaker caught a break. Since the fire George had spent half the winter without any heat, mostly sleeping in his car, and the entire year without plumbing. A lone port-a-john stood in the yard, and he showered at friends' and occasionally at our place. It had been a rough year, but he adamantly refused to find other, even temporary accommodations while Ursula painstakingly sorted out whether to rebuild.

One early May morning, he found us in our driveway amidst the blowsy pink and white magnolia petals, late as usual for church.

"Guess what?" he said, excited and oblivious to our flustered hustling of the kids into their car seats.

"What George? We're kind of in a hurry."

He started to cry.

"What happened, George?" I was worried now.

"I won a car."

"What? . . . How? Where?"

Tears streaming down his cheeks, he shook.

"At the Mohegan Sun. I won it at the slot machine."

"You're kidding, George! A real car?" Scott and I traded our "is this George story legit?" glance. "That's great. Congratulations."

"Eighteen dollars and fifty cents. That's what I spent. The bells went off and people went nuts. They had to call security because I got swarmed. Everybody wanted to touch me for luck."

"Wow. I didn't know you could win a car at a slot machine," I said.

"It's a real race car, and worth about forty thousand dollars. I'm gonna' keep it, though I should sell it."

"What color?"

"Red, bright red."

"Of course. Well after the year you've had you deserve it. Drive it in good health." We were well and truly amazed.

And what a car. A low-slung performance speed machine, it was totally impractical for New England's winter ice and bulbous roads. But George sported that car like a trophy girlfriend, reveling in the attention it generated at racetracks and car shows despite his run-ins with troopers. He considered selling it under the burden of double insurance payments (we paid him generously but never really knew how he got on), but couldn't part with his glamorous new toy. The excitement never wore off, and what a story he had to tell.

CHAPTER NINETEEN

Eating Dirt

·⊂━━━━━⊃·

IT STRUCK ME AS SOON AS I ENTERED THE BARN: a sense of unease, a frazzled energy, a whiff of panic. Bobbi is never anxious around horses, at least not noticeably, but there she stood, next to Willy in the cross ties, her hair matted down from the sweat of a recently removed helmet and a flush in her face. Elliot gave me a "Hi, Mom," and a weak smile. Then I noticed that Bobbi was putting on Willy's bridle, signaling she was behind schedule.

Cleo had a sore tendon from mixing it up in the fields with her buddies, so the plan was for the kids to ride Willy at one o'clock, Jane first then El, while Scott and I lunched at The White Hart. I would ride at two, preferring to ride without the kids around. I worried about their horseplay: nothing like Jane in tears from some barn-related mishap to raise my hackles. I had to keep my cool, especially today. Eight weeks had passed since I had been in the saddle. Various ailments were to blame. On spring break vacation in Anguilla I had whiplashed my vertebrae showing Elliot how to dive from a springy board, not unlike the one I grew up with and which, no doubt, duped me into believing I was eight years old again. I had also nursed an endless cold, courtesy of my germ magnets Elliot and Jane back at school, and had undergone a nasty surgery to correct a long-deviated septum. To be honest, I had welcomed the break. I thought I loved riding, and I wanted to master this horse

business, but the learning, the Bandicoot, and the horse farm in general had drained me nearly dry.

Since my first fall in summer, I had been dumped again in our own indoor ring over the winter. Bandi shied at the door during a trot, twisted left and bolted while I flew right, pretty much a rerun of my first airborne performance. I landed delicately, though the footing is never as soft as one wishes, and immediately I got back on. It traumatized me less than the first time, but not by much. Now I have had eight weeks of not riding to dwell on it.

But the beautiful early spring day meant an outdoor lesson—no spooky doors in sight.

"We're running a little late," Bobbi said nervously as she finished tacking up Willy.

"Oh." I said, disappointed because I had rushed through lunch, much to Scott's annoyance. "Did your morning lessons run long?"

"Not really, but Nancy wanted to finish up with a ride in the field, so Angel and I went with her. I hated to cut her short because she is such a great boarder."

This was true. Our very first customer, Nancy had been unfailingly excited about the barn, complimentary even in the midst of the ongoing construction. She and Bobbi had succeeded so much with Chase that they were on the lookout for another horse. One owner with multiple horses is ideal business-wise—reduced traffic on the road, fewer personalities to deal with, less human congestion on the property. Although technically a for-profit enterprise, we wanted to preserve the atmosphere of our own personal space and keep it low-key for people we liked. Breaking even would be enough, but hemorrhaging money forever was still a possibility if we didn't keep our business heads. Nancy had recently acquired enough skill and nerve to canter Chase out in the open field as opposed to the ring. I envied her progress and was thrilled on her behalf when Bobbi boasted about her cantering around our large hay field, not once but twice without stopping. I wouldn't have begrudged her the extra time either.

"We also had a little accident with Janie," Bobbi continued.

I heard Jane cry "Mommy" in distress from the tack room.

"What happened?" I asked, blanketing the sparks in my brain.

"Angel stepped on her foot," Elliot reported.

"I think she's fine," Bobbi added. "She'll be bruised, but she's moving everything, and we've put Cleo's leg icepack on her."

I jogged to the tack room, where Jane burst back into tears upon hearing my voice. Above the din, Jane's sitter Marie quickly assured me she'd been up and laughing a minute before. Timing is tricky for parents, and it's not uncommon for kids to re-fall apart when their safe emotional outlet appears.

"Poor Janie," I took her onto my lap and kissed her head. "Did Angel step on your little hoof? Let me take a look."

Marie had just gotten Jane's riding boots back on, hoping to encourage her to ride and take her mind off the pain. But the boot seemed tight, and I removed it to view the damage. The swelling was minimal, and Marie pronounced the bones sound. But Jane gained a fresh sympathetic audience and couldn't rally—it certainly must have hurt. We all recounted our episodes under the hooves of horses, but besides her tiny, more vulnerable feet, she also lacked her usual resilience due to a stomach virus she had weathered only two days before.

We prescribed rest and with an exaggerated groan I hoisted her up for a piggy back ride to the car. Homeward bound she brightened at the prospect of elevating and icing her foot in front of *Dumbo* and *Madeline* videos. Poor Jane: so often in tears at the barn. That her kinship with the animals made up for the occasional maiming amazed me. I gave her credit for savoring the fun and forgetting the injuries. Like her father and brother, and decidedly unlike her mother, she is a glass-half-full kind of gal.

I stayed behind to watch Elliot ride and to ready Bandi for my belated lesson. Pausing ringside, I saw Elliot comfortably confident on Willie who he had ridden only once before.

"Whoa, Elliot! Slow down that trot," Bobbi instructed. "Willie's turbocharged today."

Bobbi later told me she found Elliot's ride hair-raising due to Willy's uncharacteristic burst of energy.

"I noticed he was getting a little stiff, so I put him on glucosamine. With this supplement they advise upping his grain some, so Willie is raring to go. I'll have to cut him back."

Grain is a "hot" food and pumps the horses up with an energy boost, a caffeine kick of sorts. There is no end to tinkering with a horse's diet, including natural supplements that calm, some of which we had given Bandi. He didn't spook less, but he grouched less during grooming and tolerated cuddles better.

Elliot itched to canter Willy. It went well, if a bit fast, and Willie's big canter surprised Elliot after Cleo's delicate stride, illustrating that no two horses ride alike. Later, Bobbi rethought her decision to let him go for it. After Janie's encounter with Angel's hoof and her recent first fall, not to mention my own wobbles, Bobbi needed a break from the Bok family having adventures.

Finally my turn, I rode Bandi out to the larger ring while Elliot finished up in the adjacent dressage arena. While Bobbi, Elliot and Willy headed indoors to untack, I practiced my trotting and circles, alone and without trouble. Starting solo was risky after such a long break, but a bike ride with Scott beckoned, and I was striving to keep our relationship intact, temporarily filibustering Scott's objections to my time sink of a new pursuit.

My skills rusty, I nevertheless enjoyed Bandi again. I re-appreciated his familiar trot and even canter. Keeping him energized required steady effort, and the work strengthened my legs and kept me focused and accurate with my commands. Bobbi had recently suggested I try spurs and a whip for my lazy boy, but I was determined to muscle my will through my body to get what I wanted from him. Bobbi could do it, so it wasn't impossible. I tired quickly, but it felt a purer form of horsemanship. And I was still somewhat idealistic.

On a short break between canters, Margaret Ann strode into the ring. A horsewoman we knew from Riga Meadow, she also sold tack and gifts and dropped by to firm up plans for her kiosk at our upcoming June show.

"Hi, Margaret Ann," I greeted. "I'm almost done, maybe ten minutes, and then Bobbi's all yours."

"All right, take your time. I'll just sit on the bench here if you don't mind."

"You might get a face full of dust, but you're welcome to it." Thanks to Kenny, our ring drained almost too well, requiring copious watering in dry weather.

A teak bench divided the two rings. Margaret Ann settled down and I confidently resumed my trot, playing to my impromptu audience.

"Energize that trot before asking for the canter," Bobbi instructed. "Get him paying attention. Now sit the trot tall and left leg asks for the canter."

I had trouble keeping my butt heavy in the saddle against the trot. Only in attempting this motion did I realize how natural posting is. But if the horse feels you posting he should not, and generally will not, pick up the canter unless he is particularly generous. My usual methods of cheating included standing a little in the stirrups to keep my bouncing cheeks off the saddle altogether or leaning forward and pushing the reins forward—"Giddy-up, cowgirl" Bobbi generally joked—to make up for my weak seat. Against type, Bandi picked now to show off a too lively trot when I needed him to slow down. He's a wily character.

"Remember, the hands don't make him go, your seat and legs do. You and Elliot do exactly the same thing—flap your arms to get him to go. Yee-haw!" She chicken-winged her own elbows dramatically. "This cowboy stuff won't work. Organize yourself again, slow down the trot—not too slow—sit tall, hands give the reins *slightly* forward but quiet, and ask him again."

This time I managed it and cantered down the long side of the ring. As I approached the bench and Margaret Ann, Bandi startled, stopped short and simultaneously jumped sharply to the center of the ring away from Margaret Ann, whose entrance and presence he had distinctly noted *and* who we had already passed at a trot several times. She had not appeared out of thin air, nor had she been transformed into a horse-eating monster. Off I flew landing with a thud flat on my back just under Bandi's left shoulder. He didn't bolt this time and high-stepped to avoid trampling me while I scrambled out of his way up onto my feet. Bobbi ran over.

"Are you okay?"

I considered.

"Yes. I think I'm fine."

Unhurt, but mad. I grabbed a hold of Bandi's reins and shook his face. "Bandi! What is the matter with you? Stupid horse; don't you dare do that again."

Brushing myself off, I asked Bobbi, "Where did I go wrong?"

"Not your fault. I saw him get the hairy eyeball, but he was too quick for me to warn you. He didn't really spin, but jumped to the side. I thought you were going to stick it at first, but then sometimes it's better to bail."

"It was rather controlled and graceful," Margaret Ann said, "a slow motion ejection."

It did have that feel about it, even to me, but still I railed at having been unseated again, at a canter no less.

"Could I have stayed on?"

"Probably if you had had a little more right leg on him to curve his body away from the bench, the weight on your right would have balanced you when he jumped right."

"But wouldn't that be pushing his middle into what he feared, making it worse?"

"The idea is to curve his center body toward the spooky thing and his face and hind end away. They'll always spook away, so by curving his body like a C you not only remove his eyes from the object, but impair his full ability to jump or spin in that direction."

Sensible, I thought, but I despaired at a weight shift that was one more thing to think about on top of a perpetual consciousness that Bandi might spook at anything, even the benign Margaret Ann, or the tractor lying in wait at the edge of a field, or a rogue daytime deer, or the giddy gymnast chipmunk, or the swooping crow, or the angry wasp, or the bloodthirsty horsefly, or the revving motorcycle, or the visitor who knows nothing about horses, or the car alarm in the parking lot, or the terrifying thoughts that flit around his small, highly imaginative brain, or, or, or ... Toby even spooked at the sight of Cleo simply lying down in her pasture one day; she must have posed an unusual silhouette. He just flipped tight around and tracked for the hills until Bobbi, brave woman, forced his quivering, agitated fifteen hundred pounds right up to the fence where Cleo was sunning her belly.

"*Look*, Dumbo! It's only Cleo," I heard her urge.

He snorted his panic and danced an eight-step in place, Bobbi not allowing retreat. As Bandi and I were alongside at the time, forcing a false calm I u-turned toward the barn, leaving Bobbi to fend for herself. I was the last thing she needed to worry about. Bandi couldn't have cared less about Cleo's lounging aspect, miraculously discounting Toby's agitation, so we avoided trouble. I gave myself some credit for keeping a cool head and making a good decision.

As in life, with riding there is always something. The trick on a horse is to develop good reflexes, catch spooks early and be prepared for anything. There are no assurances in this business. Shit happens, and even if you could hermetically seal your horse environment from all possible outside influences from bugs to tractors, you'd have a totally neurotic horse who would still, I'd bet good money, find something to get loopy about. The horse term "bombproof" is silently qualified by "within reason": the horse's "reason" that is, not the rider's. Conditioning to all conditions is the lofty goal, but some horses never adjust to the things that scare them. A slant of light striping the indoor ring; a rush of wind that rattles the barn door; the harried whinny of your horse's buddy out in the field—all unpredictable and sometimes disruptive, sometimes not. I have searched for the science of this, the logic, and believe me, it doesn't exist. The only defense is a dual personality: my riderly self must stay loose, calm and relaxed to confer a sense of ease to my horse, but at the same time sit constantly AWARE, prepared for anything and everything, from the postman filling the mailbox to the cougar my horse imagines crouches in the brush as I meander, whistling a happy tune, along a wooded verge. Does this disrupt that dreamy, glamorous, magazine-quality image I stubbornly keep in my head? Well, 'er, a wee bit, yes.

"If it were easy, it wouldn't be as much fun," Bobbi liked to quip.

I *guess* so. But I hanker after that fantasy. Perhaps once my skills improve, I can enjoy my ideal ride, at least for a few nanoseconds of each experience or maybe once a year on my birthday.

So, I scolded Bandi since Bobbi repeatedly had advised me to get mad instead of scared. A rough day for her: first Jane's foot, then Elliot's speed date with Turbo-Willie, and then her boss flying through the air without the greatest of ease. Bobbi placed her arm around my sagging shoulders, made sure I was okay, and asked if I wanted to get back on. That depended on the definition of "wanted;" simultaneously I thought, *I know I should*, and *hell no*, but responded "yes" with shaky conviction. I wrangled my foot high into the stirrup, grateful for no back or hip twinges, and, with a leg hoist from Bobbi, swung my dusty, dumped self up and across tense Bandi's rippling back.

"Alright, Bandicoot, you rat, let's get with the program, boy." I tried to lighten my mood.

"Ready to try that canter again?" Bobbi probed as she returned to the center of the ring.

"Sure."

"Should I move?" Margaret Ann rose from the bench.

"No. You stay right there, as you were," Bobbi commanded, determined to see me and Bandi through this trial.

This is like parenting adults, I thought, remembering how many times I had helped my kids through a scary dream, climb a tree, or jump off our boat into the dark lake water. No matter how much you'd rather, you don't give in, but muscle them through, because therein lies the path to CONFIDENCE... or is it that deep-seated fear from which they never recover?

Bandi knew he was in the doghouse so we picked up the canter easily. As I headed for Margaret Ann on the bench, I concentrated on Bobbi's instructions so much that my brain ached.

"Keep your right leg on him and push his belly toward the bench. Let your weight drop into that right stirrup. Bend his head right away from Margaret Ann and keep him going forward. Make him focus on your commands."

My rising panic turned my head and body hollow.

"See his ears? They're turned toward you, but still up. This is good; he's listening for your instructions. Leg on, leg on... a little right rein..."

We passed the scary visitor without incident.

"Good girl," Bobbi called out. "Now ride him on, keep him going. Think gallop." Speed was the last thing I wanted more of. "Use your seat, give him some rein and look where you want to turn, then, when you're ready, ask him to trot," she continued.

Upon Bobbi voicing "trot," Bandi broke the canter without any command from me. *Great,* I thought, *he understands English but believes in monsters.* Bobbi sometimes spelled out the commands, like you'd do with a child. I haven't yet met a horse that can spell, but I'm sure one exists. *Shit,* I said under my breath; I knew what was coming.

"Was that your transition or his?"

Oh, how I wanted to fib.

"His."

"Okay, canter again and bring him down to a T-R-O-T on your command, not mine."

The next time we got it right—a canter past Margaret Ann twice around, followed by a smooth transition to trot and then to walk, on my terms. We took this tender mercy. A glimmer of confidence mingled with my disappointment at not sticking the spook. My third time in the dirt had been easier than the first two, despite my faster mph. Maybe the horsey adage was true—you're not a rider until you've come off at least ten times. Three down, seven to go.

Scott and Elliot had been wandering through the fields and missed my little drama, but I fully disclosed it later on our bikes hurtling (fearlessly now, thank you Bandi; bikes are so much more controllable), down Weatogue Road. At home that evening we nursed Jane with ice and sympathy. A blue-black hoof shaped bruise spread from her ankle, across the top of her foot, seeping down between her toes. She hobbled two days, but relieved us with steady improvement. "We should have taken more care: the parents' old lament. Scott and I re-vowed to fix at least one pair of eyes on her at all times at the farm. While Elliot and we were acutely aware of the evident dangers and better intuited the language of horses, Jane still basked in a state of taken-for-granted protection. On the one hand, guarding her safety was our responsibility until she caught us up on the learning curve. On the other, with her jump-start in horsekeeping, in expertise she will lap us in the end, and, if Bobbi is right, easy equals limited fun.

Circumstance postponed my next rendezvous with Bandi. The subsequent weekend our family missed Salisbury altogether, heading to Philadelphia for Scott's and my twenty-fifth college reunion. The kids were excited about the train, the hotel, and a hotel-supplied babysitter, a new experience. Jane's sense of adventure and romance came to the fore.

"You and Daddy met here?" she asked again and again as we approached the block of high rises at the west end of the University of Pennsylvania campus. We pointed our fingers toward the sixteenth floor of High Rise North. Elliot squirmed and rolled his eyes.

"Yes we did honey, on the very first night that Mommy moved into the school."

"Act out how you met!"

Scott and I smiled remembering our introduction twenty-seven years ago, mere babes at twenty years old. We also winced at how fast all had gone since.

"Well, I can't remember exactly, but Daddy's roommate invited me over to meet some of the people on the floor. Daddy walked in, wearing a suit and tie having been campaigning for the first George Bush, and by midnight we were all singing and dancing with lampshades on our heads."

"Lampshades? Why lampshades?"

"I know it sounds silly, but it was something we did back then to have fun." I winked at my perplexed daughter.

"From then on, Mommy and I hung around a lot together, going to basketball games and downtown into Philly to see things like the Liberty Bell that we're going to see later," Scott added, with nostalgic eyes.

For Elliot we reenacted our chants including "Sit down, Pete!" whenever our arch rival Princeton's basketball coach ventured up off the bench. The Palestra was a great place for ball, and Scott and I fondly remembered stashing our books in Rosengarten Library, only to collect them just before closing at 2 a.m. after a game date, complete with a late Double-R-Bar Burger at Roy Rogers and a long stroll through a moonlit Center City. As an insecure transfer from Monmouth College in New Jersey, I also recalled Scott's kind support as I sweated my initial grades at Penn.

The story of my path to Penn and our marital destiny is known to many of our friends though not to the kids. I had been commuting to Monmouth College and dated a classmate. It was a serious relationship, and Andy suggested we should spread our wings. We applied to NYU and Penn. I was accepted to both, and Andy to NYU. Selflessly, he persuaded me to take the Ivy League opportunity (though I barely knew what the Ivy League was). I went off on my own amidst sworn promises of fidelity. Always homesick as a kid and reluctant to venture far from home, some cosmic force propelled me west toward a deeply satisfying education and also to Scott. Just a few weeks after I arrived, I "Dear John"ed the much-too-good-for-me Andy and a twenty-seven year relationship began for Scott and me. I sincerely hope Andy found someone worthy of him. As one friend said, "You owe a lot to that guy." And so I do.

My two weeks' riding reprieve, courtesy of the Penn reunion, was welcome given my latest fall from the Bandicoot. Fruitlessly I used the time to obsess: *is this really for me if I'm so relieved not to ride?* But spring had fully arrived in our absence: the farm radiant in May's monochromatic fashion show of pale to deep greening grass and unfurling trees swishing against too-blue sky, my back and nose fully healed, and my immune system strong again. Bandi and our bursting-with-life trails beckoned like a siren's call.

BOBBI RUSHED BACK from a show Saturday late afternoon of Memorial Day weekend so we could ride. I had a test to learn for our dressage show. After my first pre-show experience at Riga Meadow, I couldn't muster much enthusiasm, but Bobbi summoned enough for us both.

"You'll be fine," she assured. "It couldn't be any more comfortable, our own show at our own barn, totally familiar territory for you and Bandi."

I wondered how a show at my horse's home could be advantageous now at Weatogue Stables and yet was disadvantageous at Riga Meadow, and I concluded Bobbi manipulated the facts toward my greater comfort. But Jane was excited without really knowing why, and once I told a reluctant Elliot that his Cleo really wanted him to show her, he readily agreed, not questioning my pony language powers. Like Bobbi did with me, I was not above manipulating my kids for their own benefit, or for mine for that matter.

I like dressage. Introductory level A and B require walking and trotting a set test pattern, hugging the wall or fence, transitioning smoothly between gaits, changing rein (or direction), circling evenly, stopping squarely and saluting the judge. Sounds easy, but you can spend a lifetime perfecting the intricate details of a seamless, elegant connection between horse and rider. A perfect circle with good form is harder than it sounds. The rider appears to just sit and take the ride: still hands, motionless legs, perfect upright balance of a graceful body void of busy maneuvering. Slight shifts in weight, eyes and thoughts, and wiggly fingers project a seemingly telepathic communication. An equine puppeteer, the dressage rider strives for invisible strings. Done expertly, the judge barely sees commands and simply enjoys the results.

I appreciate the quiet, measured pace of dressage, and the solitary act of me, the horse, a judge and a score. Of course that means judging eyes are on one rider at all times; she'll not miss any mistakes. Placement accrues from accumulated points against a tough standard calculated as a percentage of 100, rather than your ride rated against others alongside. Anything in the 50–60% range is good, 70s get rare, and you want to avoid 40 or below which signals incompetence, a possible risk of injury to the horse, so much so that the judge can actually excuse you: a slam-dunk of embarrassment. If you can avoid that, it is mostly a civilized one-on-one, the only free-for-all occurring at the warm-up when riders share the practice area. But because there is no jumping and because each test concerns one rather than multiple riders, even this progresses sanely.

My hardest task would be keeping my mouth shut. Points are deducted for talking to the horse or clicking the tongue, which I tended to do on a continuous basis at the trot in a vain attempt to keep a steady rhythm. I was a human metronome.

"Remember: no clucking," Bobbi warned.

"OH. Right," I said, getting right back to it after one pass, "Cluck, cluck, cluck."

"Bandi, tell your mother to be quiet.... Bandi says 'be quiet, Mom.'"

Bobbi was now talking both to and for my horse, a veritable equine ventriloquist.

"I can duct tape your mouth," Bobbi suggested.

"Maybe if I chew some gum." I pursed my lips into a cramp.

"Cluck, cluck, cluck."

"Just think whip instead of mouth if he needs some energy."

"Can you tape my ass to the saddle while we're planning props?"

After a few silent minutes: "cluck, cluck, cluck."

I bit my tongue through the test course a few times, feeling accomplished and eager, for once, to return the next day and hack away at it some more. Multi-taskers, welcome—about six or more maneuvers must occur at once, in varying combos: pressuring one or both legs into Bandi's sides, edging one back or forward, not too much, turning one or both feet to employ a spur, or not (just as difficult), shoulders back and down, half-halt with my outside hand (that one rein squeeze and release that keeps his attention), flex the ring finger of my inside hand (or is it the other way around?), reins taut but giving, elbows relaxed (yeah, right), hands at the withers, thumbs up, no unintentional tickling with the whip but no rapier flailing either, no crossing over the reins to adjust for poor lower body action, ugh—(that last circle was an amoeba), left seat bone down, heels down, weight into the right leg, shoulders *back* (I revert to Quasimodo style ASAP), strong belly forward, oops—missed that corner altogether, sit heavy, loose hips, tighten thighs, no—loosen thighs, change the whip gracefully to my inside hand, no sound effects... oh, and my old favorite, look where I want to go. Following the course requires enough intensity of focus to edge out any concern about spooking or falling. The concentration freed me. I toted the test score sheet back to NYC to memorize it, all fired up now about the show, thinking less often about scratching at the last minute. I did not tell Elliot that he and I might compete against one another. This was getting interesting.

After my first official dressage lesson, Bobbi, Angel, Bandi and I headed out for a trail ride in the late afternoon sun. The day ended steamy as

New England's moist spring often invokes summer's heavy heat; only last week we feared frost would harm my family's incautiously planted zinnias, delphinium, foxgloves and tomatoes. We lazily followed the farm's dirt road watching Chase and Q run flat out around their paddocks, bucking, jumping and farting so that the ground shook under our feet. Their wild speed and agility both awed and terrified me, such powerful otherness that we somehow collect and tame—almost, but not quite—that plainly broadcasts horses' retained freedom and strength. I'd rather not see what they can do in their natural state. *Can they reliably sublimate those instincts when we're on their backs?*

We turned onto the wide path that Meghan had mown through the high fields, the hay already ripe for the season's first harvest. Winding through two fields and woods, around the seventy or so acres, we enjoyed the undulations of green-to-golden grass in the sweeping breezes. Birds took wing out of the meadows, swooping to stitch crazy patterns of blue sky and white clouds. Bandi and Angel relaxed on an outing that didn't require concentration or ring-defined circling. Angel's swift walk prompted lazy Bandi and me to trot occasionally to catch up. I chatted loudly to Bobbi, my method to flush any more birds or camouflaged deer and turkeys well before we got to them, but even the bugs respected our peace.

I appreciated this ride as "one of life's wonderful moments" moment: out on my own trusty steed (well, sort of trusty), in a preserved field, on a farm approaching its beautiful apotheosis after more than a year of renovation and impatient questioning, *will it ever be done?* The dirt piles but a memory, all lumpy overgrown paddocks had been leveled off and were re-growing in various stages of baby grass, their tender blades peeking through the hay we laid to protect the seed. Ferns were feathering their tendrils and the trees, young and ancient, were popping open to full-domed shade umbrellas. My attuned senses absorbed every last detail of spring with almost paranormal awareness. Was green ever so verdant, the light ever so lucid? I floated, a light-hearted butterfly able on the breeze. The distant barn stretched long and proud, its fresh paint daring the wear and tear of a new chapter. Though we gratefully intuited Mrs. Johnson's venerable experiences etched within the old grains of these barns and the furrows of these paddocks and fields, our history on this patch of land was yet to unfold; I rode poised between El-Arabia's past and Weatogue Stables' future. *What stories await us? What adventures?*

Loud neighing roused me from my reverie. In addition to Chase, we had recently welcomed two new horses who were playing in their paddocks: OneZi, a four-year-old gelding training under saddle and his sire, Royaal Z, a sleek, twenty-two-year-old black stallion. They both belonged to Sabrina, a keen equestrienne from distant Greenwich, who sacrificed proximity for full day turn-out and a large paddock over which her "boys" could hold dominion. Three more boarders were due. In the early days, Scott, Bobbi and I concluded "if we build it they will come," and they have: lovely people and horses. With Weatogue Stables off to a fine start, I rode the land deeply moved by this rare, storybook experience. It is worth the fear, the falls, the hassle, the time management, the child worry, the spousal friction.

We rounded the bend and slow-poked home. Without warning and in an instant Angel leaped right and Bandi, in unison as if they were of one mind and body, did the same only higher and farther. A beady-eyed turkey head had popped up out of the tall grass inches from Angel's feet and skittered noisily into the woods stage left. Bobbi and I both held on, and the horses quickly settled upon reassurance of hysterical fowl rather than that dreaded equinevour. Bobbi had mentioned earlier that Meghan sometimes encouraged Bandi to chase the wild turkeys from his paddock.

"Oh great, Meghan," I teased. "Just what I need—a horse that races after turkeys."

But Bandi didn't pursue the panicked bird, and I quietly noted that each time Bandi spooked I settled just a bit sooner. During my first Bandi trail ride last summer, I awaited the worst, panic my only mode.

Over time I still worried, but also inched toward acceptance of inevitable "challenges" out in the big bad world of unforeseen circumstances; and, as in life off the trail, sometimes you stay on, and sometimes you fall off. I counted my blessings that I stuck this time, and Bobbi and I congratulated one another. It goes against my nature to look on the bright side, but I did, and the psychology worked... some.

That night, drifting into sleep, I jumped awake in my bed, as we sometimes do when dreaming of falling. But this was a leap, exactly the sensation of Bandi spooking, and it happened three times before I finally trusted slumber. I shook off my inclination to label it a bad omen.

CHAPTER TWENTY

Our First Show

·⟨⟩·

WEATOGUE'S INAUGURAL BIANNUAL DRESSAGE EVENT would take place the Sunday of the June weekend that the kids and I migrated to Salisbury for eleven weeks of summer vacation. Weekdays at the farm and no commuting on Friday and Sunday nights—what bliss. At least for three of us: Scott's work held him to the city, but he aimed for a few weeks off in July and August. It had been increasingly hard to leave on Sunday nights: the farm had morphed into our own Emerald Isle, its viridescence softening any memory of mud, machinery and workmen. It was time to revel in its glory.

Arriving late Friday night, we had little time to prepare for the event. Elliot and I had been practicing our tests the last few weekends, and enough riders had signed on that Bobbi split the Intro categories into adults and juniors. Elliot regretted that he and I wouldn't compete head on, but not me—I didn't want to win, and I didn't want to lose, either. I work hard to improve my kids' skills only to feel geriatric when they eventually best me at everything one by one—chess, throwing and hitting a baseball, swimming, running, skiing, math, riding, life.

Salisbury had already weathered ten days of rain and flooding. Sunday's forecast predicted a washout, but horse events take place rain (barring lightning) or shine. Saturday, practice day, dawned overcast. Since Bobbi was frantic setting out flowers, aligning the dressage rings and gussying up the barn for company, I soloed on Bandi. While last year

I took my maiden fall the day before my first show, this time I rode my test with relative ease. A hard-earned accomplishment: I could tack up, take a ride and untack *sans* babysitter. I knew that Bobbi, Meghan and Brandy kept one eyeball on me most of the time, but they hid it well. Elliot seemed ready too, and though showing wasn't a priority, he is a born grade-grubber keen to obtain a score on which to improve, measuring himself against himself. Generally competitive with his peers, against type he inclined to keep this aspect of his life strictly personal pleasure.

We were rider-ready and the farm was show-perfect—nearly. Despite assurances, Mike let us down: our raw fences stood unpainted though May boasted perfectly dry days. But so much had changed, transformation enough to satisfy even Scott. This time last year the grounds were patched with small lakes and islands of muck, and though Scott and I glared at the dirt piles excavator Kenny shifted around for months on end, we now believed. Our farm drained like the Mohave. We completed the barn by topping the rooftop cupola with a bespoke weathervane of a dressage horse, in full stride with gold-gilded tail and mane above the banner "Weatogue Stables," gleaming in not-yet weathered bronze. Operatic birds repatriated the renewed gazebo, and were relieving themselves with impunity on the flagstones and my new benches, tables and chairs. It does resemble an aviary, and no doubt they pegged us the intruders.

At our house a robin couple nested in the topiary outside the front door. Established before our summer pattern had us banging in and out all day every day, these surprised birds nevertheless stuck it out, keeping their four blue eggs warm. The children and I kept watch to see three of the eggs reveal the sparsely fuzzed, loose-limbed hatchlings. The indolent fourth took two more days to break out. We marveled at their metamorphoses. Over ten days, their naked cowering slid into feathery battles for space and food until, unable to stand their siblings and the close quarters any longer, they departed the nest, one by one. Our housekeeper Lourdes was especially excited. In the Filipino culture, hosting baby birds brings great fortune.

"It's good luck, Mum. Lots of money coming," she said, smiling and rubbing her fingers together.

She said the same thing about the ant swarm that engulfed our patio one day, and then, just as mysteriously, disappeared.

"Look kids: ant world," I said.

"Cool," said Elliot.

"Wow," said Jane.

"*More* money, Mum," said Lourdes, palms rubbing.

I designated these events signs of a prosperous farm, my definition being a break even on operating costs. We lost track of the renovation expenses, not really wanting to know the grand total and having never aspired to recoup these or the purchase price. Some figures are best kept hazy. Almost to confirm my new found stock in Filipino mysticism, another robin, or maybe the same one, reused the nest and reproduced the identical family unit of four eggs, again with three hatching together and the last two days later. Scott rescued one fallen baby successfully, and Lourdes shook her amazed head at the numerous portents predicting our coming windfall.

But deep down I knew that few can coax the economics of a horse business out of the red, no matter how much work, hope and love you expend, or how you fudge the numbers. With the onslaught of bills for everything from horseshoes to light bulbs, I fully understood how Mrs. Johnson's "successful" Arabian breeding farm eluded her in the end. Horses beat up everything. We had already replaced fence boards rubbed, pushed and snapped by horses with itchy butts, gates that crafty horse lips unhinged, metal stall guards that robust chests bent and cracked, countless metal latches and chains demolished by muscular bodies and dexterous teeth, and though I vociferously explained to the offenders that they cannot, absolutely can not chew on the carpentry of their stall windows and doors, they would lift their handsome heads from their labors, look at me with soulful eyes, whinny apologies as I backed away with my pointer wagging, then immediately resume— gnaw, gnaw, gnaw. Fact: a barn is only a heartbeat away from dirty, broken and bankrupt; it takes deep pockets by the owners and constant vigilance by the manager and stable hands to keep it together.

I still hadn't met Weatogue's former owner. Mrs. Johnson had undergone surgery for a brain tumor, and I had hoped her recuperation would allow her to attend our show. I wanted to tell her how much we liked the farm and how well it worked, how right the bones were set and how thoughtfully she had laid the blueprint, how excited we were, how her legacy of horses on this land would continue. I wanted to right my earlier, rash judgment of her now that I personally experienced the challenges of horsekeeping. Yet, I awaited a serendipitous introduction and shied from knocking on this private woman's door, or even writing her a letter. Would she see our renovations as crudely excessive, a recrimination? Was El-Arabia's transformation painful to her or a relief?

"I think she's happy and sad," Bobbi said. "It's hard to let go sometimes."

I suspect Bobbi was shielding me from Janet's verdict on our interpretation of her farm, sensing correctly that the guilt would eat at me: now that I so valued Weatogue Stables' reincarnation, I cared what this horsewoman thought. But this farm was traveling a course that, by necessity, relegated El-Arabia's history to deeper layers of the land under its footprint.

I would regret my hesitation: Mrs. Johnson died ten days before our event. A small service with no calling hours marked her passing. She willed her house to MIT, grateful to the educators who had empowered her to finance her passion for breeding Arabians. In the tack rooms we hung two pictured plaques, mementoes she had presented to Bobbi about the heyday of El-Arabia and her best stallion, Gwasz. I thought of her often when out on the trail gazing at the barns and her house beyond.

A nurse shared Janet Johnson's last moments: with eyes closed she laid on her bed with a full view of the farm. As she could no longer see, the nurse described the farm activity: Meghan, Brandi and Bobbi lead-ing the horses, hips swaying, tails twitching and heads bobbing from the fields into the barn for their dinner in the soft glimmer of a lower-ing sun. A lone whinny; the rhythm of hooves; a human admonishing a horse to mind his manners; feed and water buckets banging; spring renewing. A tear trailed Janet's cheek. Perhaps she was revisiting her own beloved Arabians, her singular favorites, shushing their hungry neighs and impatient kicks. Maybe she was looking into their crinkle-lidded eyes, kissing their velvet muzzles, one hand smoothing a polished neck and the other reaching deep into her crumb-lined pocket for a last biscuit. I imagined she grieved at the possibility of a horseless future, but perhaps the spirits of her husband and horses of old escorted her comfortably on. I hoped she found some satisfaction in another's equine dream that would live on in the beauty of well-kept horses experiencing optimal lives in fields and woods on a rescued New England farm reli-ably fecund with impending summer.

The morning of our show, the predicted stormy weather scattered and the novices rode in a white-grey mist. By afternoon we endured a steady downpour, but only three of the scheduled sixty riders had can-celled. Bobbi's horsey friends shouldered in against the work required to stage a show, much of which cannot be undertaken in advance. The day preceding and the day of, many hands are needed. There are entry forms to organize, entrant numbers to disperse, score sheets to label, alpha-betize and eventually tally, signs to make and post, the prize table to display, food vendors to direct, cars and trailers to park, horses to wash, brush and comb, manes to pull, riding rings to groom, a big barn to clean, port-a-pottys to situate, organizers to instruct, riders and horses to calm, and, and, and. Plus we still had our boarded horses to care for. At 10:00 p.m. Saturday night, I reluctantly left the girls atop footstools at their assigned horses' necks, braiding manes in a quiet calm. Snipped black yarn littered the floor. Mesmerized, I procrastinated leaving their night-check tasks and idle horse chatter, the low hum and soft smell of late evening in a barn.

Near dawn eight hours later the barn pulsed with activity and nervous energy. The first ride was 8:30 a.m., the last around 5:00 p.m. Bobbi perpetually stood ringside to read the test to riders who hadn't memorized their courses (most). I knew mine cold and declined Bobbi telling me where to go and when, aiming for some extra credit. Or so I thought: confused during my second test, I lost points with a wrong turn. Elliot knew that having a reader call the course out loud during the ride is benign score-wise at the lower levels and laughed at my vain attempt to get a jump on the competition.

So before my first ride, Bobbi, who needed to be in ten places at once, was not in the barn helping me prepare. Nor was anyone else. The umpteen last minute glitches kept everyone hopping, and Meghan and Brandy, in addition to calming the boarding horses who didn't thrill to the invasion of their territory, also had to sort out Toby, Angel and Q for their own rides. Orphaned, I decided to buck up and get on with it, nerves aside. Elliot and I had to dress, tack and emerge ready to warm up twenty minutes before our test times. Elliot groomed unruffled and steady, but the uncompromising deadline threw off my timing, and I stop/started several times, first running late, then too early, then a mad rush at the end.

Elliot and I rode twenty-five minutes apart. Bandi and Cleo took good care of us, taking the warm-up and the test as seasoned pros. We did well, earning four ribbons; one first (blue) and one third (yellow) apiece, a compatible tie. I also won the intro level high score overall with a 67.1% averaged over tests A and B. Friendly and encouraging to all riders, the judge, Katie Rocco, took time at each ride's conclusion to compliment and offer pointers. Worthy of her attention, we felt like real horse people. Elliot and I huddled over our test sheets to compare our marks.

"Look, Ellie," I raved, "you got lots of 7s. Your halt was 'very straight and square' and your left circle had 'nice energy.'"

"Wow, Mom. You got an 8 on your working trot, but too bad about that 5 on your free walk—'needs to cover more ground.' And that had a coefficient of 2."

At 11:00, Scott delivered Jane to the barn for her lead line walk trot class, their delayed arrival my idea to forestall their inevitable boredom. We readied the ponies. Jane's friend Keira would ride Cleo, and we wove elegant pink spray roses I somehow remembered to clip from my garden at 7:00 a.m., into her elegantly braided mane. Jane would ride Hawk who, we found by experiment, accepted her under saddle without ire. Into Hawk's wild black forelock we stuck heartier yellow daisies, better suited to his red plaid pad and western saddle. Poor manly Hawk: bad enough to have been emasculated from stallion to gelding, but to suffer a flowered coif as well? Jane couldn't care less that he still owned a Y chromosome. Indignant, Hawk shook the daisies out, but we persevered and enough held to wow the soggy crowd as they paraded the ring. The kids walked, trotted and reversed direction, playing to collective "ooh"s and "ahh"s. Keira's talented posting earned a first, Jane's attentive posture and serious demeanor won her a second, and a tiny boy perched on a big grey took third. It passed all too quickly for Jane, who pouted "That's it?" and wanted desperately to go again. Keira's parents and Scott and I photographed away with full hearts anticipating the memories this scene would long inspire.

DESPITE THE RAIN, IT PROVED A BELLWETHER DAY. No dangerous rides or falls, and the relaxed flow of incoming, outgoing, exercising horses and trailers signaled that our farm made sense physically and could operate smoothly. Emotionally our connection to animals was deepening, and we were gaining strength, agility and confidence, all within a context of hard-earned, gratifying fun. I hung around all day, helping Bobbi, running errands from ringside to the barn, watching the riders and, come evening, lingering in the fellowship of the barn.

As darkness fell, we storied the day in low voices while seam ripping the yarns from braided manes and praising our horses and ourselves for tests well-ridden and a show well-executed. I silently thanked the spirit of Mrs. Johnson and fantasized that she watched from afar. Exhausted and deeply satisfied, we already looked forward to our next show in September.

CHAPTER TWENTY-ONE

The Apotheosis

·⊂══════⊃·

WHILE WONDERFUL IN EVERY ASPECT, the show was only a preview of the delights that a summer hanging around horses and the farm would avail. The heavy construction work behind us, we tackled the domestic finishing touches—hanging curtains in the bathroom, hammering handsome saddle holders and bridle hooks to tack room walls and grooming stalls, hanging Bill Binzen's photographs (which I had commissioned to document the process of renovation), establishing routines, allocating all bits and pieces to their nooks and crannies, and, last but not least, indulging my new favorite pastime of catalog-shopping both necessary and not-so-necessary equine-related accessories. I wallowed in horse- and barn-keeping. That I was still queasy about the riding didn't diminish the myriad pleasures of barn life.

We grew to about twenty horses including the one or two who periodically boarded for a training tune-up or a rest. Hawk, Bandi and Cleo belong to the Bok family, Toby and Angel to Bobbi, and Q to Meghan with Bobbi and me sharing our "lesson horse in-waiting for Scott to ride," Willy. Theo aged 31, Katie, 29, and Glimmer, 27 are out-to-pasture retirees, and Glimmer's owner Big Jane rounded out our stable of full-time workers by early September. That left ten active boarders including our earliest, Chase; the Hanoverian black stallion Royaal Z and his colt OneZi; Symphony, a large, sweet Holsteiner Thoroughbred cross mare; the white dressage master Dutch warmblood Aram; the Danish chestnut warmblood Colombo; and Quarter Horse Eddie who has Cushing's disease and can't eat hay. He wears a muzzle basket to keep him safe from grass-induced tummy upsets when out in the paddocks, along with Hawk who blimps out if left to graze the salad bar all day. We affectionately call them the "basket heads."

There is also the Thoroughbred Monty, the blue-eyed white-muzzled paint Casper, and Chester, an ex-dressage horse that hated Florida but seems content in our New England stable. We nicknamed him "Castanets" for his nervous habit of clicking his teeth. Humble Bee, a racer on rest for a hairline fracture, doubles as a civilizing "buddy" to the young barbarian OneZi.

Already I could attest to the wonderful characters of "horse people," and Scott and I looked forward to hosting all our boarders and their spouses, along with Bobbi, Meghan, Brandy and Big Jane and various service providers like the vet, chiropractor, farrier and dentist to a dinner at The White Hart in September. We had more boarding prospects in the works and figured that growing to about twenty-five horses might enable us to operate without losses. The economics still puzzled us, however: more horses involved more staff, as well as additional wear and tear.

A family of sorts with the boarders, we were patient with one another in getting this fledgling operation through its toddler stage. Our boarders were gracious even the few times things hadn't been perfect despite Bobbi's masterful orchestration of the rhythms and routines of horse life. Rigging a shipshape organization happens according to "barn time" which is warped, and I have never known hours to slip away more quickly, not even in the whirlwind rush of NYC. I was still making excuses to my family for my tardiness returning from the horses, and other pursuits also suffered: tennis (my usual summer sport), errands, biking, and even showering and grooming myself properly. If my many suggestions of barn organization and aesthetic improvements lacked immediate attention by Bobbi, I knew it was because horses, like kids, demand to come first. Barn work never ends.

But I had succumbed to this life that generates such sweet pleasures; showers never rained down more delightfully than after a day at the farm, sometimes riding two horses a day (well, once I managed that), cleaning, organizing, grooming, grazing my horse, swapping and absorbing horse stories. The pure physicality of hard labor brought bone-deep fatigue, but also bound me in a cocoon of contentment. It took me out of my head; I transferred the fruitless static of my worry brain into the tasks at hand. If not necessarily horse-sold yet in the riding aspect, I was certainly barn-crazy. *I could really be happy doing this as work,* I often thought as I filled buckets, rolled the feed wagon or sauntered the aisles disbursing treats; *I've stumbled onto my own animal-based therapeutic program.*

The mini trail rides I increasingly risked became infinitesimally more relaxed, and I forced myself to strike out on my own (facing my fears!), if not through the woods then at least around the near field. Lazy Bandi inevitably dragged his hooves away from the barn and quickened his pace on the return. Everything bothered him—the bugs, the rustling brush, the calls of the other horses from the barn—and his jumpiness ignited mine, which fostered his, which accelerated mine, which re-inspired him and … and … and. But the land lay lovely, and viewing it from horseback allowed a slowed-down, broader perspective. Forward motion without engine or effort is a rare mobility, and the togetherness of human and animal in nature together flipped all kinds of soothing switches: it was quiet, old-fashioned, time-honored, historic, rare and empowering. And something whispered that my forced solo rides would make the training easier. Slowly Bandi and I were gaining a deeper acquaintance. I acknowledged his tics and quirks and he mine. I accepted that fully knowing my horse would take years. I believed he knew me as his "special person" if not his regular keeper.

"Bandi loves me when you're not here, but totally ignores me when you are," Meghan claimed.

"Oh yes. He knows his Mama, don't you Bandi?" Bobbi added, tickling his withers.

Feel-good flattery perhaps, but I appreciated the girls' efforts to center me in the life of Weatogue Stables even though I disappeared weekdays most of the year.

George hacked out several virgin, very windy trails (Scott protested any tree-cutting) through the prickly undergrowth of the twenty acres of woods, enabling us to ride without backtracking and to vary our routes. Our greed for more extensive wanderings knew no bounds.

"Do the horses have to take over *all* the land?" Scott asked testily.

"Well, 'er, they do keep the trails nice and clear for *our* walks," I tried.

"Can't we just keep the horses relegated to the horse farm property? I like the woods wild, the way they were."

"I'll tell Bobbi," I said, disappointed at any barrier to our expanding frontier, not that I was brave enough to travel them with a horse.

But our explorations continued, and the horses pushed at our borders—north, south, east and west. I cringed when Scott and I walked our old trail, knowing that every deeply divoted, muddy hoof print and sneaker tread-jamming pile of moist, hay-flecked manure somewhat offended him. Horses were hijacking his wife, his children, his land and his wallet. And it wasn't long before we regularly saw horses traipse around the alfalfa field out our kitchen window.

"Isn't it lovely to see them go trotting by?" I encouraged Scott to grasp the beauty, the rarity of it.

Silence.

So I became a stealthy trespasser on my own land, adding trails and land-bridges across culverts that Scott grew to enjoy despite himself, or so I convinced myself.

Our alfalfa field rested under corn that year, and though generally protective of every inch of tillable pasture, farmer Duprey obliged us, leaving an unplanted perimeter path that corralled us out of his crop. We delighted in trailing alongside the feed corn that grew eight or nine feet high by harvest, chastising the horses that snatched a leafy snack here and there. Once, Bandi walked the long way back to the stables with a bent stalk sticking out of his mouth, chomping on it occasionally, ready for a barn poker game.

The kids trail-rode regularly with Meghan on foot leading Hawk and Jane, and Elliot loose-reined and relaxed on trustworthy Cleo, trotting and cantering through the woods and fields. The day I mustered enough courage to join them on Bandi was a milestone not lost on any of us and marred only, as Elliot noted, by the absence of Scott to round out the family portrait. It wasn't quite the misty scene I had envisioned long ago—my anxiety hijacked pure pleasure—but it was good enough.

Elliot and Jane had grown confident and skilled in their riding and horse care. Elliot tacked up without assistance and favored his flying mount of leaping lightly onto Cleo while she moved forward from the mounting block.

"Remember, Elliot," Bobbi cautioned each time, "not all horses will tolerate those theatrics." He'd smile devilishly in return: he felt he knew his Cleo.

His jumping over cross rails was attentive yet relaxed, not jeopardized by the occasional fall. He and I shared a lesson on occasion, and seeing him ride the fences so easily gave me the urge to try. And he liked it all, jumping, dressage, trail rides and, since driving a horse was not enough, he also learned to operate our new John Deere electric "Gator" that transported us through the fields from our house to the farm. A cross between a miniature pick-up and a golf cart, it tops out at 30 mph, is serenely silent, and lacks the rollover dangers of ATVs. With Jane gamely bouncing along in the tailgate, Elliot practiced through forward, braking, turns and reverse. I graded him on his safety and skill, and this rite of passage was the high point of his summer. Though he participated in several day camps from soccer to theatre, he also squeezed in barn hours of mucking, cleaning, leading, feeding, sweeping and grooming. I was informed he was an excellent worker, diligent and willing, though slow initially. We raised his hourly rate once he speeded up, as agreed, but often neglected to pay him as he forgot to ask.

Jane didn't fully trust Cleo after her tumble, but forged her own relationship with Hawk. She pioneered his riding-under-saddle career since no one else, not even Meghan was small enough to test him out. Sixty pounds being Hawk's safe limit, it will be a sad day when Jane gains another thirteen. Hawk showed Jane special regard, even though she ponytailed his forelock and took donkey years to clean each hoof. He honored her carefree faith that he would take care of her. On him she learned to trot and post, not easy with his short-legged, choppy gait. What was scary on Cleo became an easy adventure on low-to-the-ground Hawk. Then she actually cantered him.

"Look Mom, I'm galloping holding only the reins..." she'd shout in passing as she craned her neck around at me and still didn't lose her balance.

"Great, Jane, but look where you're going...."

Neither Hawk nor Jane had any knowledge of leg commands so he and Jane worked out their own system. No one ever tired of watching this duo, horse and rider in perfect proportion only small, and most things in miniature captivate.

Spring and summer whooshed past, and all of a sudden we noticed the absence of Jane tears. She was managing to keep her distance from horse's hooves and cats' claws and reliably led Hawk around the barn and out to his grassy paddock all by herself. She logged many happy stall hours with Hawk, two peas in a pod. She was learning the language of horses.

One perfect summer day Jane and I made an impromptu picnic after our rides. Plain turkey sandwiches tasted gourmet to the growling of hollow appetite that follows strenuous effort. The airy shade of the gazebo refreshed us just as I had dreamed it would. Satiated, we gazed at the sunlit paddocks of horses swishing their tails and lunching on the grass, occasionally lazing over to a richer tuft.

"Mama, is there anything more beautiful than this farm?"

I let her words drift on the crystalline air and withheld my tears.

Wordlessly we both understood that no, there were few moments more perfect than right there, right then. The view of well-kept, peaceful horses out in nature, particularly in spring, is among the most picturesque known to humans who have been studying and depicting them since we lived in caves. Their elegant design of graceful power that they permit us to harness creates a beauty of form and function that stirs many of us deeply. Their sculpted musculature, the sleek sheen of the shorn horse and the woolly coats of wintering ones, the varieties of size, color, shape and personality that blended over thousands of years have yielded an exquisite creature humans should treat with more respect and honor than we generally do, whether they pull plows or carry top-hatted riders to the Olympics.

WHEN I REPORTED MY DAY WITH JANE TO SCOTT, he relayed more child wisdom from his own Jane file. An ancient "burying ground" fronts our road: a white-fenced, pine tree-cathedraled plot respectfully tended by the town, with revolutionary and civil war headstones memorialized on patriotic holidays by miniature flags. Jane questioned these "signs" and Scott explained that cemeteries hold and mark the dead.

"Oh, I see," Jane said. "When you want to feel close to them in your heart you go and visit them. You go and stand there for a while and do nothing."

It is easy to cringe at sappy thought and especially language, our taste for sentiment ruined by the cheap sound bites of Hallmark cards and emotion-manipulating movies, not to mention the thick skins of irony we don as armor against cruelty and death. But children's proclamations seem devoid of ulterior motives, pure in heart and mind, unburdened, fresh reflections of what they see. Parenting and nature experiences, when lived spontaneously and in the flesh, can still be authentically moving even within our wary, jaded adult contexts. *Relax the head and listen to the heart*, Hawthorne would say.

Jane and Elliot are still soulful little people, as perhaps children are until by necessity the world grinds childishness out of them. Or, maybe we parent them towards innocence only to relieve them of the privilege so they can cope as adults. Romantic notions aside, I know the farm has helped my family interpret and really *see* nature's beauty and appreciate its twinned gifts of constancy and variation. Tasking within nature, working the horses and the land, engaged me deeper than my hitherto passive admiration. These transcendent moments slow time by encouraging my family and me to set aside our brainy defensiveness and, simply, be. They open us. We brush a universal plain by concretely experiencing the local, the physicality of our landscape. We meld as a family connected to place. The emotion of it can be embarrassing to adults, but kids regularly smother self-consciousness. They make childlike passion fine and real, whether you are six or sixty.

Elliot and I shared some of our best moments sitting on the large rock out by the gazebo with Bandi and Cleo on long lead ropes chomping grass. Sometimes my son would hop up on bare Cleo and lie prone along her sun-warmed back.

"This feels wonderful, Mom. You should try it," he called out, his rein-free arms and stirrup-less feet dangling at her portly sides. I almost did.

Or, all three of us lying in the summer grass with the bunnies in the plastic gated enclosure from K-Mart, stroking, holding and watching them hop and pause to tenuously nibble a blade or two. We debated their cutest parts: Jane liked their twitchy transparent ears, and Elliot could barely stand it when they pawed their faces or cuddled close to lick one another clean. In broad daylight a coyote stalked us as we dawdled in the bunny pen, not twenty feet away. Healthily large, he stared us down until we rose, waved our arms and shouted him off. Jane and I convinced brave Elliot not to track this brazen creature, probably lured by the smell of fresh rabbit. Nature's dark side.

We kept our eyes peeled for the red-tailed hawk that patrols our fields, also hankering after some farm-raised chubby bunny. Eagles had repopulated our area, predators large enough to pick off our dog Velvet without any trouble, let alone two rabbits. Adventures big and small abounded if we widened our apertures and realigned our lenses, and my dream of our farm as a place that instills respect and appreciation for the land, nature, animals and people sympathetic to those ideals had materialized. Yes, I thought, this barn family was easily worth any cost; in fact, the expense began to feel a bargain.

All perfect except that Smudge, our friendliest barn cat had disappeared. Meghan searched and searched, and we could only hope that she would turn up again, mud-streaked and full of encounters we could only guess at. I held off a few days and then broke the news.

"Is she dead?" Jane asked, all eyes.

"Well, I don't know Jane, she could be."

"I bet a coyote got her," said Elliot, intent on his game of solitaire. His stoicism surprised me.

"Maybe she'll still turn up," I said without conviction. "I like to think she found a home somewhere else—maybe even as a house cat."

Shouldn't they be more upset, I wondered? I had planned on our horse business teaching us lessons of living and dying, the circle of life in its G-rated, natural, non-hyped, unsentimental version, and I suppose I got the minimal trauma I bargained for. Weeks passed and no Smudge. We concluded we had seen the last of her black-and-white smudginess flexing her claws into Scott's legs, her skulking through the parking lot, and her scaling the hayloft ladder. We began to talk about Weatogue's favorite kitty in the past tense. I dreaded discovering her as a lifeless lump along our roadside. I began to feel guilty about fostering barn cats. We spay and take care of them, but by definition good mousers are quasi-feral. Shelters won't turn strays over to barns out of concern for their safety, and feral cats murder a significant percentage of songbirds. They can be ruthless torturers and killers and are not native to our country. We had all found mouse wombs around the barn, the only body part Ninja disdained. "Yuck! What the heck is that?" Jane exclaimed as we squatted and peered. Are we exploiting cats or preserving their "felinity"?

ELLIOT TURNED ELEVEN IN JUNE, and Jane, six in July. With age and experience came some welcome freedom alongside the hard facts of lost, sick or dead animals. Elliot's skill driving Hawk persuaded us that he and Jane could responsibly cruise the fields solo. Meghan equipped them with a two-way radio, checking in like a taxi dispatcher.

"Meghan to Elliot, Meghan to Elliot, come in Elliot."

"Elliot to Meghan, we hear you loud and clear."

"How's it going out there?"

"Great."

"Where are you?"

"We're in the woods."

"In the *woods*? With the cart?"

"Yeah. Hawk jumped a log."

Meghan and I concluded they had traversed a stick and that all was well despite our concern for the cart on the narrow, curvy trail. We strained not to meddle, trusting Elliot. For two city kids whose every move is carefully monitored this gift of independence was worth a few gray hairs. And their carefree spirit spurred my memories of my own childhood invincible fearlessness. I envied their powerful optimism; that they had to *heighten* the drama with their imaginations—actually held ambition and capacity for more—kept me from curtailing their adventure. It contrasted all too depressingly to my fear and ambivalence about riding. But the kids' driving inspired me, and rather than give up, I would spend the summer in the saddle to see if I could steel my nerve.

So, I rode several times a week, except in that patch of July when the wall-thick heat had us watering down sweating horses several times a day and scurrying to hardware stores for stall fans to supplement the mammoth but still insufficient air movers in the aisles. In summer we reversed schedule: horses out in the cooler night and back in the barn to umbrella the sun. How serene to visit a full barn during the day, particularly heat weary horses content to relax in the shade and dusty slants of light, turning their broad sides to any slight breeze. Horse lethargy inferred safety and appealed to me, they were too sluggish to agitate or move quickly. I watched horses sleep on a regular basis, many of them lying down.

Before one scheduled lesson, I arrived to find Bandi flat out on his side, catching some Zs.

"Meghan, what do I do? Wake him up?"

"Well, you can... but Bobbi never does."

I looked at my watch: I had limited time. I looked at Bandi. His head rested on the floor in the shavings near the stall door and his protruding belly gently heaved, so I sat down in the aisle, leaned against the edge of his stall and stroked his nose and ears. His eyes fluttered, never fully closing for long, his tail half-heartedly swished away a few flies, and his breathing labored some because his massive body compressed his lungs, but he was mellow enough that my attentions didn't alert him. I admired him dozing, amused by the string of drool that puddled under his hanging lower lip. How charmed I was to be so near a huge animal in repose, and though I missed my ride, I happily traded it for a little piece of horse heaven. I loved my kids all the more having surreptitiously watched them sleep—quiet, safe and at peace, marveling at the design of them, and now Bandi was dearer to me, too.

TWO DAYS LATER BOBBI HAD A SURPRISE.

"Why don't we go into the jump field today?"

"Um, okay, I guess," I replied in my customary conflicted state, game and wary at once.

Our jump field is a larger grass paddock with a variety of man-made obstacles—low and higher white fences, round half-barrels, rectangles that mimic stone walls. These also grace the riding ring but the big difference is in the footing—artificial versus natural. The grass jump field decidedly lacks the soft rubbery dirt graded and pitched to perfection of the ring. There are subtle, irregular gradations that I hadn't noticed; I actually thought it quite flat until I got in there atop four legs instead of two. Lots to worry about: slippery grass, divots and lumps, rocks and wet spots, the menacing tree in the corner, the thoroughfare of woods and brush along the one side, horses running and squealing in the paddock next door, and, and, and....

Negotiating this uncontrolled environment, I half-expected the dump and run. We trotted a few clumsy passes around the jumps. I picked up a canter. Bandi was forward today, excited in this new territory. *Slow down, boy.*

"Keep his motor going up the hill and half-halt on the way down to slow and help him keep his balance weighted behind," Bobbi cautioned.

His motor seemed just fine to me, so I relied too much on the reins, but I was doing it, actually cantering the intimidating jump field, through the divots and lumps, the rocks and wet spots, the menacing tree and the long row of brush, and impressing the well-behaved horses next door so much that I began to relax and enjoy the ride. We had excised the course of all unknowns. I smiled. As I sailed past the now kindly waving tree in the left corner, Bandi hairy-eyeballed a threat, dropped his left shoulder, spun, left me to fend for myself, and bolted like an escaped convict clear across the paddock and through the open gate toward the barn. Feeling the ground shake beneath the entire length of my splayed form, I marveled at the speed and power of receding Bandi's rippling haunches and the glint of four silver-soled hooves as he thunderously fled. *What awesome power,* I thought. *Thank God I'm not riding that!*

Bobbi claims experienced horses know it is wrong to dump their riders, and Bandi's a smart horse. No longer running from the tree, this frightened, naughty child ran from Bobbi and me, evading his punishment. Laid out sideways in the grass, I registered my disbelief at the speed of my fall while taking account of body parts: *Back feels okay, head didn't hit the ground, arm bends, hip works, no pain—stand up, shake it off, track down my horse. Been here, done this.*

I shook out my legs and stamped my feet. Bobbi brushed dirt and grass from my back as we turned toward the barn.

"I hope he doesn't run into the road. I think the main gate is open," I said, as we hustled along Bandi's getaway route.

"He'll probably head for the barn but stop for some grass on the way. You know he's a chow hound," Bobbi assured me.

Meghan came running.

"Are you alright?" she panted.

"Yes, yes. Pride damaged, nothing else," I said, quite the veteran of the dump and run now.

"Where is he?" Bobbi asked, nonchalant, with that same brave face I don with my kids after a close call no matter how petrified I am.

"He stopped to eat some grass before he got to the barn, and Brandy caught him easily enough."

"That's Bandi alright, never one to pass up a free meal," Bobbi and I exchanged a knowing look.

Brandy walked a high-stepping, reluctant Bandi back into the jump field. I squinted him the evil-eye, and his agitated whites flashed in all directions of his jerking head.

"You can't keep doing this to your mother, Bandi. You've been out here before. You're too seasoned for this." Bobbi tugged the bridle at his guilty, frothy cheek.

"Bandi, I'm too old to keep landing in the dirt. I love you, but you have to stop. That tree is not a monster, and we passed it about six times." I talked right into his face, spitting my anger, *mano-a-mano*.

His half-dollar sized baby browns registered cognition of his fault, "*mea culpa*," or so I imagined, and a determined Bobbi did what she had to do. She hoisted herself up and pushed the Bandicoot through his paces, working him tightly, forcing him to focus and snap to. She was stronger with him than I'd yet seen, though nowhere near cruel. At Bandi's slightest boggle, she kicked him hard or yanked the reins. Closely in control, she used every fiber of her arms, torso, hips, legs and feet, immediately body-checking his every excuse to ignore a command. She didn't give him an inch. In this test of wills, I bet on Bobbi. Sure enough, my chastised soldier fell in line. I sat stone petrified on one of the jumps and tried to quell my thumping heart. *Don't piss him off,* I thought, because I knew what was coming.

"Okay, are you ready to get back on?" Bobbi asked after their intense ten minute session. She maintained a firm grip as she halted in front of me. Bandi's wild eyes avoided mine.

"Do I have to?" I whined, knowing I'm the one he must respect.

Bobbi boosted me up, and breathlessly I clambered through some trot work and two canters. Bandi sweated but behaved.

"Okay, bring him down to a walk."

The Good Bobbi showed mercy; it's over.

"Feel like doing a little jumping?" Bobbi added, smiling, as if it were the most natural question in the world. Clearly, she had moved on.

"Um, not really. . . ."

What can she be thinking?

"Will he be okay?" I wanted to be a good soldier, too.

"Let's just do a few," she suggested.

I circled around and trotted the first little jump. Well, Bandi pretty much stepped over it.

"Keep him going, faster trot. *Think* canter, and if he canters afterward just ride him straight to the next jump and stop."

Lacking the much desired ability to disappear into thin air, I did as I was told. I didn't chicken out, but I was so, so close. Internally, my anxiety about anxiety warned me a balk might end my riding career. Admitting fear out loud makes it real and more incapacitating. I swallowed my protest, and Bandi jumped the rails, landing with a quick sideways shift, almost a spin.

"Good girl," Bobbi enthused, "You caught him. He was going to do it again and you got him!"

At first, euphoria: *Yes! I contained him.* Then, *Wait a minute. The damn horse tried to do it again.* I slumped. I lacked the energy to fight this on a regular basis. He was testing, and winning—Bandicoot: four; Bok: one.

"Go around again and take both jumps. Let him canter between them if he wants to," Bobbi pushed.

I managed the two jumps with my heart in my throat, not once but twice, each clearance a little tidier. Bobbi determined it a quality finish. I knew she was architecting my confidence, but I didn't trust its efficacy. In fact, I deflated in the afterglow, having the time to repeatedly analyze Bandi's instinct to flee, how powerfully unconditional it was, and unstoppable. A canter is a cakewalk compared to a bolting horse. The reverberation of the ground as I lay in the grass imprinted my body memory from my scalp to my toes. Bandi's retreat grew to mythical, biblical proportions in my head in the dead of that night; I pictured those chariot-pulling, overly muscular, rearing horses in Italian renaissance paintings, and the frantic-eyed, foaming, bulging-veined Roman war steeds cast in marble and stone. Inhuman power and might—how could I, a mere simpering mortal, dominate it? What right do we have? We deserve what we get.

Normal people don't obsess like this, I thought to my wimpy self at 3 a.m. in my warm, safe bed. *Why on earth am I doing this, and am I nuts to encourage my kids to take this ride on the wild side?* I was back at square one: that green—literally and figuratively—novice that barely made it through the Riga Meadow show after being thrown the first time. Worse, I registered that Bandi's first pre-show jitters dump was not a fluke but the tip of the iceberg. *Why can't I learn to focus on the successes and not be such a chicken shit? What compels me to keep at it?*

I tried to reason it out. Maybe I chose horses the way some people do sports cars as a mid-life crisis go-to: a romantic nostalgia trip of wind-in-the-hair escape to youth and the past. Horseback as an early mode of transportation was central to American historic process and identity. We have always been a largish country, spread out, and before the combustion engine the horse with attachments settled us and our stuff across it, like so many glacial pebbles, enabling us to explore all our borders: "A thoroughfare for freedom beat across the wilderness" as the anthem goes. Sounds good—in a song. Unfortunately, we now are slavishly dependent on Ford and GM. The SUV craze capitalized on this yearning to trail-blaze, and many of us sport over-equipped suspensions gas-guzzling across groomed highways. Thus, our equinous skills have rusted. We like to think we could swing up on the bare back of a wild stallion and yee-ha for the hills like the Native American boy in the animated Disney movie *Spirit*, but even if the romantic mind is willing, the body (the irony to top all ironies as we age) is weak, and a convertible can serve just as well.

Yet riding persists as a psychic, pioneer spirit sound bite from the Lewis and Clark days; a man or a woman on a horse, no motor noise, no asphalt, no exhaust—well, except for manure and methane—through woods, fields, winding trails, over mountains, through rivers, deep into canyons, along impossibly narrow paths on the edges of cliffs. Indulgent landowners even forgive trespassing for the magic of "The Hunt." And our farm's immediate neighbors are delighted through their parted curtains to glimpse Weatogue equestrians crisscrossing their cornfields. They ride vicariously. Not many of us take advantage of such neighborly *largesse* on foot, but with a horse the possibility of borderless exploration is there. And the horse makes all the difference. I rail at the SUV with New Jersey plates rolling through my alfalfa field to shine the deer (though I might have done the same thing in my in-search-for-adventure, property-less youth), but HORSES crushing my tender new grasses, and farmer Duprey's baby corn, render me starry-eyed.

From novels and movies I yearned after those Victorian sidesaddle heroines riding feverishly alongside their *beaux* or to be the rugged, endlessly forgiving horse gal in a Western movie scene involving a sunset, a handsome cowboy in fringed chaps and lots of rough, dusty love: *the way life used to be*. Well, sort of. At least my farm is a legitimate recreation: not a movie cam in sight, no Chaps (the brand)-clad legs riding a taxi up Madison Avenue. For us actual riders that style of glamour is certainly eclipsed—the grime, the falls, the challenging horse, the cost, the just plain hard, endless work—but still the ideal beckons. Tweaking our dormant, tougher core of old, the whole riding *tableau* is delightfully, compellingly picturesque.

The devotion horses inspire is seductive. Strong men have shed plentiful tears upon the deaths of their devoted, hoofed partners. That men weep over their totaled Porsche highway warriors just can't compare. Horse crazy lieutenants under General Patton risked men's lives rescuing Polish Arabians from slaughter behind starving enemy lines during WWII to preserve superb ancient bloodlines from extinction. And most people are gaga even about their all too imperfect, garden-variety nags, as I was becoming about Bandi. I wanted so badly to *know* him, yet the horse species remains tantalizingly remote. Any connection we do manage borders on the miraculous, addicting us greedily to reach for more. That we can motivate all fifteen hundred pounds of them to work with a leg push, and dance with a ring finger squeeze on the reins is quite something.

But motor heads wax eloquent about their reliable, fine-tuned engines, and the convertible cruising west on the open road also is an iconic American nostalgia trip that Kerouac romanticized, and that Thelma and Louise took to a dramatic, postmodern *denouement*. But it really all began with the horse, that long trail ride morphed into the internally combusted escape, our more modern method of going west, checking out the national parks, lighting out for the territory, heading for the hills, going for "it"—freedom or bust. I may never, but just knowing I *can* traverse more rugged, remote terrain is fulfilling, even if I stick to the dressage ring with my imagination trotting me the rest of the way. Unlike us, horses have changed so little. They are the living scrap book that embeds us into our history. How about a safe electric golf cart, you say? Yeah, maybe, but few people with any sense of style, adventure or history would place the cart before the horse.

But this horse business is a challenging quest. The canon is encyclopedic with more "material," physical and psychological, to learn than I could have ever guessed. The latent scholar in me despaired. After one and a half years of pecking, I had barely nicked the surface. The required knowledge is endless, and though I owned a horse farm, I lacked the advantage of the full-time student. Plus I was old with limited years. What I wanted was that youthful thrill again, like falling in love, or being moved for the first time by classic literature. Who wouldn't want more of those highs? Are they still possible for the creaky and stale? Could horses spark those plugs again?

What I got was a good grounding in the basics—daily care, the tack, the bodies, the ailments, the personalities, and the traumas, the risks, not to mention some little bit about the actual riding. I had developed an appreciation of the species based on active acquaintance. Plus, I was surprising myself—the base note in any learning experience—by testing my mettle and staying power. I was, and still am, prideful and disappointed at turns, having to summon bravery and stare down cowardice often in the same day or even during the same ride. And when I hearkened back to my initial anxiety at simply standing in a stall with Bandi, or leading him in from his paddock on my own, I measured progress, and it was rich enough, even if modest, to gratify.

So after my fourth dump and run I knew that I would forge ahead, and accepted that I was both a veteran and a pointless worrier.

I also knew that it would be a cold day in hell before I set foot in that jump field again.

CHAPTER TWENTY-TWO

Summer Wanes

BY AUGUST THE FARM HAD LULLED INTO A LAZY RHYTHM, and with melancholy I counted down my idyllic days. Soon I'd be transplanting myself and the kids back to the hard surfaces and sharp angles of NYC. On one late-afternoon bike ride I felt, with the force of an epiphany, my good fortune of having landed on this particular spot of earth. My customary twelve-mile ride absorbed me like an old friend, its familiarity breeding ever-expanding comfort over the years. Yet it never tarnished: each ride was as sterling as the first. I passed our farm to cruise the length of Weatogue Road—waving to my neighbors, shushing their dogs, mourning the fresh road kill—and hugged the slow, mud-thick Housatonic River along an ox bowed meadow that showed off distant views of patch-worked New England.

Warmed up and breathing deep, I skirted charming colonial farmsteads along sleepy back roads of few cars and manageable hills. The cerulean sky pushed bleached clouds, and the fine air filtered my lungs and thoughts clear and clean. The secretive river mirrored the breezed branches that waved their greetings, cooling me without impeding my forward motion; a whiff of damp vegetation from the fen's deep and the scurry of a startled deer. As I exited a patch of woods, I squinted into a trenchant sun that immediately drew sweat from my arms and back. Undersized mountains spread reassuringly long and low behind open fields, bluish lavender in a gauzy haze: "purple majesty" indeed;

metaphor made real in rock, soil and foliage. Imagine the movement of earth that carved, so definitively, such horizontal and vertical dimension—the flat so even, the hills jutting in exclamation. I felt good. I had already ridden Bandi without incident, and my body, loosened up by his trot, moved younger than its years.

My kids were happily occupied. Jane was at a YMCA day camp paddling the lake, napping in tents and wild raspberry-hunting. Elliot was up in Lenox, Massachusetts, learning scenes from *Hamlet* in Shakespeare & Company's Riotous Youth program. I surged with serenity, a delicious rush. My eyes moistened at the severity of someday departing this town, its landscaped and wild beauty, this farm, these animals, these neighbors; a grief similar to that inspired by the imagined deathbed good-byes to my husband and children. Salisbury as home superseded sheer geography, instilling connections that rendered place a life partner, and I relished its every mood and mourned any transfiguring change. A love of place can feel like family, the parting almost as sorrowful. Soon my drenching in country pleasures would reduce to the weekends, but what a boon. I thanked any God that I shared this blissful pocket of nature's best, even as I railed at its, or more accurately, my evanescence.

BUT MY LIFE AND MY SUMMER ODYSSEY WERE NOT OVER YET.

"Good morning. Would you like to ride Angel today?" Bobbi casually asked as I hurried past the horse-filled grooming stalls to collect my tack.

My head and eyebrows shot up as I glanced around to see who she was addressing. Meghan and Cindi eagerly nodded their heads at me with wide-eyes and toothy grins like Bobbi was offering a magic mushroom I couldn't possibly refuse. Bobbi does not let just anyone test-drive her always impeccably shined, muscularly fit, deep brown mare with the white blaze between her intelligent, long-lashed eyes. Angel's model poise rendered Bandi a frump: sturdily inelegant. My mind spun as she disappeared smiling to collect the proper tack and allow me to recover. My first thought was: *No way—that's expensive, precious real estate. I couldn't possibly....* My second thought was: *Would I stay on that lively, forward creature?*

"You have to do it, Roxanne, she's truly amazing," Cindi struggled to say while man-handling her own mount "Wing" into submission in the cross ties. "Stop it, you brute," she admonished, with affection.

"You'll learn so much by this ride—I did when I rode her," Meghan added, shovel in hand, scooping the manure freshly dropped by Q. "Angel's such a good teacher."

"But what if I mess up? Do something wrong?"

"Bobbi wouldn't offer if you weren't ready. You'll get a good taste of what you're riding for and find skills to use on Bandi," Cindi concluded.

I looked doubtful and stood paralyzed.

"Just do it," they said in unison.

I went for it, mainly not to insult Bobbi who was willing to take a chance on me.

Carefully tacking and leading her outside, I whispered apologies to Angel for my inadequacy with a quick nuzzle before I hoisted myself oh so gently up on her fine body. Because she is so prized, and perhaps because she is a mare, I thought of her as delicate somehow and feared my poor riding might break her.

Bobbi, Angel and I ambled into the ring.

"Have a nice walk around and then pick up a trot. She doesn't need much prompting to get going, unlike your Bandicoot, so the trot may seem a little fast. Don't worry, she won't take off on you," Bobbi casually said as she wandered away to rake up some ring poop.

Angel stepped lively without rushing. Her steady pace relieved any pressure to use my heels or cluck her along. It was lovely, and I immediately sat tall and proud, a real dressage rider. Her trot was equally transporting, purposeful and rhythmic, musically light as air.

"She's so forward and eager to go," I said, genuinely amazed at how push-button she operated.

"She's a good girl, and she likes her work. This is what you should expect from Bandi. He may never get there, but you can get closer to it," Bobbi coached.

I lightly pressed my inside leg to guide her in the corners and along the rail, and she so tuned into the aids that hardly any pressure or rein was needed. Struggle free, I immediately sensed the difference between expecting correctness with Angel and anticipating problems with Bandi. My corners on Angel were a revelation: I was in close and neat, no dragging required. Her impulsion was vertical and bubbly, champagne in a fluted glass, as opposed to Bandi's, flatly heavy with gravity. I could concentrate all my energy on myself, free to maneuver my posture, arm elasticity, calm hands, long legs with heels down and accurate commands. I even began to imagine collecting this horse on the bit.

"She's a model of engineering," I cried. "The Ferrari of horses."

Bobbi instructed me through serpentines and circles—both twenty meter and fifteen, and into a tight conch shell spiral and back out again. The riding was practically effortless.

"I want her. How much is a horse like this? Can I get one?"

Bobbi laughed; no doubt she has heard that before. And I was joking—sort of. I pictured a riding life of ease upon such a gifted horse, and how good I could look with a lot less sweat. But then I remembered why Bobbi disallowed spurs for a long time, and why I had to fall off a few times, and why (besides the expense) I didn't have a super-trained horse: I had to learn to ride, not just sit and go. Only once my legs strengthened and I learned how to use them did she graduate me to spurs and a whip. Only when my arms elasticized to the feel of a horse's mouth, did she fit Bandi with a stronger bit affording me better control out in the fields and over jumps. From falling off, I learned balance, control, concentration without anxiety (still working on this one) and how to anticipate a horse's movements (yeah, well, this one too). Now that I'd gained just enough skill she offered up Angel, who pointed me toward a loftier goal. I saw the prize now, distant and glowing, and Bandi would make me earn it. The girls were right; in forty-five minutes Angel had educated me far beyond what instruction on my graceless lug could accomplish. I resolved a new attitude with Bandi—no longer defeatist, I would expect and pull more out of him.

I walked Angel back to the barn, beaming, and the silent girls slid me a look of shared privilege: sparkling eyes being the best acknowledgement of Bobbi's Angel gifts that placed us in a sorority you appreciate only as a member. Beatific, I couldn't restrain myself from telling anyone it made any sense to. I had been admitted to an inner circle and earned the right to effuse.

"Guess what I did today, honey?" I said to Scott the minute I got home, grinning from ear to ear like a village idiot while skipping around the kitchen. "I rode Angel!"

"So?"

But Elliot and Jane understood. "Really, Mom? Wow, I want to ride her. You're sooo lucky."

Brandy was impressed as was Chip, who dropped by the barn the next day for a quick hello to Bobbi, the wife that he hardly saw anymore.

"Yeah, I'm about tenth now after the horses and the dogs, but at least on I'm still on the list," Chip said cheerily, giving Angel a deep, satisfying shoulder scratch that arched her neck and pursed her lips in pleasure.

"Oh honey, you know I love you, too," Bobbi teased, giving him a squeeze.

They had known each other for ten years, married nearly six, a union plotted in animal heaven. On their first date of dinner and a movie, Chip picked up Bobbi in his mud-splattered truck loaded with drooling, hairy dogs. It smelled of a test—love me, love my beasts—and Bobbi didn't flinch. On their third date she took Chip, who had ridden as a child in France, on a three-hour trail ride. Agile and sporting, she knew he was the one when he called her later that night thrilled that his sweater smelled like horses.

"Guess what, Chip?" I sang. "I I I rooode AAAngel!"

Chip got it. He and Angel have a close relationship. She whinnies at the sight or sound of him and agitates until he nuzzles her. He knows all her favorite itchy spots and regularly enjoys the patented Angel head massage, something the rest of us receive only on occasion and then never with the same dedication. She clearly loves him so intensely I was taken aback when Chip admitted he doesn't care to ride her.

"Whenever I rode Angel, she'd turn this way and that and make all these moves I didn't ask for."

"But you did ask for them, Honey. She's so good it doesn't take much. You ride cowboy style, kicking away out into the sunset." Conspiratorially Bobbi whispered, "He isn't a dressage rider."

They giggled and argued good-naturedly about his riding skills.

THAT NIGHT I TREATED Bobbi, Meghan and Brandy to a delayed celebratory dinner at The White Hart as thanks for their hard work during our first show. I wanted to know Meghan and Brandy better, and I relished a few hours of horse talk cleanly dressed and comfortably seated with a drink and some good food as opposed to the quick conversations held amidst donuts shared with horses over cross ties in a barn.

I was richly rewarded, much more so than they despite their voluble appreciation of a night out. I knew I would enjoy Bobbi's company, sharing the same stage of life, but I suspected the younger Meghan and even younger Brandy might be bored. They have boyfriends and youth; would they just be appeasing the boss? If so, it didn't show. They are excellent young women, possessing a specialized knowledge but also smart, mature, boisterous and funny. They were chock full of interesting talk, and eager to share it with me, an empty vessel thirsty for horse lore. Four hours later we parted, drunk not on wine but on stories of past horses, scary rides, other farms and the rewards of horsewomanship.

We compared horsekeepers to the young investment bankers at Scott's firm arriving the coming weekend as our guests at the Inn. For several years now as a popular annual event, the hardworking, fresh-from-college analysts enjoy a weekend of free food and drink and some coveted days off. Usually Scott schedules a long bike ride, but the increasing numbers and my fear that some of the less-experienced riders would get run over (old enough to be their mothers, I felt responsible), this year we planned a hike up a local mountain followed by lunch at the farm. We invited Meghan and Brandy to the dinner because they were roughly age equivalent if incongruous in profession and lifestyle—horse versus blackberry, breeches versus suits, rural versus urban.

"I'll take them on," Brandy exclaimed after I described their long days at the office in a weak attempt to justify their hefty pay scales. "When they're bored to death in their offices I'll be lovin' my job and my horses."

After my summer apprenticeship, the term "barn help" or "stable hand" seemed a paltry misnomer to the skill sets these women possessed. Like teachers and nannies, they are chronically underpaid. Bobbi and Meghan impressed me not because they lack fear; on the contrary, their healthy dose of it is evident after each and every "episode" with a horse. Fearlessness would render risk easy, working through fear on a continual basis is hard. I told them so.

"Well, no one does this unless they love it," Bobbi said, staring intently into her coffee mug.

"I couldn't imagine doing anything else." Meghan's eyes envisioned offices and subways.

"There's no way I could sit in an office all day or live in a city," Brandy stated with conviction.

I snooped about their boyfriends, teased them about the eligible young bankers at Scott's firm and suggested that they plan a casual jumping demonstration during the lunch under the gazebo. They were hesitant, out of shyness and humility, but I was eager to pit their skills against these machismo banker types. I also had this vague romantic notion of playing match-maker. They sensed my not so deft subterfuge.

"I'm never getting married," Brandy protested.

"Me neither," Meghan agreed.

"Good idea," Bobbi and I advised, two wise old mares hitched for life.

THE NEXT WEEKEND, rain soaked our hikers but slowed in time for lunch. The bankers survived Scott's fast-paced climb despite a late night of heavy drinking and gathered in the gazebo to enjoy the farm scenery. In the ring, Meghan and Brandy exercised and jumped Toby and Bandi to enthusiastic applause. Little did we know, one member of the group, Santiago, had been on the equestrian team at Yale and spent the better part of his Mexican youth around horses. Several years had slipped by since he last rode, and Bobbi immediately sensed his itch to get back in the saddle. We set him up. A little rusty, he nevertheless took a few jumps on Bandi much to the amusement of his colleagues who phone-photographed his prowess with plans to email them around the office. His colleagues truly impressed, Santiago's ride served as a point of connection between the urban and the rural bipeds.

At dinner, the day's events provoked much horse talk. Still charged from his unexpected ride, Santiago discussed everything equine with Meghan and Brandy through the cocktail hour and beyond. Scott and I left to put our tired old bodies in bed as the bankers invited the girls to visit their vertically stacked stables in the concrete and steel paddocks of NYC. Having to rise for the 7 a.m. barn work, Meghan and Brandy responsibly departed while the urban refugees drank The White Hart dry. Scott and I enjoyed merging these two worlds, horsekeeping and financial dealing. We hung out with talented, delightful young people, and it prompted us to imagine what our own children might achieve, be it in a high rise or a barn.

AT THE END OF JULY, Bobbi and I stood by the paddocks, in despair at our still raw fences. The painter never had shown up.

"We should give up on Mike and get someone else," I said.

"I asked around but everyone's booked this late in the season." Bobbi pulled a thorny thistle from the base of a post.

Just then a cowboy-booted, jean-clad, thumbs-pocketed stranger sauntered down the path into Weatogue Stables.

"Howdy, ladies. Beautiful day," he greeted, tipping his hat. "Know anyone with fences that need paintin'?"

Our eyebrows shot north, and we summoned that creepy Twilight Zone music: *doo doo doo doo, doo doo doo doo....*

"Um, yeah," we both stammered. "We do."

Our Kentuckian smoothly "yes maam"ed us into paying his first price, not that we had any negotiating room. Facing another winter of exposed wood, we hired this unknown feller's theoretical crew as the manna from heaven they might be, arranged a fast, weekend cash deposit half expecting a jilt, and crossed our fingers. Our southern gentleman was the real deal: his team delivered the oily black paint and sprayed like crazy, and it was good, except that the horses ignored the "Wet Paint" signs.

For several weeks we dealt with sticky, painted bodies, and good-natured boarders who agreed that happy, outdoor-paddocked zebras were better than cranky indoor-stalled horses. Pints of baby oil helped dissolve the abstract artwork from the horses' faces, butts, necks and legs. No wonder these fences already showed wear, breaking and bending with unfathomable regularity; we now had visible evidence of every horse's scratch, rub and push against them. Late in September itchy-butted Cleo was still managing to find damp recesses of posts and rails, but how wonderful to complete the last major job and finally declare the farm officially finished. And what a satisfying, if latent, transformation: the wood of thirteen large paddocks going almost black from sandy brown outlined, as ink enhances a pencil sketch, our farm's etching. "It's beautiful," our watchful neighbors expressed, and we swelled with pride.

The construction phase of Weatogue Stables drew to a close and so did my glorious summer.

On Labor Day, just hours before my family's annual migration to NYC, Bobbi arranged a swan song summer ride. In preparation for the remaining events of the season, she, Brandy, Cindi and I took three horses to Riga Meadow's show-ready jump field. *Oh-oh*, I thought, *another jump field*. But my summer's work emboldened me. Brandy's new *beau* Jason tagged along to explore exactly what his girlfriend did for a living. I found myself expounding about everything equine.

"I heard you should never walk around the back of a horse," Jason said as I saddled Bandi, tied loosely to the horse trailer.

"Well most people do the exact wrong thing when they do," I explained with some authority, trying to bolster my own confidence and take my mind off the jumps spread across the slippery, uneven grass.

"It's important to let the horse know you're there by laying a hand on his butt as you go around. Don't try to sneak in the hopes of not surprising him." I demonstrated, and Bandi, surprised, scooted forward two paces.

"And the distance is important. It's tempting to allow just enough space to get walloped good and hard. You should either stick really close to limit the momentum of any kick or allow a wide distance that puts you out of reach."

It felt good to recite technique that I understood from actual experience, one that bucks intuition and that I coached myself on many a time. I still fought my inclination to arc that dangerous one or two feet away from the back end, and because my knowledge was so hard-earned, I felt compelled to wax eloquent to Jason, who was as green as me a year before.

"There's telepathy, a communication of touch that develops between you and the horse after a while. You learn how to move around each other—a two-way comfort level that makes it safer."

As I spoke those very words I lost focus on my task at hand, forgetting that I was not in the confines of grooming stall walls with cross ties.

Bandi shuffled sideways away from the trailer and high-stepped his back right hoof down hard on my left three littlest toes.

"OUCH," I cried as I jumped back, pushing Bandi's butt over and pulling forcefully to extricate my foot. Pain sweat instantaneously broke from my pores. I wrenched my toes back but my boot tip remained wedged. Luckily he didn't fully settle, unpinning me as I shoved him away, but not before crunching my toes enough that I assumed they were broken. Nausea gathered in my stomach.

"Here I am explaining how not to get kicked and then I get stepped on." Red-faced, I tested my toes slowly.

"Well, he moved pretty quickly," Jason graciously conceded.

"Yeah, he's quick alright," I muttered, my smug expertise gone. "He's a Quarter Horse, bred to be the fastest horse over the quarter mile."

My toes were bruised, and my pride too, but the humble rest of me rallied. I proceeded to jump five small fences in a row, badly, but I did it—three times. Brandy took the course spectacularly on Toby, and Jason and I cheered (quietly, so as not to spook her horse) her command of the oafish, overly "happy" (Bobbi's euphemism for "dangerously excited") Tobster. But everyone recognized it more as a milestone for scaredy-cat, over-the-hill me, who had previously dredged up any excuse against Bobbi's suggestions of equine road trips in general, and we slid it in just under the wire, the last official day of my summer vacation. Exiting the season on such a high note made it that much harder to ride only once a week and learn at the much slower pace of my kids' school year. There was no substitute for daily hours in the saddle. And in those long winter months I really missed my horse; I mooned over his photo front and center on my bulletin board and day-dreamt of him running, in the early morning light, across the frosty paddocks.

CHAPTER TWENTY-THREE

The Scene of the Crime

·❮━━━━━❯·

A YEAR HAD PASSED since I first showed Bandi at Riga Meadow, where my beginner's luck had won me my only blue ribbon one day after my toss off Bandi, both events hair-raising personal firsts. Bobbi and I decided our barn should enter Riga's September show again.

Bobbi bucked my automatic reluctance to join in the "fun" once again. "This will be old hat now. You've come so far."

She was right. With a full summer of riding under my belt, I was an adequate, if not fully secure, equestrienne. My ride over the jumps on Labor Day boosted my confidence, and though the memory of that first show still weakened my knees, this year I slept soundly the night before and awoke eager rather than a quaking wimp. This time, three members of my family were participating. Jane was hoping to improve her lead line walk/trot fifth of five finish, and Elliot would debut. His four classes and my three brought cantering and jumping cross rails into the mix, so together we faced new territory.

Weatogue Stables was well-represented: early Saturday morning Bobbi trailered our seven horses, in twos, the eight miles to Riga Meadow. To avoid a fourth trip, she wedged the mini Hawk sideways in the tack compartment of her trailer, strictly admonishing Bandi and Willy to behave. Packing for and moving seven horses and nine riders was complicated: in admiration I watched the girls remember everything from Showsheen—a mane and tail beautifier—to treats, crops to bridles, saddles to hoof oil. They had been up since 5 a.m. and at the barn until midnight Friday bathing horses, braiding manes, polishing and organizing tack, but they couldn't fix the weather. Three to four inches of rain fell on Friday. Saturday morning I cut through the early morning fog and arrived at Riga Meadow to find a soppy outdoor ring with two small lakes windrippling at the far end.

"No one can ride in this," I told Bobbi, assuming a collective retreat.

"Oh, this is nothing. You should see some of the hunter pace shows—it's hard to tell the horses from the riders everyone's covered in so much mud. Horse shows take place no matter what."

We found Bobbi's friend Cindi and her niece Kaylee both set to ride, and Terri, who kindly came as groom to choreograph this dance of Weatogue pairs crisscrossing overlapping events. Unlike in dressage competitions, there are no predetermined riding times at hunter jumper shows, only a sequence of classes simultaneously run on two fields that unfold as they may. We had to watch and be ready. Though Bobbi was not riding until late, she had eight riders to baby-sit; being the oldest, I couldn't monopolize her. Elliot and I nodded at our instructions where to be and when and settled into preparation. I paid our fees and from the organizer's tent collected our black numbers on white cardboard that we strung around our waists. I drew forty-seven, my age, which I hoped signaled luck. Elliot helped me tack up Bandi, and we headed outside.

"Good luck, Mom."

"You too, El." I took a deep breath and saddled up.

The grounds were not as busy as last September, the weather good for something at least. My warm-up went well both in the ring and on the slick grass. Elliot played photographer and Bandi and I hammed it up; we laughed and relaxed. During the ring practice Bandi sloshed unperturbed through the water both at a trot and a canter, at ease and willing to go. He enjoyed showing and picked up his game in response to my aids.

Our appearance certainly shone more professionally this time. I remembered those posh kids from last year and stepped up to the plate.

At Manhattan Saddlery earlier that week I had spent a small fortune on fancy new gear from show pads to gloves. It paid off: Elliot looked grown up and handsome in tan breeches, a white collared shirt and his navy school blazer. His smooth skin glowed late-summer ochre and his skill with our horses testified to a vacation well-spent. Our slightly uncomfortable show duds reminded us this wasn't our daily, schooling ride. In vain we tried not to soil ourselves as we groomed.

Later, when Jane turned up after her soccer match, she was equally handsome in beige show breeches, shiny black Ariat paddock boots (I drew the line at show boots for the kids with the way their feet were growing), and a pink satin helmet cover set off by a black ribbon above the visor and little embroidered horseshoes scattered across the crown. I shortened the arms of Elliot's outgrown dark green blazer to Jane's size and splurged on a white, stretch-cotton, choker collared show shirt and pink and black gloves. I gathered her abundant, root beer-shaded hair into a black cotton snood, crocheted and beaded with a rhinestone bow, tasteless glitz in the real world but a nice touch here. Bobbi hunted down an English saddle small enough to fit Hawk, and Jane (no western saddles allowed) and I bet this compact elegant duo would surely win on cuteness alone. But Jane's skills had improved since last year when, on Bandi, she declined to trot.

Alas, looking the part was less than half the battle, and Elliot and I had a rough day. In my easiest class of walk/trot I took a green, sixth out of the seven entrants, the same class I had won the year before. Adding the canter in my next event I improved but broke to an unintentional walk in a tight turn when I foolishly attempted to space myself from the large, looming ever closer, possibly bucking butt of the horse ahead. I placed fifth of seven. I considered chickening out of the cross rails event but gathered my nerve despite having practiced it only twice. Four cross-railed jumps, about a foot high at the lowest point, were arranged across a rectangular course to be taken twice at either a trot or a canter. The direction was given to take the course left, and I usually always jumped right. A wave of dyslexia set in as I reoriented my plan, but at least I would be riding solo in the ring, able to concentrate on myself.

An awkward start: I cut the corner into the first jump and trotted instead of cantered, but then everything smoothed out. Bandi, my seasoned coil of a leaper, knew exactly what to do. I gave him his head, raised my hind from the saddle into my two-point, kept my heels down and my back slightly concave, my head up, eyes straight ahead, allowed him some more rein and, last but not least grabbed some mane just in case my show-off went big. No need to have worried. He gave just enough to clear all eight, safely and, being Bandi, without expending any excess energy. I was balanced and calm. It didn't feel as clumsy or sound as thunderous as it seemed watching previous rides. Bandi's hooves to dirt in the canter no doubt pounded the same gaited *galumph, galumph, galumph*, customary jerking landing and flying dust as the others, but our ride was level, clean and silent to my ears. Once airborne, an exhilarated concentration edged out all anxiety. I didn't stop thinking, but thought fruitfully, a basketball coach would say "I got my head in the game."

We placed second. It was curious to do better at the least practiced task and, newly confident, I wished I could redo my earlier ride to better honor Bobbi's valiant effort teaching me to trot, canter, steer and hold Bandi to those damned corners.

But poor Elliot and Kaylee atop Cleo and Willy! Elliot finished dead last and then fifth, and Kaylee only slightly better. By the end of the second class Kaylee's eyes cascaded tears. Our usually "mild mannered enough to trust little kids and someday Scott on him" lesson horse Willy had morphed into a wild man, strongly forward enough to petrify Kaylee as he galloped the course and preferred not to rein back. To her credit Kaylee kept her wits and hung on throughout. She fared better later in the day with a controlled ride on steady Cleo to high placements in some of the hunter classes out in the grass field. But with Elliot on Cleo in the ring, she kept breaking her trot, and he, already unnerved by his earlier ride, had the added misfortune of following a bucking appaloosa. This naughty pony's antics stopped Cleo fast in her tracks and almost sent Elliot flying over the front of her neck.

As he exited the ring I met him straining back tears. His head was down, his face red.

"Elliot, don't be a sore loser," I chided.

He shook his head but couldn't speak without the dam breaking. I lectured him some as we walked around since poor sportsmanship raises my hackles, especially in a kid who performs brilliantly at most things without much effort. Too quick to judge, I talked when I should have listened.

"NO, Mom. It isn't that. I'm scared. That horse freaked out, and Cleo seemed to be leaning to the right after that and I think she hurt her leg," he croaked.

Cleo was not lame; Bobbi and Meghan would have noticed before he would.

"Oh, Ellie," I said and rubbed his back. How could I not have anticipated his fear given my own that I indulged so readily?

"How bravely you did the exact right thing! You kept your distance from that crazy appaloosa, and Cleo also did the right thing. She stopped and didn't take off or spin. You held on and didn't come off. You were perfect, and her legs seem fine."

Kaylee's Mom was strenuously applying similar damage control not too far away. And I had to admit to feeling a little more sympathy for Kaylee: Willy truly acted the brute, almost dangerously so. Elliot's episode seemed rather small beer in comparison, but then, he's less experienced, and fear is fear, rational or not.

"I'm not doing the cross rails," he declared.

"But you'll be fine in that one. Cleo is such a good jumper, and you'll be alone in the ring." I felt compelled to push him. "It's so much easier that way, just like at home."

"No way."

He stood his ground despite more cajoling. Bobbi and I trusted Cleo implicitly, but we weren't the ones riding her.

This was a tough call as a parent—do I let him off the hook or recast him for another try? On the one hand, ending on a sour note could bode poorly for his riding future and confidence in general. On the other, due to a cold his batteries weren't full strength. But I suspected he would perform better, and if not, getting through is almost always better than quitting…unless of course, he got hurt, a possibility more likely with revved up nerves. I chewed my lip considering, while Elliot wiped his eyes. My gut: *get him through the cross rails class*; my heart: *give the kid a break*. I defaulted to some tough love that had worked for me once before and that I incidentally discovered by losing my patience. Instead of pushing, I pulled.

"Okay Elliot, you're right. I'll scratch you from the event. What's your number?" I spoke in neutral tones and reached for the number strung to his back.

He twisted away from me. "No, Mom…Wait. I'm gonna' do it."

He was digging deep for confidence. I knew that effort.

"Let's scratch. I'm not sure you're ready."

"NO, MOM. I'm gonna' do it," he shouted, annoyed.

Angry is better than scared, I thought.

I paused, to help him really want it.

"Okay Elliot. I think you're making the right decision, and you're going to be fine. Take some deep breaths and keep your heels down."

Elliot took third place and Kaylee second. I considered both solid victories given the pre-game show, and though Elliot downplayed it, he smiled more and accepted the congratulations I sincerely piled on. We agreed that scratching his last event, the pleasure pony group class, was a good plan. Taking this breather, we relaxed. Almost immediately Scott arrived with a tearful Jane, fresh from her first soccer game with a bee sting on her finger. Her puffy face as she piggy-backed Scott dramatically expecting a sympathetic fuss, sent me reeling: *Oh no*, I thought. *I cannot deal with another fragile child right now.*

With hours before Jane's event, a rest and lunch revived us. Scott took a drained Elliot home while Jane retold her yellow-jacket tale of woe to her barn friends who turned up to support her and the beloved Hawkster. Soon I had five or six girls with me in Hawk's stall, grooming and firing dozens of questions about the next procedure. At one point I believe the girls levitated our poor mini, picking all four hooves simultaneously. But Hawk bathed peacefully in the attention and nobly suffered their ministrations, always the perfect gentleman.

Hawk and Jane elicited audible admiration as they approached the ring, captivating even this veteran horse crowd. With a screen star grin Jane directed leader Meghan to walk, trot and canter her and Hawk around the field to warm up. She knew all eyes were already on her. It was her big moment: this time she was ready.

Eight entered the short stirrup walk/trot, a big group. And they all looked perfect—girls with pink satin-ribboned braids and polished ponies; blazered boys atop over-sized, sweet-tempered horses; trusted trainers leading them who, along with the judge, couldn't help but serially smile. This low pressure respite of pure enjoyment was appreciated by all. Allotted ample time to circuit, the kids reversed direction and received individual, studied attention from the judge. Their serious faces registered the import of their precious time under her professional gaze. Jane maintained her bolt-upright posture and, in her new show duds, posted like she'd been born in a saddle. With heels down, her head and thumbs up, and all silliness gone, she slightly frowned in concentration as Meghan subtly prompted her. So impressed by her gumption, confidence and beauty, I blinked back tears of gratitude that I made Jane.

"All line up, please," the judge commanded.

Janie gave me a not-so-surreptitious thumbs-up and a toothless smile that overflowed those threatening drops down my cheeks. *Can't she stay this age forever?*

The judge walked the line and took up the blue ribbon.

"First place goes to Number 48, Jane Bok riding Miller's Red Blue-eyed Hawk."

Our sizable Weatogue crowd cheered, and all arms collectively shot up into the air. I pumped a double thumbs-up to Jane who clutched her blue ribbon and her embossed winner's cup with the pride of knowing she had nailed it. Exiting the ring into her bevy of admirers, she glowed until sundown. It was Jane's moment alright, a highlight in her little life so far, and a reparative end to our show day of ups and downs.

On the whole, Weatogue Stables performed well, sweeping events out in the jump field with Cindi on Bandi, Bobbi on Chase, Kaylee on Cleo and a jittery Brandy debuting on Toby. Only Meghan trailed, finishing dead last on Willy in her only two events. This bit of news helped cheer Elliot who learned that even experienced riders have bad days. We also learned, from Willy's behavior, that a good lesson horse does not necessarily make a good show horse. All told, we returned to our barn happily depleted with arms full of ribbons.

Yet the rewards ran deeper than satin medals. The effort involved just to get there was immense (only five miles away for about nine hours but it may as well have been further and longer), loading up horses, equipment, outfitting ourselves body and mind: and then to actually compete—multiple animals, fifteen rides, the emotional roller coaster. To emerge whole at the back end of such a unique and thorough sensory experience exponentially satisfied. Winning was fun, and we plumbed those moments when they came our way, but underneath I settled on the firmer foundation of vocation that matched, even exceeded both the logistical hassles and the thrill of victory. The shows periodically and publicly marked our progress with our horses, yet there would always be more, harder work, not always under our control. And this day-by-day, side-by-side effort was both the whole point and a large part of what Bobbi meant by "if it was easy, it wouldn't be much fun."

Already Elliot, Jane and I understood it is all about spending time with your horse and going for your personal peon best in this sport of

kings. Experienced equestrians around our farm talk about each ride—
what went wrong, what right—and their horses first and foremost; their
placement, if it is mentioned at all, is an afterthought. "We came in last,"
someone will say, "but my horse didn't break the trot and was soft in
my hand the whole time." For our crowd, at least, the shows are mostly
an excuse to justify our horsiness, the internal, self-indulgent, intensely
compelling gratification of it, both to ourselves and the outside world.
If we bragged about a first or a second, it was always underscored by the
fact that it speaks more to the hours in the saddle, the collective years and
decades spent grooming and befriending your horse, the truly enchant-
ing "work" that surrounds those few minutes of judgment. Once hooked,
you're done for. But, don't lean upon accolades. More process than result,
any winning goes hand in hand with more losing. Few people who do not
actually participate themselves will ever really understand the compulsion. You'll probably alienate family and friends. And forget the money.

By evening our road trip was far from over: all hands were enlisted to
unload, clean tack and unbraid manes. The rest of the horses still wanted
their stalls cleaned, their dinners served, their fly sheets fitted and their
escorts out to paddock. Though exhausted, no one complained. The not-
to-be-rushed culmination of a show day was praising, feeding, grooming
and turning out our show companions into the late summer night, and
rehashing the events—our fears, revelations, disappointments and surprises of the day as the crickets chirped and the sky embered down from
orange to dark night blue.

As I drove home, I acknowledged that my nerve had been returning
over the last several weeks; that now I honestly looked forward to riding and began believing in my own invincibility again; that I could fall
and not paralyze myself; that Bandi was more steady when I was confident; that I could catch him in the dump and run and would improve
with practice (after all, Brandy, Meghan and Bobbi managed him); that
it was foolish to waste this rare opportunity to really know horses by
dwelling in a state of fear. This was not racing or bronco-busting but

well-executed, measured control of carefully-trained animals. My perceived huge boulder of risk chipped down into more manageable rocks. I envisioned grinding them into smoother pebbles, maybe even innocuous sand. An endless beach, years of riding pleasure stretched ahead. I looked to that distant horizon and settled in for a long trek.

THE NEXT WEEK WE HOSTED our own second Weatogue Stables dressage show, pretty much a repeat of our first in June but doubled in size: two rings and two judges. Once again we skirted the predicted heavy thunderstorms and lashing wind with only mist, humidity, and a few brief downpours. A cloud-burst during my first ride rocketed Bandi through our free walk, the section of the test requiring a slow, relaxed pace and a loose rein, usually Bandi's best mode that I expected would boost my score. Elliot, Jane and I all moved up to training level this time, and we rode well, but not great.

By the end of the day I had a hard time recalling exactly where in the middle of the pack Elliot and I placed, but my memory remained scored by other details of a great day—Elliot's controlled canter into the corners and his circular twenty meter circle (one of the hardest skills to perfect); Jane's confidence on Hawk and the kisses she lavished on his neck with her friends all gathered around; the focused faces of the young Weatogue riders working their skills and Meghan's pride watching them; Bobbi, as conductor, centered between the two rings calling the tests as needed and, by walkie-talkie orchestrating every aspect of this complex ballet of a show, grateful for the coffee, coke and water we ferried to keep her going; the lively movement of riders, horses and spectators shifting between the barn and the ring; all this against the lush green backdrop of a renewed farm.

I had arrived at the barn by 8:00 a.m. and planned to return home after Elliot's last test at 1:30. By 5:00, I still could not drag myself away from the afternoon's higher level rides. The heavy weather had ceded to bright and breezy, with a nodding sun glinting rays off the few top-hatted experts strutting their regal paces around our well-draining, not-soggy ring. As masterful horses fancy-stepped their distinct silhouettes against the stadium wave of the luxuriant maples, a few of their leaves portending autumn, I mourned this coda to a transformative, vanishing summer. I draped my bone-tired frame over the fence, cooler now in the long shadows of the day, intently watching the exquisite *pas de deux* that years of fine-tuning can cast between horse and rider. Looking into both their faces as they waltzed past I saw such utter concentration coupled with their stately strides, human and animal confident in their abilities, and in tune only to each other. Their eyes may have stared vaguely out, but their focus was turned deeply inward, monitoring and refining every body part and its movement, their very skin alert, striving for grace and accuracy in the spaces between every second, and in the air between footfalls. Their wordless communication of thought and motion energized through seat, legs, fingertips, muscles, bones, sinews and brains was so compelling that I already yearned to be back up on my horse so, together, we could do better.

As I reluctantly turned to my car and the pull of home, Meghan unabashedly paraded Angel around the grounds in the green fleece "Weatogue Stables" embroidered cooling sheet that they had won as a team in June. A preening close to our successful event, her "billboard" promoted both our farm and Bobbi's accomplished horse that Meg had just ridden at a high level test. They both shone in the sun's golden beam. I was filled with goodwill and sheer joy as they passed by.

"Show off," I teased, and then sincerely noted, "You two looked great out there."

"Oh, I made plenty of mistakes, but she's teaching me," Meghan humbly replied, patting Angel's sleek neck. She slipped me a sideways smile that transmitted our shared, silent gratitude for this horse life.

"Wasn't that you and Bandi cantering in the field all by yourselves yesterday?" she asked with a nod toward our back pasture.

"Yes it was," I responded proudly, "just Bandi and me."

CHAPTER TWENTY-FOUR

End Tales

·◁══════▷·

IT IS ALWAYS SOMETHING WITH HORSES, usually something that costs money. Just when I thought I had purchased all possible *accoutrements*, more treasures tempted me. The basic must-haves—bridle, saddle, stirrups, a pad and a spare whet my appetite for the irresistible and just plain fun—that fifth saddle pad in mint green with diamond quilting, duotone piping and micro-tricot lining that wicks away moisture, or the baby blue anti-pilling, breathable polar fleece cooler designed with a tapered chest and hook and loop closures for a close fit that matched my riding vest. A sucker for all the cleverly advertised "necessities," that I coordinated my clothing to that of my horse was vaguely disconcerting. But who could argue for trapped sweat, a poor fit, weak fabrics or careless color combinations?

I figured I had Bandi pretty completely outfitted, but then he changed shape. His expanded girth shouldn't have surprised us: all summer his head inclined toward the grass, unlike his comrades who occasionally came up for air, and as a result my gently used Pessoa jumping saddle "bridged" Bandi's shoulders causing him to shudder these weird spasms when I tacked him up. Bobbi consulted "Wolf," a robust German saddle expert to determine whether we could "reflock" my old saddle, but the verdict was a thick "Nein!"

I had discovered the comforts of a dressage saddle during my Angel ride, so I shopped for two new saddles—at several thousand dollars a pop. Either I ante up or put Bandi on a more restricted diet. But we had already cut him to a cup of grain a day, slender rations for my poor boy who lived for his chow. It broke my heart. They term such horses "easy keepers" but I would prefer a metabolic machine able to put away the groceries without portliness, one I could lovingly over-feed with the best of Jewish mothers. To certify that Bandi's pudginess did indeed derive from gluttony, we tested for Lyme disease and a thyroid problem.

"Good news and bad news," Bobbi said. "Bandi's tests were all negative. He's healthy—just fat."

"Oh no," I replied, fearing the next slimming step. "He'd be so unhappy as a basket head."

"Let's just hope he trims down over the winter."

"I thought your motto was 'fat and happy, lean and mean,'" I joked.

"Yeah, but cellulite is rippling on his neck." She pinched his inches. "There *is* a limit, you know."

"Policing food is hard enough with my kids; I was hoping I'd get to indulge my horse." I patted his padded rump and sighed.

So my education continued. Bandi and I settled into a compatible relationship, and our trust deepened. I began to physically manage, not just intellectually understand, that he calmed when I calmed, and I aimed to maintain this virtuous circle. Sensing my budding confidence, Bobbi lobbied me hard to join her on an upcoming hunter pace. While I felt more inclined than before, I still chickened out. This horse business is a marathon, not a sprint. As with Yoga, there really is no *there*, there, and it takes "many lifetimes" to attain "expert." Almost every trainer I meet still works with one more experienced. It is nice not be in a hurry for once; so much of my daily existence is taken at a gallop. Elliot however, thrilled at the idea of a pace, so he and Cleo ran wild with Bobbi and Bandi, taking a very respectable team sixth. All four love to canter, and I consoled my ego with the facts that Elliot made a more sporting companion and Bandi had more fun under Bobbi. I envied Elliot's spirit of adventure and did not want him to leave me behind, but was proud of his courage and his growing passion for horses.

Janie forged ahead as well. Bobbi rescued a "free" pony—an oxymoron if ever there was one—named Peaches. Bobbi just can't help herself when it comes to sad-sack cases, and I thought that Peaches looked the wrong side of useful. At eleven hands, our new pony fit in between Hawk, whom she outgrew, and the nearly horse-size Cleo. Although ribbed and mangy, Bobbi espied an inner-Peaches, a sandy blonde dappled cutie with a long mane and matching tail the peroxide color and texture of Barbie hair, an attribute that endeared her to my daughter and set me wondering whether the dolls were manufactured with real horsehair. To seal the deal, Bobbi outfitted Peachy with a pink halter and Jane with a matching riding crop in the shape of a glittered hand that sparkled in the sun.

"I don't have a daughter," Bobbi justified, "so I get to spoil Jane."

Peaches needed serious TLC, but she was sturdy, had a promising trot, and was supposedly good with kids. Elliot and Jane immediately adopted her into our Weatogue fold, so I hoped for the best. Our family grew—we added ponies in between our ponies.

Petite Meghan was just slightly big for the job so Elliot first cantered and jumped the rehabilitated Peaches to test her fitness and safety for Jane. How exciting that Elliot's broadening skills enabled him to play the trainer. We joked that Peaches "breezed" (track-speak for a short speed test) the same day as our resident Thoroughbred racer Humble Bee breezed in her return to Belmont. Both performed admirably. Soon Elliot and Jane were regularly playing tag on horseback, a strategic game that Meghan introduced to develop balance, steering, speed and brakes. The ponies undertook all with equanimity.

Bobbi kept life interesting at the barn. Jane and I looked forward to our first "bling" party, right up my material girl's alley. Barn friends were invited to arrange beads and jewels into patterns that Bobbi's crafty friend Cynthia would encrust into leather brow bands for our horses' bridles and into matching belts for us. *Who thinks this stuff up,* I wondered?

"But Bandi is a boy. Well, sort of still a boy," I protested, disappointed because it sounded like so much fun.

"Doesn't matter," said Bobbi. "Pick masculine colors. Toby has one."

So I brought a chocolate mousse cake from The White Hart, and Bobbi cooked up her famous chili, and while Scott and Elliot kicked off the first ice-hockey practice of the season, Jane and I ran back and forth to test out variations of color and style across the brows of our dozing, unimpressed horses, creating equine jewelry in the company of new friends in the cozy tack room.

Oh, and the best news of all: a minor miracle, really. On Friday the thirteenth of October, Bobbi was driving home after night check. A half mile from the barn a black-and-white blur sped across the road.

"Can't possibly be . . ." she thought, but stopped her truck to climb out into the darkness.

"Is that you, Smudge?" she called. "Here Smudgy, Smudgy."

An approaching car allowed her one more cat call, though she already convinced herself she was mistaken.

"Smudge? Come on now."

As she started to withdraw into the warmth of her truck, disappointed yet again, a meowing Smudge emerged from the tall grass and into her arms. Bobbi returned to the barn cottage and surprised a pajama-clad Meghan with a joyous, midnight reunion. Thin and hungry enough to scarf down a can of food and look for more, Bobbi warned an effusive Meghan to go easy. The next morning Bobbi called our house bright and early.

"I have great news but I want to tell Elliot first," she sang happily.

I passed Elliot the phone and stood by, all ears.

"You're kidding. That's *awesome*," Elliot shouted, smiling broadly. I ran to the extension to hear the whole story.

After we hung up, Elliot repeated it to me again, and we picked over the details before sharing them with Scott and Jane.

"You know, Mom, I would often cry about Smudge at night before I went to sleep," Elliot admitted.

I am not sure what mortality lesson this taught us, when the dead resurrected. But we willingly took the boon. Smudge moved in with Meghan, a cottage cat now much to her chagrin, since we could not convince Scott to add her to our house family. If Smudge couldn't meld with Boomer and Meghan's eclectic gang, we would find her another good home.

Speaking of home, our neighbor Ursula finally rebuilt her house and returned Thanksgiving of '06, fifteen months after the fire. Rumor had it she wasn't happy, but how can a two-hundred-and-fifty-year-old school house and forty years of living in it ever be recreated? She and George had a falling out, and he relocated, but continued to keep up our yard work. In late January '07, I heard Ursula was in a nursing home battling cancer. I bet against the disease.

Also in January, Weatogue Stables suffered two, this time irreversible, good-byes. Katie, an out-to-pasture thirty-year-old mare, lay down in her paddock for several hours the day before our first real cold snap of the winter. The girls pulled, slapped and pushed to get her up, but she reclined again in the barn, in and out of mild distress throughout the night. Meghan spent the first night with her, and Bobbi the second, walking her around the indoor ring in the wee hours to give her a fighting chance. By 5 a.m. she died peacefully in her stall. Katie's next door neighbor, Meghan's Q, uncharacteristically dumped all his manure close to their common wall as if, by keeping his back to Katie, he afforded her privacy. Bobbi warned off all the two-legged boarders, borrowed a truck and recruited Big Jane's husband and three more guys for muscle to remove Katie for burial along a picturesque, wooded border of our farm.

It is neither a pleasant spectacle nor an easy task to move such bulk, but they managed with all possible dignity. As much as my family would mourn Katie, I remembered that Bobbi's daily, loving care had spanned fifteen years. And Barbara had owned her for twenty-eight, longer than many marriages I know. Purchased as a two year old, Katie went consistently lame at sixteen, and Barbara secured her a top retirement, first with Bobbi and then with us. We appreciated her gentle spirit and often acknowledged that she would have made a perfect mother. Peaches, her most recent paddock mate, thought so too: she ran the fence line for two days looking for her.

Two weeks later, in the midst of the bitterest of cold spells, Bobbi had to put down old Theo, her one-eyed rescued Thoroughbred. Young Theo's first act of gratitude upon moving in with Bobbi was to repeatedly buck her off, so she quickly retired him. Despite his failure as a riding companion, she lovingly maintained him for over fifteen years. Theo coughed persistently all winter with Robitussin getting him through, but soon after Katie's death he stopped eating. Hand feeding him carrots and grain did not tempt, and his nose oozed green gunk. Disoriented and increasingly miserable, Theo convinced Bobbi he was done with living. She led him in his last walk across the pasture, telling him he was a good boy, stroking his neck and offering him treats. The vet administered an injection, and he crumpled into his pre-dug grave. She arranged his body and said good-bye. Thirty-two years is old for a horse, but he was appreciated to the end.

Grieving Bobbi thanked me for having allowed Theo a room at the farm in her company amongst the Weatogue action. We all grew fond of the old man, and he alone owned the privilege of trekking back and forth from paddock to barn untethered, moving along at his own pace, occasionally side-stepping off-parade for a look-see elsewhere. Some loud calling of his name would bring him back in line. Bobbi, Meghan and I believed he died of grief at the loss of Katie, his companion of fifteen years, but the vet pegged it more likely age and the weather. I wonder. Old people seem to die off in the winter, but they also tend to follow their spouses. The pain of such parting I am beginning to comprehend: after twenty-five married years, Scott and I both acknowledge that once old, we would choose to die first rather than be left. Happy trails, Katie and Theo.

Epilogue

·⬡━━━⬡·

NEARLY THREE YEARS HAVE PASSED since these events took place. The barn is comfortably broken in and well-gnawed. Weatogue Stables is full with thirty-five horses in residence, only two stalls empty. We would break even as a business if Bobbi and I could only stop sprucing up the place. Much to Scott's dismay, we've added run-in sheds for each paddock, mirrors to the indoor ring (so riders can check their positions), and exquisite, though extravagant dust-free outdoor footing that cushions the horses' legs and doesn't pollute the trainers' lungs.

Bobbi probably misses the early quiet days as I do, the times when she had time to think and I knew well all the horses in residence. But the farm bustles with good-natured people and creatures, though early friends have come and gone. Brandy and Jason went west to California. Big Jane went back to gardening. Meghan chose to sleep in mornings, waitressing nights at a local restaurant. Old Tuxedo moved on with Meghan and shortly thereafter his marathon life finally expired. Currently two abandoned black-and-white cats cower in our tack room, in training to join Ninja as barn cats. The sisters hiss in fright (who knows what their histories held), but we await their trust and are patient in their rehabilitation.

Our staff has grown to eight, and we welcomed tall, lissome Jen as assistant trainer, along with her massive, handsome, black rescue Don Nero. Seventy-something-year-old Arthur puts us all to shame with his strength and energy, and dedicated, can-do Juan from Mexico lives in the cottage. Our caretaker George slowly drifted away. Ursula survived many setbacks, but in true Yankee fashion came back swinging. She is back in her new house and recently called the contractor to shout "I'm not dead yet, so I need some bookshelves!"

We eventually purchased Mrs. Johnson's house from her estate, fixed it up and rented it to one of our boarders, Heather, ensuring a horse friendly neighbor. We saved two wooden couches from Mrs. Johnson's place to remember her by, which now hold pride of place in the center of the barn. For the cushions I splurged on Ralph Lauren equestrian print fabric, my thoroughly impractical nod to the ideal aspect of my dream—probably as close as I will get. While we are ever too busy to sit, Jen's aging terrier Jenga and Juan's new rescue pit-bull mix Cody embed the polished cotton to snore away the afternoon hours. When Heather moved in across the street, her younger corgi, Buddy, abandoned his family for AWOL adventures across the street. A third to Jenga's and Cody's brat pack, such happiness radiates from "barn Buddy" that even Heather smiles at his disloyalty when she arrives to drag him home to be "house Buddy" each night.

Yes, Scott just rolls his eyes at the new footing, the mirrors, the dog-draped Ralph Lauren couches and the revolving door of in-need animals. Yet he did accept, if not quite welcome with open arms, another house pet. On horseback last November, Bobbi found a starving, shivering kitten with an ugly abscess on its neck in the manure pile at the edge of the back field. He freaked out in the car en route to the vet and bit Meghan who promptly named him Spaz. He is polydactyl, otherwise known as a Hemingway cat, with twenty-five toes. Despite his travel aversion, his social intelligence stole our hearts as he recuperated and grew large in the tack room. In December, we took him home to New York, and he has been with us ever since.

While Spaz made the cut, Bandi did not. In January 2007, the day Barbaro died, I decided to find my horse another home. Just after I bought those two new, non-bridging saddles! But the Bandicoot subjected me to three dump-and-runs in one session of riding, and though I stuck them all, the salient fact was that this awkward dance between the two of us was not going to go ballroom. He is a jumper, and more and more I was staking my claim in dressage. Bandi hated those endless circles going for elegance; he needed release across the fences and through the fields. Though he had made great strides in his suppleness, he would never be a happy dressage horse. Terrific in so many ways, he deserved a loving owner who would work him to his skills.

I didn't know if I could actually part with Bandi. The week after my decision I visited him in his stall. Leaving his hay and walking right over, he nuzzled me in recognition. He knew, after our year and a half together, that I was his special, if often absent, "little person" (as Meghan termed horse owners). It is agonizing to send an animal you love into the unknown. We toyed with leasing him, but Bobbi made a few calls and found two young girls who appreciated him. At a financial loss, but content with the barn and trainer that Bobbi knew, I let him go. The two girls feel lucky to have him. He has not misbehaved; thus, I conclude he is happier leaping with the young and nimble. We keep track of him, and I maintain a contractual right of first refusal against a sale as a way to control his future.

Still, it was tough. Pitying my turmoil, my hard-boiled husband said: "Would it help to keep Bandi *and* get a new horse?"

My heart swelled at his indulgence, but I was thinking just the opposite—instead of two, perhaps no horse. I even sported a new sweatshirt that read "I do not need another horse, I do *not* need another horse, I do *not* need another horse." So what did Bobbi and I do? Bought the first horse we looked at. But this time the connection was immediate: like in love, I just knew. That his birthday is the day before mine surely was a sign. Leonardo (sire Michaelangelo, mare Durona) is a highly schooled, fourteen-year-old Dutch warmblood gelding that Bobbi will be riding at Prix St. George level this summer. A bay with a white star, he is all sweet lover boy who, when I lower the stirrups before mounting, places his head on my shoulder so I can kiss his closed eyes. Though a fancy dancer surpassing even Angel, he generously teaches me the basics and trail rides safely. I have had him a year and a half; I haven't come off him yet, though I expect I will. But I'm not too worried: when he startles he takes me with him—a sideways little leap, not too fast—and he never bolts. He does crib: that is, he chews on fences and rails to intake air for a quick high, but nobody is perfect. I love him more each day.

So I plowed into dressage with my new vehicle. There are six levels to reach Prix St. George, a respectable halfway house to the top, or Grand Prix. Within each of these early levels are two to four "tests" or courses to be followed to the letter, literally: black letters posted around the dressage ring designate direction for maneuvers of military precision. From Prix St. George, there are two levels of Intermediare to perfect before glimpsing the territory of Grand Prix, a rarified atmosphere few horses and riders get to breathe.

By the fall of '08 I had worked through Introductory and Training levels, more or less to satisfaction, only to be confronted by a major fact that I had somehow, despite my saturation in horse, missed.

"What do you mean all trotting is done 'sitting' at the upper levels?"

"That's right. There is no posting after Training level," Bobbi said. "You're going to learn to sit the trot."

"Leo's bouncy trot?"

"Yes, maam. We'll get you on the longe line and loosen up those hips, don't you worry."

"Eight years of yoga hasn't succeeded, I doubt you can crack me. But if I'd known how hard this gets, I might have stuck with jumping—just hang on and go."

I am trying to get this sitting trot thing down, and I despair until I remember back to when I couldn't ride Bandi into a corner, or even stay in the ring for that matter. Inch by inch I progress though I still get humbled, jostled and last summer, again stepped on: it took two months for my big toenail to fall off. The disguising red polish I wore helped us locate it in the pool when it finally gave way over Christmas vacation. I waited a year for it to fully grow back in. That wasn't pretty. But, it wasn't until attempting the prolonged sitting trot that I realized how natural posting is and why it was invented. Oh, that first sitting trot lesson! Afterward, I took a pee and writhed in pain realizing the raw and... well, all of this is more information than you need to dispel the glam horsey image. Nothing a little cream and time can't fix.

Jane and Elliot are solid riders now and thoroughly at home around horses. Elliot had competed at Training level with me and just completed his sixth hunter pace with Bobbi. (Yes, I'm still too cowardly to join them). He outgrew his beloved Cleo, but is now the proud owner of Sundance Sonata, a palomino sixteen-year-old gelded Draught-Quarter Horse cross that he fell in love with at first sight. Bobbi and I tended toward the more dressage-schooled, fox-hunting Baxter, but Elliot stuck to his first choice, and he was right. Though we adult worrywarts distrusted Sunny's forwardness according to Bobbi's "Whoa is better than Go," Elliot loves to gallop and can both handle and rein in his horse's "happiness" when need be. Boy and horse are *simpatico* whether in a lesson, alone out in our fields, leading or following in a hunter pace. Sunny is not a dressage horse, but that's fine—Elliot just wants to have fun. His consistent dressage flat work under Bobbi gave him a safe "seat" for the wilder stuff. That Sunny has not misbehaved once earned our trust in him and in Elliot's instincts.

Jane worked tirelessly with the restored Peaches and won her first dressage show. Untethered from the longe line she took the blue in Introductory level against mostly adult riders. We were so proud of both horse and human; they had come such a long way. Jane, too, is already outgrowing her second pony, but trusty Cleo stands ready to teach her the next skills. Currently she rides both, a real horsewoman. That my kids are so brave and increasingly skillful is ten times better than my reaching any of these milestones. Jane, Elliot and I appreciate the riding and the barn life of horsekeeping more and more, though we have